GUTS GLORY AND BLUNDER

NOREUIL, 1917
the forgotten fight

Big Sky Publishing Pty Ltd
PO Box 303, Newport, NSW 2106, Australia
Phone: 1300 364 611
Fax: (61 2) 9918 2396
Email: info@bigskypublishing.com.au
Web: www.bigskypublishing.com.au

Cover design and typesetting: Think Productions

 A catalogue record for this book is available from the National Library of Australia

Title: Guts Glory and Blunder. Noreuil, 1917 the forgotten fight
ISBN: 978-1-923144-13-2

Front cover image: Australian troops in a sunken road leading past Noreuil Australian Cemetery into the ruined Noreuil village. (AWM E02021)

Back cover images: (L-R) Allan Johnson, Arthur Funnell, William Hoggarth, Oswald Griffen and Harold Hughes (AWM P09291.040, AWM P09291.280, AWM P09291.126, AWM P09291.052 and AWM H05570)

Main back cover image: Noreuil Australian Cemetery, 2 April, 2023. (Andrew Faulkner)

GUTS GLORY AND BLUNDER

NOREUIL, 1917
the forgotten fight

BIG SKY PUBLISHING
www.bigskypublishing.com.au

ANDREW FAULKNER

GUTS
GLORY AND
BLUNDER

NORFUL 1977
the forgotten fight

ANDREW FAULKNER

Contents

Introduction

'One of the most ... gallant fights that has been fought by Australians in France.'
Charles Bean, *Daily Herald*, 15 June 1917

This story starts at Gallipoli, but this is not another Anzac book. The stage is the Western Front, but this is not another story about trench warfare or attritional stalemate. Or futile 'over the top' charges. Or mud and rats and all the other Great War tropes. It begins at Anzac Cove, but Gallipoli is merely a portal to this largely untold epic of Australian valour in World War I. This story takes place in a far-flung corner of the map, nowhere near the Somme and a long way from Ypres.

This is the story of an Australian battalion's valour on a single day in 1917. Of hardened Anzacs and green rookies fighting side-by-side in a battle of manoeuvre. Skirmishing and flanking and fighting in the open in an action that ebbs and flows like the tides. Of hand-to-hand combat. Bomb and bayonet fights. Men carrying on against enormous odds. Audacious rescue missions. Counterattacks. Human shields. A Victoria Cross stunt. Of fragging and friendly fire. Of men killed in cold blood. Of a battalion teetering on a precipice between victory and defeat.

This book was born at Anzac Cove, for that was where Private Arthur Blackburn – later Brigadier Arthur Blackburn VC – and his 10th Battalion scouts scrambled ashore from one of the first boats to ground on Gallipoli's stony shingle. As I researched my biography of Blackburn, *Arthur Blackburn VC* (2008), I was drawn to a battle two years after the Landing at Gallipoli. I was intrigued by how Blackburn's Anzac mates survived Gallipoli only to die at a place I couldn't find on a map, let alone pronounce. For this is not another Pozieres story, nor is it about Bullecourt, Passchendaele or Fromelles. Those grand stories have been well told, and will continue to be told.

Beneath the famous campaigns emblazoned on standards and memorials and etched in our national consciousness are dozens, scores, hundreds of largely forgotten fights. This book is about one of those fights, and the men who fought. It is a diggers' trench-eye view of the battlefield. And they looked through trained eyes, for in this, the third year of their war, the humble digger knew something about fighting. More than some of their generals, and decidedly more than those generals who betrayed them in this marathon battle. It is about the forbearance of the soldiers' families in waiting for news of their fate, or keepsakes after death. It is about how we remember brave men, and how memory has faded into sepia. It is about persistence in the face of adversity, courage under fire and how the dread of letting your mates down was more terrifying than German shot or shell. It is about carrying on, no matter the cost. This is the story of the Hungry Half Hundred's dawn attack at Noreuil, France, on 2 April 1917.

1

The first step on a bloody path ...

They watched him die in the first Anzac Day's fading light. He staggered. He fell. Slowly he rose to lurch a few metres before falling again. Rising. Setting like the Aegean sun. The brigadier's entourage watched in silence from the facing hill. They watched him rise again to strike out for that setting sun. Here, at The Nek, the last, fatal, bullet's impact spreadeagled his arms into the shape of the cross – just like Archy Hamilton in *Gallipoli*'s frozen final image. Made a plum target, up on the skyline, backlit by the sun. Perhaps he was dispatched in an early display of Turkish compassion at Anzac. From his headquarters on the other side of what would soon be known as Monash Valley, the brigadier gave the last rites. 'Poor devil.' Went the day well? This unnamed digger never knew. Just as we'll never know his name or anything other than this account of his lonely death on 25 April 1915.

That we know even this much is thanks to Private Henry

Cheney, who spoke about the incident later. If our unknown soldier is Mark Lee's Archy Hamilton, then Cheney is Mel Gibson's Frank Dunne. Sent down from the front to try to stop the men on the lower slopes unintentionally firing on their comrades up on the ridges, Cheney scuttled down the hill, all the way under fire. Whether his desperate mission was accompanied by *Oxygene* is unknown, but it was certainly redolent of Dunne's dash near the end of the *Gallipoli* film. 'Shots came buzzing ... but I never gave them time to train a rifle on me,' Cheney said. He stumbled across the brigadier's headquarters. 'I went to him and told him of my mission. When I concluded my disjointed narrative, he vouched no answer, only to tell me to rest a little.' Cheney did as he was told and watched the brigadier direct the battle. When his adjutant reported the position of a Turkish gun, the brigadier opened his map and calmly, 'as though he was ordering lunch', said, 'tell the *Queen Elizabeth* to put a few 15-inch [shells] into X', giving the map reference to be relayed to the British battleship's gunners, who duly sent a 900kg missile screaming into the Gallipoli hillfolds.

Cheney, 24, a driver from Mitcham in Adelaide's southern suburbs, was in the first wave at Anzac Cove. His 10th Battalion landed in the centre of the line 'at the very spearpoint' of the attack. On battle eve the Australian official historian Charles Bean wrote: 'Some of the positions tomorrow I believe have to be taken "at all costs" – I believe that is an order to the 10th Battalion.' Cheney's platoon was told to capture a Turkish gun; after that he and his comrades were, like the rest of the 'covering force', supposed to get well forward to screen the rest of the 1st Australian Division from Turkish counterattacks. But first they had to get ashore ... at least one man drowned when his boat capsized; another rode a destroyer's wake while clinging to a providential rope.

Henry Cheney (AWM P09291.129).

Shrapnel shells from the Turkish guns at Gaba Tepe splintered boats and bones as Cheney's C Company neared the shore. But Cheney's boat was spared, and its 37 soldiers vaulted into the chest-high sea. 'It was truly a baptism of fire and water,' he said. Holding his rifle high, Cheney laboured over the slippery cobblestones to the beach. He dropped his pack, as ordered, and fixed his bayonet, also as ordered. There would be no shooting until daybreak – friendly fire was feared in the dark.

'Everything was disorder now. Excitement running very high. No-one gave a thought of what we had been told to do. We had been told we had to dig them out with as little noise as possible, but that was cold blood teaching. Now we were at fever point, and they just made as much noise as they possibly could. In two seconds after, I was lost in the wild mob, in the wildest of charges that I think was ever made.'

The enemy fled before the 'cold steel' of the Australian bayonets, Cheney said, adding a Turk's-eye view to his narrative by pondering the terrifying effect of attackers coming on in waves, up-hill through 'rifle, machine-gun and shrapnel fire' – all without firing a shot back. 'Out they went of the trench at the top of the first rise,' he said. It was now light enough to shoot, at last. 'We poured a fire into the retreating figures.' Onward and upward went Cheney's platoon, up over a 'few more hills' to a 'high plateau about a mile from the beach'. They had arrived at the northern end of what would be known as Johnston's Jolly, on the second ridge.[1]

Private Wilfrid Jose was one of the first ashore. He and his fellow 10th Battalion scouts were almost certainly in the second boat to ground in the Anzac shingle. The shooting started when they were about 30m from the beach; a man took a bullet through his mess tin and another through his peaked cap. Bullets passed between seated men but no-one was hit. They landed near the centre of Anzac Cove, fixed bayonets and started scaling the steep slopes to Plugge's Plateau. 'The way our men went at it was sight for the gods,' wrote one of Jose's comrades. If the gods were watching – after all, Troy's just down the Aegean coast – then they would have approved of Jose. For Jose was an Australian Apollo.

Wilfrid Jose (AWM P06431.002).

Contemporary pictures of Jose show a strikingly handsome young man. His smouldering eyes are windows to his deep intellect and character. Only just turned 20 when he landed at Gallipoli, Jose looked younger than even that tender age. Born in Ningpo, China, where his father was an Anglican missionary, Jose was educated at Adelaide's esteemed St Peter's College, at an Oxford private school and Adelaide University. He was Saints' school captain and dux of the school. He was vice-captain of the first XVIII, played intercollegiate tennis and captained the First XI. 'At the University he has already shown his cricketing prowess in the cricket eleven,' reported the school magazine in 1914. 'He bids fair to hold a position equal to that of AG Moyes and CE Pellew, who were his predecessors as captain of the school cricket team, and are now members of the University eleven.'[2] Johnny Moyes was selected for the 1914 Australian tour of South Africa (cancelled because of the war) and Pellew was in the South Australian Sheffield Shield side. So we can assume the athletic Jose was in the vanguard of the race up the slopes in the opening minutes of the battle. He and the other 10th Battalion scouts were among the first to reach the heights above the beach. There they formed a line and went at the Turks with the bayonet.

While the force's prime directive – get forward at all costs – was a vague order, the scouts had been given a specific task. A battery of Turkish guns was somewhere up on what would be known as 400 Plateau. On the eve of the battle British sailors had shown the scouts how to disable a field gun. Jose and his comrades crested the second ridge and fanned out looking for the guns. At last, a corporal found them in a hidden valley, and, together with a platoon of the 9th Battalion, the scouts captured the three German-made Krupp guns. Private Joseph Weatherill was awarded the Distinguished Conduct Medal for his bravery in the attack, in which he seized two prisoners. 'The poor Turks did 100 yards easily under evens,' Private Weatherill said.[3] Weatherill was a 'good scout', the 10th's commanding officer wrote in his award recommendation.

Before the dawn, the destroyer *Scourge* slipped into its place in the line of British ships, and Lieutenant Noel Loutit, 21, a short and stout engineering student from St Peters, shepherded his platoon of D Company, 10 Battalion, into its boat; no easy feat in the dark, but the men had done this dozens of times in preparation for this moment. It was still dark when Loutit's boat neared the shore but the Turks were finding the range. A bullet tore through a soldier's neck and blew out the back of his head. Three men were dead before the boat grounded halfway along Anzac Cove; Loutit eased a mortally wounded bugler onto the beach then turned to organise his men. Like the others, Loutit's platoon wasted no time in clambering up the slope. When they crested the ridge they saw Turks running up the other side of Shrapnel Gully, so plunged down to overtake their quarry. What came next is not often mentioned on Anzac Day. The Turks surrendered – and were shot. Charles Bean excused the Australians by saying there were 'too many to capture'. In a letter from the front Loutit wrote: 'Everywhere were mad Australians with fixed bayonets – we gave them hell.'[4]

After another hard climb Loutit's party was atop Second Ridge. With the orders to get forward at all costs foremost in his mind, Loutit led his little force across the next valley to the Third Ridge. Stopping on a spur of the range, he beheld Turks swarming on a hill 350m away. He ordered his men to take cover and open fire. Desperate to make sense of the tangled terrain, Loutit took two men and skirted to higher ground to the left. Here they caught a glimpse of the objective – the Dardanelles Strait. There was no time to admire the view – Turkish bullets scythed through the low scrub and one of the trio was hit. Loutit and his other companion carried the wounded man back to the main group. Other Australians were rushed up to bolster Loutit's thin line, which was taking heavy fire from a vastly superior enemy force. It was hopeless. When Turks started working around – and behind – Loutit's left flank he gave the order to retreat. What came next was probably his best bit of work for the day: he led his men back across the fingerlike ridges to the north, close to the Turkish force, because he knew the men could give covering fire from the low ridges, and the shallow gullies afforded the best cover. Without Loutit's leadership they would have been swamped and wiped out. As it was, only 11 unwounded men of his force of 32 made it back to the Australian line then coalescing on the second ridge. Loutit led his men up a broken gully, Wire Gully, from where they climbed a steep gutter running up to what became known as Johnston's Jolly. Here they dug in to form a post 40m in front of the main Australian line.

Noel Loutit: Gallipoli's intrepid inland adventurer was among a handful to make it to the Third Ridge (VWM 12814).

As they scraped away at the dirt, their D Company comrades provided covering fire. Lieutenant David Todd, 23, a clerk from Thebarton, was barking orders as his 13 Platoon dug in above Loutit's men on Johnston's Jolly. Compared with many other units, the 10th Battalion maintained reasonably good order – Cheney's C Company was digging in alongside D Company[5] – and now held an almost continuous line from Owen's Gully to the northern lip of the Jolly.[6] As soon as Loutit and the rest of the forward parties were driven in, the Turks went to work with their rifles, machine-guns and, most deadly of all, their artillery. With their observers overlooking the shallow Australian shell scrapes, the gunners rained shells up the line and back down again. Fire for effect? The effect was terrible. The Anzacs dug for dear life in this their first battle. Some baptism of fire. This was the sternest of tests for tough men. Tough men such as Corporal Esson 'Tom' Rule, 20, a blacksmith from Burra in South Australia's mid-north, Private Charles Hendry, 21, a Port Adelaide labourer, and Private Sydney Wills, 24, a heavily tattooed miner from Broken Hill. The casualties mounted but the men of the 10th held on.

Cheney's C Company platoon scratched at the gravelly ground. Some of the men were exultant, thinking their job done. They had seized the beachhead, as per their orders, to screen the main Anzac force. How wrong they were. 'We had only been digging in about 10 minutes when the Turks opened up a deadly fire upon us,' Cheney said. 'It was only courting death to continue digging, so we had to take cover behind the little we had dug.' As Cheney said, 10 minutes digging with an entrenching tool does not amount to much of a hole. 'It will be simply useless to try and describe what we went through that day. To call it Hell appears to me to be very inadequate. They poured every sort of conceivable fire into us. The day seemed as though it was never coming to an end – every five minutes seemed an hour.' Overlooked from the front and the main ridge running up to the north-east, and with Turks firing at them from the flanks and even the rear, the Australian casualties quickly mounted. 'Our nerves were strained to an intense degree,' Cheney said. 'Not so much by the noise of battle, but by the sights we had been compelled to witness, made more horrible by the fact that most of them were our mates who we had been in constant company with for over eight months. It was one long, continuous cry for stretcher-bearers, first from flank, then from another, and next it would be someone near to [us]. The stretcher-bearers simply could not cope with the work, and many, many men laid [*sic*] for over a day without getting any attention.' Herbert Bice, 21, a butcher from Broken Hill, was shot through the hand; he was evacuated to a hospital in faraway Birmingham.

Bice's C Company had a strong Broken Hill contingent. More than half – 126 of 238 men – of its complement was from the frontier mining town in far-western NSW.[7] These were hard men well accustomed to hardship and to digging. Private James Wilson, 33, was an Aberdeen-born adventurer who had served two years in the South African police force. He was driving trains at the mines when he joined up. Private Henry Steuve, 20, was a miners' cook. His regimental number was 300; number 301 was Private Alfred Bridley, 28. Bridley excelled under the heavy fire. When his section ran out of water, he gathered their water bottles and broke cover to fill them from a soak in the rear. 'When ammunition was running short he assisted in bringing up supplies, and several times delivered and brought back important verbal and written messages under heavy fire,' the citation for his Military Medal reads.[8] The rough-and-ready diggers shared dugouts with city boys such as Lance Corporal Royce Spinkston, a 21-year-old clerk from Clarence Gardens in Adelaide's southern suburbs.

After landing from the *Prince of Wales* in the first wave, B Company was largely intact when it reached 400 Plateau, but it suffered terribly once it was there. After taking its place on the right of the battalion line, one by one its officers were hit until by late afternoon only one remained unwounded, and he could not hope to exercise effective control from his position in a precarious outpost well in front of the main line. Without their officers, NCOs filled the breach and privates stepped up. Privates such as William Hoggarth, 25, a civil engineer from Hawthorn, Adelaide, and Joseph Waine, 26, a salesman who listed as his next of kin a brother in his native England. B Company did a lot of dying that first day but it also did a lot of learning.

A Company was next in line, up the hill on B Company's left. It was also almost complete when it arrived on the ridge. Yes, there had been losses – men were swept overboard when their boats were swamped as they were towed by their destroyer *Foxhound*. In an almost catastrophic case of mistaken identity, the company commander was very nearly bayoneted by his own men soon after he landed. But the company gathered into some sort of order and the men gave a cheer as they started up the hill. A heavily camouflaged Turk sniper – standing in a hole just deep enough to bring his head level with the scrub canopy ('pretending to be a bush as hard as he could'[9]) – missed the company commander from point blank range. A digger sprang up and clubbed the bush so hard he smashed his rifle butt as well as the Turk's head.

The men of A Company dug their shell scrapes between B and C companies. The Turk gunners wreaked their havoc. An officer and a sergeant thought they were done for when an overhead burst showered them with ball shot. However, the pellets were made of clay, not lead – a dodgy Turkish munitions contractor had saved their lives. As the casualties mounted, lieutenants acted up to do the role of captains; sergeants filled their roles and so on down the line to privates such as Charles Long, 28, a photographer from Hyde Park and Rupert Francis, 25, a Murray Bridge mason. Both men were born leaders, as we shall see.

Needless to say, stretcher-bearers were in very high demand. Private Patrick Auld, 20, an insurance clerk from Norwood, landed with his comrades of the 4th Field Ambulance on the evening of the 25th. The 1st, 2nd and 3rd Field Ambulances were already ashore but couldn't possibly cope with the enormous casualties, so the 4th's bearers, minus their officers and doctors, were sent to help. With the beachhead far from secured, Anzac Cove was a dangerous place. Loaded up with all manner of equipment, the bearers were aptly named as they clambered into their little boats. 'They took with them three days' "iron" rations, which consisted of a tin of bully beef, a bag of small biscuits and some tea and sugar, dixies, a tent, medical comforts, and, for firewood, all the empty cases we could scrape up in the ship,' the 4th Field Ambulance's commanding officer wrote. 'Each squad had a set of splints, and every man carried a tourniquet and two roller bandages in his pouch. Orders were issued that the men were to make the contents of their water-bottles last three days, as no water was available on shore.'[10]

Captain Harold Seager, 21, was a bank teller when he joined up, but there the parallels with Private Frank Pike end. Joining the senior cadets at 15, he served with the old Adelaide Rifles, which made the precocious sergeant a 2nd Lieutenant soon after he turned 18. Seager was one of the first officers to enlist in the 10th and was given command of C Company.[11] But Seager did precisely no fighting on 25 April 1915. Recovering from serious pneumonia, he had a grandstand view of the action from the troopship *Ionian*. (A fortnight before battle he had arrived at Lemnos bearing £18,500 in cash to pay the troops; he must have been a popular man.) The *Ionian* (or as the diggers called the pongy vessel, the 'One Onion') was soon pressed into service as a hospital ship, such were the casualties. 'Never again do I want to be on a temporary hospital ship,' Seager wrote in a letter to a friend. 'The poor mangled, quivering pieces of humanity were placed on the decks, in the saloons, cabins, boat decks, and even down in the holds.' Seager attended his wounded and dying comrades with great tenderness all the way to Alexandria, where, once the blood was washed from the decks, fresh troops marched up the gangway and the ship steamed back to Gallipoli. Seager was sent straight up to command B Company. After some time in the line he earned the sobriquet 'Daredevil Harry'.

Bright young leaders such as Seager were in high demand to replace the bright young leaders killed in Gallipoli's opening days. The Landing's casualty figures are notoriously ropey, but we know at least 13 of the 10th Battalion's 29 officers were killed or wounded in the first five days of battle, which roughly matched the unit's overall casualty rate of almost 50 per cent. The Queenslanders of the 9th Battalion on the right were shot up more than even the 10th; they lost 19 officers and 496 other ranks. One by one the 9th's officers fell, until command of the battalion fell to the officer commanding A Company, Major Alfred Salisbury, 30, of Sandgate, Queensland.

Salisbury was working in a bank at the outbreak of war but if Seager was no Pike then Salisbury was certainly no Captain George Mainwaring. Salisbury had nearly 10 years' service in the militia, having risen to captain in his Queensland battalion. After being one of the first to land, Salisbury led his company onto Plugge's Plateau, from where the Queenslanders followed the 10th men in their pursuit of the Turks fleeing up Shrapnel Gully.[12] 'For the rest of that day, until the 9th Battalion ceased to exist as a fighting unit, it was this young officer that commanded it,' Bean wrote of Salisbury.[13]

Standing at 185cm, Salisbury was a strong man and he was also a silent type of officer. What he said he meant and when he spoke men listened. He was not on familiar terms with his troops; he exercised his command in a detached manner and was respected for it. On the morning of 25 April, he led his company and half another company of the 9th up onto 400 Plateau, where they started digging in on the right of the 10th Battalion. Then away on the far right, on the lower slopes of the Third Ridge, came signs of a Turkish counterattack. Up the Turks came, in ranks as if on parade, marching up the spine of the ridge before dispersing into battle order. The Australians were impressed with their training and discipline. The Turks wheeled left, plunged into Legge Valley and came straight at the Australians on 400 Plateau. The brigadier ordered Salisbury to meet the counterattack head on. The men of the 9th kitted up and disappeared into the scrub. And were all but wiped out. Salisbury was shot in the hand but remained in command, only attending a dressing station after nightfall. Salisbury is a leading figure of Anzac.

Major Alfred Salisbury took command of the 9th Battalion on the first day at Anzac (Australian Dictionary of Biography A110519).

As Salisbury headed back to have his wound dressed, he might have passed Lieutenant-Colonel Harold Pope going the other way. Pope, 41, was leading his newly landed 16th Battalion up to the key sector, the hotly contested ridges at the top of Monash Valley. This was the apex of the emerging front; the extreme eastern point of the semi-circle of the ANZAC line from Fisherman's Hut to the foot of Bolton's Ridge. It was also the most unforgiving country of one of the most confounding battlefields in the war. Pope led his men into the breach.

Soon after his force arrived at the front line, Pope sent a small party out to make contact with the Indian troops in the hillfolds and on the ridge, Russell's Top, to his left. The Indians were duly found, whereupon Pope was summoned to a conference. He clambered through the low scrub and perceived figures around him in the darkness. Pope was suspicious. Rifle shots followed him as he dived down the hill. He was right to trust his instincts – the 'Indians' were Turks. Three of his men – his adjutant, a lieutenant and a Tamil-speaking private – were captured by the imposters. Pope set about digging in on the hill that ever since has borne his name. 'With his confident bearing, strong face and kindly eyes', Pope was a popular officer and endures as a prominent figure in the Anzac story.[14]

Withdrawn from the line on the 28th, the exhausted men of the 10th Battalion assembled at Shell Green and counted the cost – 466 killed, wounded or missing. Men drawn into other fights or bewildered and beaten by the terrain dribbled back in the ensuing days. And those lightly wounded such as Private John Hunt, 21, joined their comrades in the firing line when the battalion was sent to man the trenches on the right of the line, overlooking the beach. As the stalemate solidified, the battalion was moved up to the trenches snaking down from Lone Pine. This is where they spent most of their time on Gallipoli. This is where the men of the 10th learnt the art of trench warfare.

* * *

The big guns boomed as 2nd Lieutenant Harold Armitage's shipload of reinforcements approached the fatal shore in early June 1915. 'I am hopeful of pulling through ... tomorrow we land,' Armitage wrote in what he feared would be his final letter to his father Henry. 'Army' Armitage, 20, was an erudite and thoughtful schoolteacher from Millicent in South Australia's south-east. He had an acerbic streak and a fatalistic bent. In the event he was killed, he instructed his father to distribute his badges and trinkets – including an ivory elephant bought in Colombo – among his family, and asked his father to connect with his surviving comrades after the war. 'At all times I have endeavoured to do my duty to you, and struggled hard to be a credit to you,' he wrote. 'Thank God that I have parents who brought me up in such a way that I have a bit of backbone.'[15]

Armitage's contingent of 10th Battalion reinforcements included Scottish migrant Private Ralph Mann, 27, Private Clifford Goode, 21, from Richmond in Adelaide's inner western suburbs, and farmer William Woods, 24. Private Nicholas Herring, a labourer from the Adelaide Hills town of Lobethal, presented an early challenge for 2nd Lieutenant Armitage: just turned 19, Herring was a hard case – he was forever having pay docked for offences including being absent without leave, urinating in the lines and general insubordination.

Greater man-management challenges awaited ashore. Armitage was posted to command a C Company platoon of rough around the edges-types, mostly from Broken Hill. 'My platoon has a history – and according to history and reports on conduct sheets – they "made history" in Cairo – but so far I've had no trouble with them.' The fresh new subaltern was regaled with tall tales of the Landing, including how a group of Australians disappeared under the water when tipped out of their boat, only to surface in fighting order after having 'fixed their bayonets while underneath'. The philosophical stoicism soon faded from his letters – Armitage was too busy trying to keep his men alive. He quickly found the best means of achieving that was encouraging them to keep their heads down. 'I have already had some close shaves,' he wrote on 2 June. 'One's hair rises now and then to hear "ping" – "thud" – just above one's head in the bushes.'

Hair-parting rather than raising was the problem for Private Charles Long in the early fighting. 'Gun Shot Wound scalp,' his official record reads. Long must have raised his head a fraction too high. Bill Hoggarth took a bullet through the shoulder and was evacuated to Cairo. Henry Steuve was shot in the left arm on 19 May – the day the Turks launched human wave attacks along the Anzac line. Eleven men of the 10th were killed and 23 wounded that day. Steuve was out of action until July but Long and Hoggarth were back at the front by June.[16] They were among a flood of wounded men returning to the unit about that time. On 13 June Armitage wrote that the 10th was almost back to full strength. It wasn't and it wouldn't be again at Gallipoli. Exposure, heat, flies, poor food and rudimentary sanitation combined to make the beachhead a land of plague and pestilence. Of the men we have come across so far, only Bridley, Waine and Pope did not succumb to illness severe enough to force their hospitalisation and/or evacuation to Mudros, Malta, Egypt or England. The sick parade reads thus: Cheney (August, dysentery), Jose (August, diarrhoea), Loutit (August, diarrhoea, then enteric and ophthalmia), Todd (October, typhoid fever), Rule (August, influenza), Hendry (September, gastroenteritis, dysentery), Francis (September, septic foot), Wills (July, hand and leg infections), Steuve (August, influenza), Auld (July, malaria), Seager (September, influenza), Spinkston (September, diarrhoea) and Salisbury (August, influenza)[17]. Private Joseph Peebles, 31, who landed in the first wave before being seconded by the mules corps, was one of the very few men of the 10th to remain on the peninsula for the whole campaign.

Without its reinforcements the 10th would have ceased to exist as a unit let alone a fighting unit. Five drafts of 150 men – three-quarters of a battalion – were landed on the beachhead from May to September. Lieutenant Charles Moule, 35, an electrician from Gilberton in Adelaide's inner-east, joined the battalion in the line on 30 May. Moule was an experienced militia man, having been commissioned in 1909. Moule's mob included Private Walter Wood, 26, a brickmaker from the copper mining town of Moonta, and Private Ernest Fishburn, 20, a tall and lean Broken Hill fireman who perfectly matched the Anzac ideal. His experience after being shot in the leg in early June was instructive of the medical logistics supporting the fighting troops: he was evacuated to Mudros, then Gibraltar, and finally Bristol, before being sent back to Egypt when declared fit.

Second Lieutenant Murray Fowler of Norwood was yet to turn 20 when he arrived in early August, but he already had almost two years militia experience. Richard Wilton, 22, was a St Peter's old scholar seen as a man on the rise. Soon after arriving with his 7th Reinforcements in September, 2nd Lieutenant Wilton trekked from the 10th Battalion's trenches on Silt Spur, in a southern sector of the line, to the valleys north of Plugge's Plateau to visit friends from the newly arrived 27th Battalion. Some walk in some park.[18]

The 7th Reinforcements was the last draft to join the battalion on the peninsula. It included one of the youngest 10th Battalion soldiers at Gallipoli – Private George Barrett gave his age as 18 years and one month when he enlisted in March 1915. It also included probably the only Indian-born man in the battalion: Private Charles Khan, 30, whose complexion was described as '(Abor) Dark'. Khan was of the few to answer the 'have you ever been convicted by the Civil Power' question on the enlistment papers: 'Yes, Unlawful Possession of bicycle.' Moonta-born miner Thomas Murrin, 33, was another exception: 'Yes, Drunkenness Fined.'[19]

For Barrett, Khan, Murrin and their fellow 7th Reinforcements, Gallipoli was a subterranean world of deep trenches and deeper tunnels. No advances on a broad or even a narrow front. Private Keith Tamblyn, 22, never set foot in no-man's land, which by this stage of the campaign was strewn with used bully beef and jam tins – a crude early warning system for both sides. The most dangerous 'job' (Tamblyn's word for any army task, including pitched battles) entailed two-hour shifts on one of 56 T-shaped fire steps in the frontline trench, firing the odd not-so-angry shot – a Turk opposite Tamblyn waved a shovel to signal misses like a marker on a rifle range.[20]

Lieutenant David Todd (far end of the tunnel) in the labyrinth that was the 10th Battalion's fortress at Silt Spur (AWM A02160).

The 10th Battalion supported the Lone Pine attack in August and waged war with illness and the Turkish snipers. James Wilson took a bullet through his left arm on 1 October. He was evacuated to Egypt and never returned to the peninsula. When the battalion's 8th Reinforcements arrived in the Middle East in early October, only 2nd Lieutenant Jim Churchill-Smith was sent to Gallipoli. Already an evacuation was being considered.

Another of the Broken Hill crew, Private William James, shares his page of the embarkation roll with a Norwegian, a Dane and a Finn. Prior to his December 1914 enlistment, the Finn, Karl Ljung, sought and received confirmation of his bona fides from the Russian consulate in Adelaide – Finland then being part of the Russian empire. The 6th Reinforcements included Private Joergen Jensen, 24, a Danish migrant who was labouring in the steel city of Port Pirie when he enlisted. Swede Andrew Johanson, 26, landed with Armitage's contingent in June. So much for the bronzed boys from the bush Anzac myth; 202 of the original 10th were born in the British Isles, 12 in New Zealand, 12 in 'various parts of the British Empire', and 10 in 'foreign countries'. It was a broad church, the 1st AIF.

Private Oliver Winter, 20, better fitted the Anzac ideal. Born and bred on a station at the mouth of the nation's greatest river, the Murray, Winter had travelled too: he listed his 'last unit' as the '5th [Eyre Peninsula] Battalion Volunteer Defence Corps' – the Eyre Peninsula being several days' ride from the Murray Mouth. Winter was a country lad; he allowed some enterprising photographer to tart up his studio portrait with a bucolic stage backdrop of faux post-and-rail fences and trees. No number of props could hide that he looked 15, 16 at best, under his slouch hat and inside his ill-fitting tunic.[21] Little wonder when he fell ill it was measles. After a month in the trenches Winter was evacuated ill in August. After a spell in an Alexandria hospital he was back in the line in October.

Oliver Winter (SLSA B 46130/542).

He returned to a veritable fortress. The 10th had turned Silt Spur into an intricate network of tunnels reaching to listening posts and sniper nests in no-man's land. Three lines of deep trenches stood between the Turks and the sea. All around were field kitchens – one per company – officers' dugouts, command posts, ammunition dumps, aid posts and signallers' stations. A catapult post added a medieval flavour and confirmed that this was a siege. As did the order and complexity – the Turks weren't getting in but the Anzacs sure as hell weren't getting out. Not in an easterly direction in any case. The 10th Battalion left the peninsula for a rest on 22 November, the same day the British generals decided to abandon the Gallipoli misadventure.

Every man named in this chapter is an Anzac. Every single one of them survived Gallipoli. And every single one of them found death, glory, ignominy or despair on another battlefield two Aprils later. For them, Gallipoli was the first step on a bloody path that led to a ruined village in northern France. This is the story of their plunge into death's shadowy valley; of their descent into hell. Of their bloody, pyrrhic victory. And of their crosses of bronze, stone and wood.

2

The hungry half hundred

The officers' mess was heaving. Foaming ale was flowing freely and some enterprising soul had scrounged band instruments for the musical accompaniment. 'Rather a noisy one,' reported Pat Auld of the night. Toasts were made and speeches given. Four new commissions had come through. They included Auld, whom Harold Seager and Noel Loutit had headhunted from the stretcher-bearers. Auld and Bill Hoggarth had risen through the ranks to earn their commissions. They and the other new officers gave their 'entering speeches' before diving into a night 'hideous with revelry'. There was much to celebrate. Surviving Gallipoli, for a start.[1]

For this night of great cheer was at Tel-el-Kebir, Egypt. And while 10th Battalion stalwarts Seager and Loutit had recruited Auld, this party was not in the 10th's officers' mess. It was in a brand new battalion's mess. To explain: most of the veteran battalions had been split. Half of each became the nucleus for new battalions. Both the old and new battalions would be backfilled with reinforcements fresh from Australia. This is how the 10th begat the 50th Battalion. Led by the 10th's former second-in-command, decorated Boer War officer Lieutenant-Colonel Frederick Hurcombe, the daughter or pup unit had the same colour patch as the 10th, purple and blue, but in a circle instead of a rectangle. The restructure was a seismic shift but was achieved without too much fuss – each battalion was divided, half the men marched out to a new camp and their replacements marched in. Hey presto – 16 new infantry battalions comprising 50 per cent Gallipoli veterans and 50 per cent raw recruits. The 50th Australian Infantry Battalion was born on 26 February 1916, at Habieta, Egypt.

Leaving their original units and their mates was a great wrench for the men, but the change was completed efficiently. Hurcombe's battalion was informally described from the start as a second 10th battalion; that or Hurcombe's Hungry Half Hundred, Dirty Half Hundred, the Ups and Downs (because the 10th's purple and blue colours were inverted on the 50th's shoulder patch) or the Deep Thinkers (because the latest recruits had thought long and hard before joining up).[2] Whatever the moniker, the 50th Battalion was built upon a hard base of Anzac bedrock and around thick pillars of Anzac steel.

Loutit, now a captain, was the new battalion's adjutant, Charles Moule was its quartermaster and Dick Wilton its machine-gun officer. Seager was appointed to command A Company and Harold Armitage C Company. Seager said the replacements – mostly South Australians earmarked for the 10th Battalion – were 'a fine lot of chaps and as keen as mustard – the discipline is excellent ... we are a very happy family and everything points to a battalion equal to the original one'.[3] Hoggarth, Wilf Jose, Murray Fowler and Jim Churchill-Smith were platoon commanders. Tom Rule was made a company sergeant major before being commissioned in July. Hurcombe further bolstered his already impressive stock of leaders when he persuaded David Todd to also join the 50th. Privates who excelled at Anzac Cove entered the 50th as non-commissioned officers: Joe Weatherill was a warrant officer class II, Henry Cheney and Alf Bridley were sergeants and Charlie Long was now a corporal. Cheney's younger brother Edward was the battalion's inaugural regimental sergeant major. The veterans set about training the raw recruits, including some who had never shot a .303. 'The new hands look up to the Anzacs with awe and the old hands play the part of veterans to perfection,' Seager said.

One of the freshest new hands was Private Hurtle Harvey, who when he enlisted gave his age as 19 years, even.[4] He was probably younger as 19 was the minimum age for enlistment in the early months of the war. Even then, the farmer from Prospect Hill, south of Adelaide, needed his parents' permission because he was aged under 21. 'We are willing for our son Hurtle Ralph Harvey to go to the front,' they wrote. When Private Harvey, regimental number 3347, sailed in October he did so with Private Harvey, regimental number 3349. Ernest Harvey, 27, was also posted to the 50th Battalion. Brothers in arms.[5]

Angus and Tom Boston were issued numbers 3249 and 3250. They were allocated to the 10th Battalion, sailed on the same ship, and were both posted to the 50th in January 1916. Angus, 26, left wife Cecelia and three children in Naracoorte in SA's South-East. Brother Tom, 22, left his job as a baker and a mother, Hannah, fretting about farewelling two sons on the same day.

Temporary Lance Corporal John Edwards, 27, was a newspaperman and put his trade to good use soon after arriving in camp. Edwards fired off a dispatch to Port Augusta's *Transcontinental* to say how the country was not unlike the land traversed by Australia's east-west railway. 'We are training now with full packs on, so that we will be in good condition for next Friday morning when we start on a 40-mile march,' Edwards wrote. Reports such as Edwards' sowed the seed of the Anzac legend back home. 'The opinion among the people here and in the press is that better fighters do not live today than the Australians. Get them away from a place where they cannot get drink and give vent to their boisterous spirits and they are the healthiest, strongest looking and most humorous lot of fellows I ever saw. God help the troops that come into contact with the Australians. When the Prince of Wales passed through this camp our fellows rushed out of the mess hut where they were having lunch and cheered so lustily and waved pieces of bread and jam, jam tins and mess tins so frantically that the Prince got frightened. Kind regards to all.'[6] Fighters, drinkers and terrorisers of the monarchy – meet the emerging digger.

Dedicated servants of the Empire or proud sons of Australia? The diggers' regard or otherwise for the monarchy was a complicated matter. The future Edward VIII's visit brought out both competing views. To not inconvenience the troops, the young prince did not demand a formal parade of the men; rather he rode through the tent lines as they went about their daily work. 'Attired in the simple khaki uniform of a captain, and wearing a pith helmet, he was distinguished from his suite (of attendant officers) by only the Prince of Wales feather,' a

50th Battalion private wrote. 'As he passed along the desert pathway, he received the spontaneous cheers of our fellows.' However, when he neglected to salute one group, the men registered their displeasure in the tried and true Australian way – they counted him out. 'One, two, three, four ... nine, out!' Puzzled by this unfamiliar practice, the prince asked a member of his entourage what it meant. When told the dashed impudent colonials were abusing His Royal Highness, he rode back to the men – not to order 'orf with their heads' or even to put them on a charge. He saluted them. They cheered. And he rode on.[7]

As did the 50th's officers. When Loutit challenged Seager to a horse race in April, Fowler and Captain Frank Hancock, another old 10th man, demanded to be included. Each of the four put a pound on themselves in the 'Serapeum Cup', run over 'About Three Furlongs' on 20 April. Seager was on Beachy Bill and Hancock rode Mr Booze '(Out of Condition by No Beer)'. Fowler beat Seager by half a length, with Mr Booze a close third. Loutit didn't finish. Grave fears were held for the hero of Gallipoli when his horse did a 'complete somersault' early in the race. But he emerged from the dust cloud to walk to the finish line, nursing little more than a nosebleed and minor cuts. Tough man, Loutit.[8]

Sport broke the monotony of camp life in the desert. The men marked the first Anzac Day by holding a carnival in the Suez Canal to 'celebrate the action of the boys in jumping into the water at Anzac and swimming and wading ashore'. The program was reported by an anonymous correspondent and published in an Australian newspaper. 'Greasy pole contests were reminiscent of the slippery Turks, and foot races reminded some of the boys of the sprints they had after the elusive followers of Mahomet. Altogether a most enjoyable day was spent.'[9] Gauche in the extreme? Yes. Nevertheless, they were *the* Anzacs and it was their story to commemorate.

As April rolled into May, the heat intensified. Battalions new and old browned under the desert sun. Anzacs taught the replacements how to shoot, how to march and how to stick an enemy with a bayonet: In! Out! On guard! Water was so scarce they were issued a mess tin per day. Little wonder a man in another brigade, mad with thirst, shot an officer before killing himself. Others died on route marches. 'The boys were nearly flogged out,' Armitage wrote in June. 'Many of them nearly broke down. I was very glad to see the grit they showed then. On the desert marches it did one good to see each platoon in step and to hear them singing a marching chant. Each platoon has a "songster" and singing made those marches much easier.' There was a spring in their step when they marched 15km to embark from Alexandria in early June. '[They] simply yelled their songs,' Armitage wrote. 'Many of us "old hands" are beginning to hanker after powder again. This life seems too slow.'[10] The 50th Battalion sailed for France on 6 June 1916.

One of the new platoon commanders, Lieutenant Max Gore, 21, a clerk from St Peters, left with desert bugle notes echoing in his ears. 'At 10pm each night ... first a bugler from a unit close at hand would sound "Last Post", then perhaps one from ours, then another and another ... away, away into the distance, then almost alongside, and finally one so faint that it could only just be heard. In imagination I can hear them still; always one is reminded of them when the call is sounded. One wonders if Gabriel's Reveille will be like that.'[11]

Max Gore (State Records of SA GRG26/5/4).

Plenty were about to find out. Mouquet Farm, or Second Pozieres (August/September 1916), was a hell of hot metal that forged a battalion in fire. The novices proved themselves to the Anzacs. Gore was awarded a Military Cross for his bravery leading the battalion bombers in this his first battle. Artillery did most of the killing here: Gore saw 'a dozen men in their death throes' after a single shell hit his trench. Churchill-Smith received a Military Cross for his work commanding hard-pressed troops in a key forward post. Auld's Mouquet Farm MC was for 'conspicuous gallantry ... although wounded, he led his men forward to reinforce part of the line ... he set a splendid example to his men'. Rule's 'coolness and bravery under fire' earned him an MC recommendation but it went no further than that. Edwards, the newspaperman who wrote that 'better fighters do not live today than the Australians', backed his words with actions. Sergeant Edwards was awarded the Military Medal for rallying his men during the worst of the shelling and for rescuing men buried by explosions. The Swede Johanson, now a lance corporal, commanded an isolated and undermanned post that held out against counterattacks. 'It was only due to his fine example and cheerfulness that the position was retained,' the citation for his Military Medal (MM) reads.[12]

Just as Loutit had set a record for roaming the furthest inland at Gallipoli, the battalion boasted the first man to set foot on the ruins of Mouquet Farm. Hoggarth – disorientated by the foggiest of war fugs – inadvertently reached the objective before, like Loutit at Anzac, pulling back because the position was untenable. Mouquet Farm was a quintessential World War I battle where the generals talked big and the men felt very small indeed under the weight of enemy shell. Typically, the men would attack behind a creeping barrage, seize what was left of an enemy trench, repair the trench as best they could, before it and they were blown to smithereens by the enemy gunners. Armitage described it as being hit with the entire complement of Essen and Krupp munitions factories at once. Shells hit his trench 'every 10 yards every five seconds'. And that was 'before starting work' – the trench in question was a communication sap leading to the frontline. Buried by a shellburst, Gallipoli veteran Private Thomas Murrin was dug out by his mates and evacuated with shellshock.[13]

The battalion suffered about 500 casualties at Mouquet Farm. Joergen Jensen took a chunk of shrapnel in his left shoulder. Hoggarth might have been the first to set foot on

Mouquet Farm but that did not save him from being shot in the backside – by an Australian rifle. 'He was hit by a rifle bullet and sustained a jagged, oval, gaping wound in the left buttock,' a medical board in England ruled of the 'friendly fire' incident that kept him out of the line for three months. After being shot in the left arm at Gallipoli, Sergeant James Wilson was hit in the left shoulder at Mouquet Farm. Private Oliver Winter was out of action for six weeks after suffering an unrecorded wound on 16 August, the day the battalion recorded 105 men killed in action or died of wounds.

Hurcombe never returned after Mouquet Farm. His first battle in command of the 50th was his last. He was evacuated with severe shellshock. 'It broke our old colonel, poor fella,' Corporal Keith Tamblyn said. 'It broke his heart.' Seventy years later Tamblyn said Hurcombe was a wonderful man but at age '60' was too old for combat. Hurcombe wasn't that old – his birth year is variously recorded as 1859, 1867 and 1872 (it is likely he lied about his age at enlistment); nevertheless, he probably was too venerable for such a brutal and unforgiving war.[14] Hurcombe commanded troopships for the duration. The men keenly felt his loss. He was replaced by Major Alfred Salisbury, the hero of the 9th Battalion's doomed advance across 400 Plateau at Gallipoli.

The hero whose name was given to the treacherous Anzac hill he defended, Colonel Harold Pope, was, like Hurcombe, a victim of the AIF's heavy casualties in its 1916 battles on the Western Front. When his 14th Brigade was wrecked by a lethal combination of British generalship and German machine-guns at Fromelles, Pope was accused of being drunk and was sacked. 'Pope ... rather disgusted me by the boastful way he talked –

I think he had been refreshing himself after the strain,' Bean wrote in his diary on 20 July.[15] Bean was more discreet in his *Official History of Australia in the War of 1914–1918*, writing in a footnote that Pope was 'returned to Australia … on disciplinary grounds'.[16] Pope denied he was drunk and Brigadier Pompey Elliott sympathised: 'I am sorry for him. He did well in the fight, but next day it is said he was so cut up that he took some drink and he was in such a state with his nerves that he was incapable of commanding his men if there had been a counterattack, and so he was sent home.'[17] Pope immediately agitated to clear his name and return to the front.

Harold Armitage (AWM P09291.100).

Several heroes of Anzac were delighted to have an impromptu rendezvous on leave in London in October. After visiting a tailor, Armitage became lost until a policeman suggested he lunch at the Trocadero. As he entered the crowded restaurant a voice yelled an Arabic phrase, which Armitage at once recognised as 'a pure Anzac cry from Egypt'. It was Murray Fowler, who was sitting with a large group enthusiastically celebrating Captain Arthur Blackburn's Victoria Cross and Captain Bill McCann's Military Cross. Both were original 10th men and both had been decorated for their heroism at Pozieres. Armitage folded into a throng that included Jose and Moule. The lunch bill was a small fortune – more than £9 – but Armitage said 'Blackburn doesn't get the VC every day'. Afterwards they quickly went through another half a dozen quid at the Hippodrome, but 'McCann doesn't get the MC every day ... I remember joining in with the song "The Perfect Day". It was a perfect day too ... the best and first time I have ever been "perfect" in all my life. But it was worth it. For you can't imagine how pleased we 10 of the old 10th were to be together once more'. Armitage 'very penitently' went to a service at Westminster Abbey next morning.[18]

One hundred and thirty-three men of the 50th died at Mouquet Farm. They were killed in action or died of the wounds they received in their two battles; on 12–16 August and 2–5 September. These were large, brigade-strength operations on a broad front. Many if not most Australians have heard of Pozieres, even if they might not have heard of Mouquet Farm, which is on the same field and was essentially the same battle. The 50th's next big fight came at a place few have heard of, let alone visited. Forgotten battle? Noreuil was never remembered in the first place.

3

That's the stuff to give the bastards

As the ground thawed after an especially cold 1916/17 winter, the diggers emerged from the trenches, blinked, stretched their stiff limbs and found the enemy was gone. In one of the most startling strategic strokes of the war, the Germans had pulled back from the Somme to a heavily fortified network of trenches about 20km to the rear. The Hindenburg Line was a zig-zagging rent in the French countryside running 160km from Arras in the north to Soissons in the south. It shortened the German frontage by hacking off the salient bulging out towards the Somme. Shortening the line meant the trenches could be more thickly manned in a war that was all about numbers.

The fortifications comprised three lines of trenches, forbidding redoubts and deep concrete bunkers, all behind thickets of barbed wire. 'This line is a beauty from what I hear,' Harold Armitage wrote on 23 March.[1] 'Anyhow I wouldn't mind having a look at it.' As they pulled back, the Germans cratered the roads, blew up the bridges, felled the trees, torched the villages and poisoned the wells. The French locals were marched away but there really was no need as the Germans had made their land all but uninhabitable.[2] Let off the leash at last, the Australians deployed the Light Horse in its intended role. The horse soldiers rode out onto the scorched earth in pursuit of their quarry.

They trotted out rather than cantered because by setting ingenious booby-traps – a pencil blew up in one digger's face – the Germans put a price on the land they were leaving. Snipers and machine-gun nests marked the way to the Hindenburg Line. The nearer the pursuers came, the stronger the resistance became. The Australians learned caution was their friend. Scattered before the new German line was a string of villages bristling with machine-guns and garrisoned with fresh and experienced troops. One such village was Noreuil (pronounced nuh-RAY), a hamlet in a shallow valley that ran down to the Hindenburg Line. At Noreuil, the Australians succumbed to haste. Ordered by British General Sir Hubert Gough to 'push on', the 2nd Australian Division made an ill-conceived and underprepared attack that cost it 330 casualties for no material gain.[3] Gough complained that the Australians were tardy in bringing up their artillery to support the infantry. The pursuit was over – from now on any advances needed to be well-planned and backed by the guns.

After a long stretch out of the line, training and reorganising, the 50th was in fine fettle. By the end of March the battalion strength was 21 officers and 826 other ranks,[4] with each of the four rifle companies approaching its notional complement of

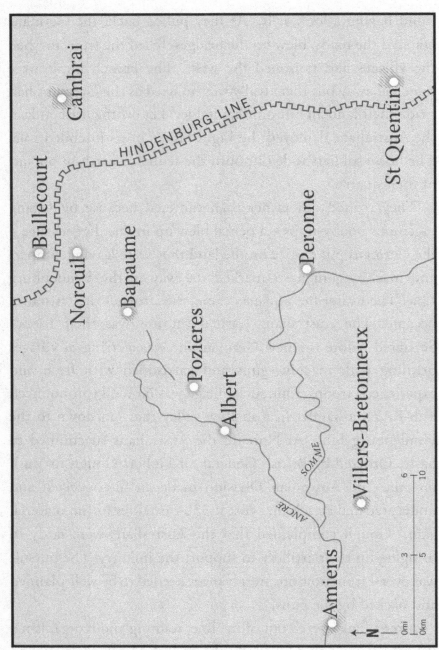

To the Hindenburg Line.

more than 200 troops.⁵ Some of the Mouquet Farm wounded were still trickling back to the ranks six months after the battle. Men such as Sergeant Herbert Bice, who, after being shot in the hand at Gallipoli, was shot in the thigh and the back at Mouquet Farm. While convalescing in England, a drunk and disorderly Bice was arrested, found guilty of bad conduct and stripped of his stripes. The thrice-wounded original Anzac was a private when he rejoined the battalion on 1 April. He was a handy man to have in the ranks with a battle brewing.

Anzac original Royce Spinkston was promoted sergeant soon after returning from hospital – a Mouquet Farm shell had peppered his face, right hand and leg with shrapnel shards. Sergeant Joe Peebles, who was 'made like a sieve about the arms and legs' by a German shell, had recovered and was back, as was original Anzac Sergeant James Wilson. Armitage was grateful for the provident return of his NCOs ahead of the next big push: 'Everyone has got his punch – tails well up, chins well out, noses up … in fact we are not only like Johnny Walker, but also Viceroy Tea.'⁶

Private Nick Herring's war to this point was colourful to say the least. The Gallipoli veteran had been disciplined multiple times for a range of offences: starting with going AWOL for 12 days in Egypt, insubordination and wilfully disobeying an order – topped off by him telling the officer involved to 'go and get fucked'. That little incident landed him in an army prison in Egypt for five months. Arriving in England in late 1916, he again went AWOL and was jailed again for urinating in the company lines. Perhaps the authorities gave up – instead of fighting them he might as well fight the Germans: he re-joined the battalion in early February.⁷

Corporal Bewick Vincent, 26, was in the pink when he rejoined the unit from a school in March. So healthy was the section leader, his men told him he had grown fat while he was living it up in the rear. 'If they give me any cheek I put them on guard or on fatigue,' he wrote to his wife Sylverea[8] on 16 March. 'If they don't do it when I tell them, in the clink they go. So you better be careful what you say to me when I come home or in the clink you'll go, quick and lively. Don't forget to have a good Christmas dinner ready for me, I will be home before that.' After dutifully reporting he had taken confession that evening and was attending church at 7 in the morning, Vincent signed off by saying he would say a prayer for his beloved and his son, 'my dear little Willie'.[9]

Corporal Bewick Vincent (AWM P09291.060).

Private Roy Houston arrived with a batch of reinforcements in mid-March. The strapping McLaren Vale labourer, 21, had no issue with the rations – 'bacon for breakfast, stew for dinner, and bread, butter, cheese and jam for tea'. Although he did admit to tiring on the long march through Bapaume to the front. The men bore a heavy load: rifle and bayonet, 220 rounds of ammunition, steel helmet, two grenades, three gas helmets, full water bottle, a tin of bully beef and six biscuits, groundsheet, blanket, waterproof cape, overcoat, spare clothes, towel, shaving gear, field dressing and sundries. They stopped in a sodden field where they were dusted by a light snowfall and harassed by desultory shellfire as they ate a meal at the end of a two-day, 30km march to the front.[10]

The men filed into a chain of posts on a long, low ridge above Noreuil. The supporting troops lived in hollows scraped out of the banks of the sunken roads[11] etched into the undulating farmland. The first green shoots of spring were stymied by winter's last gasps; the men huddled as the rain fell on their groundsheet shelters. Out in the advanced posts, they huddled also against the shellbursts.

Lance Corporal Norman Gates, 24, had been shelled before. Up on Russell's Top and in the hills north of the Sphinx. A Wimmera farmer, Gates enlisted in a Light Horse regiment, one of the units sent to fight as infantry at Gallipoli. Perhaps the infantry life agreed with him, as he transferred to the 50th in Egypt. He and a dozen men of 14 Platoon were in an outpost above Noreuil when they were seen by German artillery spotters on the morning of 28 March. The gunners zeroed in on the Australians in their shallow weapon pits. About 4pm a round killed Gates outright. He lay there until sunset, when he was carried out under the cover of darkness. He was buried in a gully or quarry just off the Vaulx-Noreuil road. A little white cross was placed over his grave. 'Gates was very well liked by all who knew him,' his platoon sergeant, Frederick Chapman, said. 'He and I were great friends.'[12]

Private Edward O'Toole, 43, was killed the same day. He had been with the battalion eight days. O'Toole, a labourer, intriguingly gave two incongruous addresses when he joined up – Oodnadatta out beyond both Bourke and the Black Stump, and St Peters, the leafiest of Adelaide's leafy inner-east. Presumably O'Toole was also killed by a shell but the official records documenting his life are scanty. Sergeant Peebles served for the duration at Gallipoli but was one of the first to die at Noreuil. He was also killed on the 28th. How and where is a mystery, but this time the records are blameless – he has no known grave.

The German gunners had found the range. The next day, at about noon, C Company Second Lieutenant Alfred Sheard, 28, was hit in the shoulder. The barrage was too heavy to risk carrying him to a dressing station in broad daylight. In any case he said it was little more than a flesh wound. 'Goodbye, lads, I hope to be back for the attack,' he said as he was stretchered out after nightfall. His 'flesh wound' was akin to that of the Black Knight's: Sheard was dead inside a day – a shrapnel pellet had sliced into his spine. 'He made so light of his wounds,' Private James Michael said. 'Even when the stretcher-bearers were carrying him away, he wished to get off the stretcher and walk.'[13]

That Sheard hoped to be back in time for the attack perhaps shows the officers had been told they would soon be going over the top. But much needed to happen before the attack could be mounted. Brigadier-General William Glasgow was gathering intelligence upon which to base his plan. He needed to work quickly, because the British generals had ordered the outpost villages be seized immediately. Once they were secure, the 4th Division was to mount a 'diversionary' attack on the Hindenburg Line at the village of Bullecourt, 2km north of Noreuil. That battle was designed to draw enemy attention away from a British/Canadian hammer blow in the north, at Arras and Vimy Ridge. The dominoes were lined up and Glasgow needed to get cracking.[14]

Enemy trenches showed out clearly on aerial reconnaissance photos, but bunkers and machine-gun nests were harder to pinpoint from the air. So Glasgow issued orders for patrols to sortie into no-man's land forthwith. A five-man patrol crept out before dawn on the 28th and returned after being fired upon by a machine-gun at a barricade on the Noreuil-Lagnicourt Rd. The strongpoint was duly marked on the brigade and battalion maps. An NCO and four men went out at about the same time and returned safely after reporting movement in the sunken road that led from the ridge down to the south-west corner of the village. The intelligence was duly recorded in the brigade diary. A 28 March battalion diary entry says so much in five words: 'Noreuil still held by enemy.' This suggests the Australian brass expected the Germans to complete the last stage of their long withdrawal and take the final hop from Noreuil to the safety of the Hindenburg Line. The fresh evidence contradicted that assumption; it appeared the enemy would stand and fight.

Back in his headquarters in Vaulx, 3km south-west of Noreuil, Brigadier Glasgow pored over the information and framed his plan. He decided it was the 50th's turn to crack the Noreuil nut. The battalion would go in at dawn on 2 April, with the

51st Battalion on its left and the 52nd on the right. This would be the 52nd's first big fight under a new commanding officer – Lieutenant-Colonel Harold Pope had persuaded the army to give him another chance after he was bowler-hatted at Fromelles. The price of his second chance was dropping from brigade to battalion command.

Up in C Company's frontline trenches, 10 Platoon Lewis gunner Private Irwin Coad, 22, from Kingswood in Adelaide's southern suburbs, felt the cold rain blow in late on the morning of 29 March. As he sat yarning with his mates, he pulled his greatcoat over his knees to keep his legs dry. Bang! A kick in the ankle. The revolver in his greatcoat pocket had accidentally discharged. Coad was evacuated to hospital – and charged with deliberately shooting himself to escape the fighting. When he had recovered sufficiently he was brought before a Court of Inquiry that heard witnesses including Company Lewis Gun Sergeant Syd Mortimore, 10 Platoon Sergeant James Wilson and CSM Alfred Bridley, the Gallipoli private whose Military Medal was won at the Landing. Bridley told the court Coad was a fine soldier with a clean conduct sheet. Coad said he had loaded the pistol at the previous night's stand-to and could not understand how it had discharged when it was not cocked. He was absolved of all blame; the real fault lay with the army, as it had not issued him with a holster for the pistol, which was why he was carrying it in his greatcoat pocket. It might have been worse – when not in his coat pocket, he tucked it into his belt.[15]

The battalion continued to probe the enemy's defences. On the night of 29 March Lieutenant Wilf Bidstrup led a patrol down the hill to a machine-gun post in a barricaded sunken road. Bidstrup's men pulled the pins on their Mills bombs, hurled them over the parapet, and scarpered back to their lines without waiting to check the results of their lightning raid. One man was wounded during the rapid withdrawal.[16] Meanwhile, the Germans continued to lob shells at the ridge. Company cook Private Charles Khan copped a lump of shrapnel in his side on 30 March. The wound wasn't serious but it underlined how no-one was safe from the German guns.[17]

Six more patrols went out on the night of 31 March/1 April. All encountered Germans: two groups were fired on by machine-guns; a grenade was flung at another patrol; a fourth saw troops moving in the dark and a fifth saw riflemen in weapons pits. The sixth patrol discovered the Australian gunners needed to adjust their sights – their shells were landing in the wrong place.

Lieutenants Pat Auld and Max Gore each led one of these patrols. Gore's little group crept out of their shell scrapes on the far right of the line, where the 50th's right flank met the 52nd's left. Gore's men counted their steps. A hundred straight ahead. Then they cut across to the right until they came upon the Lagnicourt-Bullecourt Rd. Using the sunken road as their guide but not entering it, they crept another 300 paces down the hill 'straight towards the enemy'. They were now closer to the German lines than they were their own. Indeed, they were probably behind the enemy's forward posts. But on Gore went, like an intrepid deep sea diver, going deeper and deeper as his diving bell creaks and groans. 'We advanced two fifties, then four twenty-fives,' he said. Crack! Crack! Crack! A machine-gun opened up but the bullets streaked harmlessly overhead. 'In the stillness that followed we watched and waited with beating hearts,' Gore said. What to do now? None of the other patrols had gone this far but Gore considered going even further. After lying doggo for 10 minutes, Gore decided to 'worm' his way back to the lines. He marked the machine-gun post on a map, handed his report to a runner, and went to bed, satisfied with a job well done and perhaps wondering if he might receive a bar to the MC he won at Mouquet Farm, or failing that a mention in despatches.

How wrong he was. Because Lieutenant-Colonel Pope said Gore's machine-gun post did not exist. A Company commander David Todd gave Gore the bad news in the morning: 'The CO of the 52nd Battalion said that the machine-gun position could not possibly be where you said there was one, because that is where his left flank rests.' The fact it was April Fool's Day is noted without comment.

Glasgow's plan was explained in detail to the brigade's senior officers. Three companies of the 50th would charge straight down the hill, seize the village with bayonet and bomb, and then turn right to fight to the Lagnicourt-Bullecourt Rd on the eastern side of the town. Churchill-Smith's D Company was on the left of the line, with Armitage's C Company in the centre, and Todd's A Company on the right. A Company had been handed the key role – and the hardest task. The entire operation depended on A Company timing its right wheel at exactly the right moment, as the other companies would pivot on its axis. Turn too early and Todd would lose touch with Armitage and Churchill-Smith … too late and a gap would open between the 50th and the 52nd Battalion. Todd's company was 'thickened up' with a platoon of the battalion's reserve, Seager's B Company. The brigade password on the eve of battle was issued to all ranks. It was Churchill. 'I feel quite bucked for stunt,' Churchill-Smith wrote in his diary.[18]

Captain James Churchill-Smith (AWM H06219).

Gore described Glasgow's plan as 'one of the most grandiose and stupid ever drawn up'. It certainly was complex. As well as the 50th's frontal attack from the south, another blow would fall from the west. The 51st Battalion would skirt Noreuil's northern edge before meeting up with the 50th on the eastern side of the village. On the right, part of the 52nd would advance down the hill and connect with Todd's company in the valley floor. The topography added to the complexity. The 50th had to deploy in a long, strung-out line on the west-east ridge before attacking down the hill, up and over a low railway embankment, then ford the L'Hirondelle River.

All this would be done under fire and without much cover: the country was almost treeless; sugar beet and other crops were

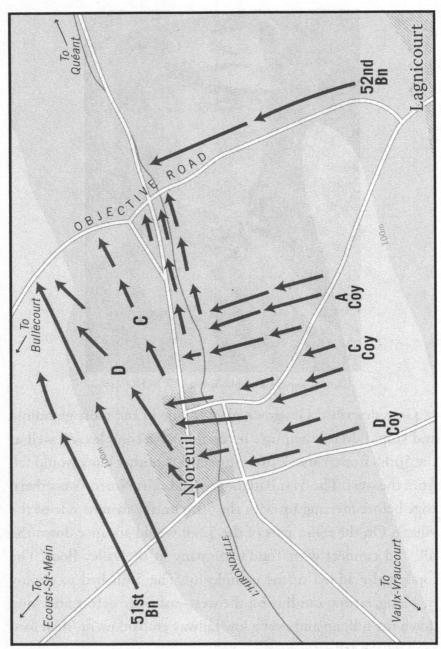

The Noreuil plan of attack.

grown in fields around the village. Two sunken roads ran down the hill, each leading to a southern corner of the town. The Germans had built barricaded machine-gun emplacements in both roads; mortar teams and designated grenade men would silence these. Squads of moppers-up would follow to clear houses and cellars.

The artillery would 'muffle' the enemy's strongpoints, Bean wrote. Once at the objective – the Lagnicourt-Bullecourt Rd about a kilometre east of the village – the men would dig in and light flares to declare both their success and their location to friendly planes. 'Not to disclose it to the enemy artillery – oh no!' said Gore. 'The aircraft would signal OK, and then the glorious cavalry – because through jealously their officers were dying to demonstrate how it was done at Balaklava, what! – would charge through, and, Bob's your uncle, the enemy would fly like chaff before the wind.'[19]

Yes, the cavalry officers and their squadrons, rendered supernumerary by machine-guns, artillery, barbed wire and sundry other products of the latter industrial revolution, were itching to get at Jerry. Whether Jerry would indeed wilt before the might of Empire was another matter, as the night before zero hour, the Germans attacked an Australian forward post. Unsuccessfully attacked, but attacked all the same. The Bosche are doing what? Don't the damned fools know they're supposed to be falling back! Behind the Australian lines a booby trap blew up a battalion headquarters, killing four and wounding two. A mine blew up the Vaulx-Vraucourt town well.[20] Four enemy planes cruised over the Australian trenches. The diggers skulked under the German barrage.

As the cold but clear night fell, six officers convened for a battle-eve chinwag. The six friends were all old scholars from rival

Adelaide private schools, St Peter's and Prince Alfred College. Lieutenants Wilf Jose and Pat Auld were among them. They 'had a bite of bread'; Last Supper comparisons are irresistible. All around – in forward posts, shell scrapes and bunkers cut into the sunken roads – the men chatted as they checked their rifles, ammunition and grenades. They would bear a heavy load into battle; as well as their personal weapons and ammunition, there were extra drums for the Lewis guns and each rifleman was ordered to carry a shovel tied diagonally across their backs. They wore wool lined leather jerkins under their tunics, and waterproof ponchos against the forecast snow. Battalion quartermaster and original Anzac Charles Moule praised his men while passing the ammunition.

Gallipoli veterans such as Moule gave the battalion a core of experience but also something else; they were revered, the men of the Landing. The Gallipoli privates were now leaders of men. Jose (C Company) and Auld (A Company) would lead platoons in the looming fight. A Company sergeant major Rupert Francis had landed at Gallipoli as a private. A Company Sergeants Henry Haythorne, Ernest Fishburn, Andrew Johanson and Bill James were Gallipoli men. B Company was commanded by Captain Seager, who had Lieutenant Rule leading one of his platoons. Armitage could rely on men such as Sergeant James Wilson – the Aberdeen-born hard man who was driving Broken Hill trains when he enlisted – in his C Company: like the old C Company of the 10th, Armitage had a lot of Broken Hill men and hardy country types under his command, including Ted Lamming, a stockman from Nackara on the Peterborough to Broken Hill railway line. Lamming, 27, was regarded the best bushman in the battalion.

The left flank: Churchill-Smith's D Company had to charge down this slope, knock out the enemy strongpoints in the sunken road on the left, fight its way through Noreuil, make a quarter-right turn, and race across the open fields above the village to the objective (Andrew Faulkner).

Original Anzacs Hoggarth, Waine, Steuve and Wills prepared to lead D Company into the fray; Hoggarth and Waine as platoon commanders and Steuve and Wills as NCOs. The leavening of Anzacs reached deep into the 10–15-man sections, such as the one featuring Lance Corporal Percy Foster, the Dane Joergen Jensen and the baby-faced farmer Oliver Winter. Anzac Allan Brown – who copped shrapnel in the right shoulder at Gallipoli and a bullet in the right arm at Mouquet Farm – was made lance corporal in February. 'Thank God I've got good NCOs,' Armitage wrote in a letter to his family. 'Most of them were in the old 10th at Gallipoli with me. If we go over the top they'll all go – and go hard too – for we have a lot to make up for our fallen mates.' So proud was Armitage of his regiment, he thought of it as a second 10th Battalion: 'Of course, the 50th is a twin of the 10th, so we rank as equals ... just imagine a 50th or 10th in the 43rd or 32nd!'[21]

While Armitage trusted in his men, Private Bert Adcock, 21, a clerk from Croydon in Adelaide's western suburbs, took succour from his Baptist faith: 'I am trusting God to help me through this battle, but if He wishes otherwise, I am still trusting.'[22]

As zero hour neared, the 'left out of battle' men marched to the rear. It appears C Company CSM Bridley was in this group: a nucleus of veterans and specialists around which the battalion would reform in the event of disaster.[23] Up on the ridge, men of the attacking waves were pulled out of the line for an hour's sleep. That was Major Loutit's cue; Gallipoli's inland adventurer crept forward to lay tape from where the men of the 50th would start their day of days. At 2.30am they dropped into line like coins in a slot: D Company, then C and A, the attacking waves spread along 650 metres of the reverse slope.[24] The B Company platoon supporting A Company was the last to file into place. It was a cold but windless night and all was quiet – the heads thought a preliminary barrage would forewarn the enemy (Of course, no-one ever attacked at dawn). Private Gilbert Jacob loaded his rifle, fixed his bayonet and lay still. 'I watched the red moon set. It sank slowly among a few thin clouds, then, for a little while, the night was darkest before the dawn … there was a strange stillness now – a hush in the darkness.'[25]

Like the landscapes they dominate, hills stand tall in military history lore: Bunker Hill. Hill 60. Pork Chop Hill. Hamburger Hill … Valleys? Not so much. No-one made a movie about seizing a valley. We laud those going up, not down. We don't conquer valleys 'because they're there'. Be it Gregory Peck scaling sheer precipices in *The Guns of Navarone*, or lantern-jawed commandoes swinging grappling hooks to get at Norwegian heavy water plants, martial popular culture likes its cliffs sheer and its hills high. *Combat's* seminal two-part episode wasn't called *Hills Are for Heroes* merely for the alliteration. And Obi-Wan didn't tell future Darth Vader: 'It's over, Anakin. I have the low ground.'

The 50th Australian Infantry Battalion had the high ground on 2 April 1917. From their extended line stretching across the plateau, they had to advance almost a kilometre downhill to seize an unseen village in the valley beneath. The Anzacs knew much about high ground. High ground such as Plugge's Plateau, 400 Plateau and Battleship Hill. As they lay on the frozen ground, did the diggers ponder why the hell they were plunging into a valley?

Filling the time with random thoughts, Private Gilbert Jacob's mind was on mountains, not valleys. He drew on Shakespeare and thought wistfully of home. 'But look, dawn with russet mantle clad walks o'er the top of yon high eastward hill,' he intoned.[26] 'I only wished there was some great hill, some Mt Lofty, in the east over which the day would dawn.'[27] At 5.13am a shell instead whistled over from the west to burst unseen in the void below. Then another. The 5th Australian Artillery Brigade's third shot was the signal to go. Jacob saw flashes like summer lightning in the west. Soundless lightning. 'There was a rush of shells, a flash in front of us, and the sharp burst of shrapnel. No-one even winked. We knew they were on our side. The battle had begun.'[28]

More than 700 men of the 50th Battalion rose and marched towards the shellbursts. Bayonets were fixed but this was no charge – they kept time with the 50 yards (46 metres) a minute creeping barrage.[29] As they marched they beheld the pyrotechnics playing in the pre-dawn: flashes of red and streaks of blue and then the green of the Germans' SOS flares summoning their own artillery. And then, as the men descended into the maelstrom, white wasps of German tracer spitting through the night. On the left, Captain Churchill-Smith's D Company took machine-gun fire from the front, flanks and in lethal crossfire from posts in the two sunken roads running down the hill, a cemetery near the foot of the valley and ruined houses in the village.[30] One of the diggers called it a beehive.[31]

Firing their .303s and Lewis guns from the hip (a dangerous practice discouraged in the training manuals), the 50th Battalion plunged into the storm. Men of the first wave began to fall. A bullet thwacked into original Anzac Lance Sergeant Sydney Wills's leg. He was left for the stretcher-bearers. On the diggers went, hurling bombs and lobbing rifle grenades into the barricaded strongpoint on the left sunken road. The fire from that quarter ceased.

It was quickly clear that their leaders had underestimated the enemy's strength. The cemetery position near the foot of the valley was protected by wire and a high bank. More men fell. Private Allan Johnson, 25, a gardener from Hermitage in the Adelaide Hills, was riddled with machine-gun fire. Lance Corporal Jack Brakenridge, 31, was 'killed instantaneously by a machine-gun bullet' according to Sergeant Bernard Ryan, although Sergeant Ernest Smith said Brakenridge lived long enough for his mates to call for stretcher-bearers. Perhaps Ryan was softening the blow for Brakenridge's parents: they received full details from a 50th Battalion corporal. 'I myself being his brother have written home and told them everything about his death,' Corporal Hamilton Brakenridge, 22, told the Red Cross.

Lance Corporal Jack Brakenridge (AWM P09291.111).

The first man into Mouquet Farm never made it to Noreuil: as he lay dying in the ruined village's faint dawn shadow, Lieutenant Bill Hoggarth shouted 'go on, go on' when his men went to their stricken leader's aid. Go on they did. Killing Germans with bullet, bomb and bayonet, what was left of Hoggarth's 16 Platoon rushed through the cemetery to cross the fireswept valley floor and start up the facing slope into the village, 'going very fast so that the Germans had no more time than to bolt into the next house, or hedge, or sunken road, before they were routed out of that also'.[32] Captain Churchill-Smith and Lieutenant Waine led the second wave into the village, leaving Wilf Bidstrup's bombing platoon to deal with a second strongpoint in the sunken road on the left. 'I don't know how I got through,' Churchill-Smith said of the machine-gun fire. 'One bullet went right through my haversack.'[33]

Lieutenant Bill Hoggarth (AWM P09291.126).

Like Hoggarth, Private Robert Haines, 25, also urged his comrades to go on without him. He was dressing a slight wound to his arm when a big shell screamed in. Killed instantly by the tremendous concussion, he was found without a mark on him, save for the slight arm wound. 'Don't feel like going over,' Haines wrote in his diary on 1 April. 'Hope come out alright.'[34]

The D Company vanguard slogged its way through the foot of the ruined village to confront Germans emerging from their dugouts now the barrage had passed. Determined to avenge their dead mates, the diggers went to work with their bayonets. Although Australian training rather than bloodlust accounted for an unfortunate German killed by a soldier shouting a mantra imparted on the parade ground: 'In! Out! On guard!'[35]

It was a street fight straight out of the Wild West: Churchill-Smith shot two of the enemy with his revolver as he scurried through the village. There was no time to check whether his victims were wounded or killed, although Churchill-Smith said it was the latter: who would argue – the standard issue Webley might not have been the most powerful hand-gun in the world, but its .455 slug was larger than Dirty Harry's .44 Magnum.[36]

It appears officers of both sides drew their pistols in this close-quarters fight: German company commanders Lieutenants Eisenhardt and Steinhilber were killed in the village.[37] Two company commanders meant the Australians were up against at least two companies. This was no token German rearguard.

Emerging from the rubble, D Company burst into the open ground above the village and wheeled right as per the plan. The diggers dropped to their knees to shoot enemy troops fleeing across the fields to the German support line; those of the enemy unwilling to suffer such a fate were captured. D Company linked with the West Australians of the 51st Battalion on their left and pressed on for the objective road, some 550 metres distant.

Strongpoints and bunkers were not the only features missed by the pre-battle patrols and reconnaissance fly-overs. Approaching the objective Lagnicourt-Bullecourt road, Churchill-Smith's men came upon a shallow trench not marked on their maps. The 51st Battalion on their left was already deepening the part-finished trench, so Churchill-Smith told his men to do the same. The pick and shovel work was done under fire; Private Patrick Sheehan, 33, was shot in the stomach. The fire was too intense to risk hauling him out – he was too badly wounded to be moved anyway.[38]

It was now almost 6am and Churchill-Smith was anxious to tell Salisbury his company was digging in 100 yards (91 metres) short of the objective. But sending men back across the fireswept ground was to send them to their deaths; in any case, two D Company runners were shot at Churchill-Smith's side in the trench. D Company dug in, engaged the enemy to its front, and waited for Bidstrup's bombers to bolster its thinly held line.

They never came.

Lieutenant Bidstrup's platoon was reinforced by a few 'mopping-up men' detached to follow the attacking waves. Private Patrick Bennett, 26, a teamster from Millicent in southeast South Australia, was among them. In the advance he and two companions stopped to help Sergeant Hurtle Ayres, whose left shin was smashed by machine-gun fire. Seeing a group of hard-pressed Australians further down the hill, Bennett intrepidly – or perhaps blithely – joined them by crossing the sunken road via the enemy barricade. As he crossed he saw 40 Germans in the strongpoint below. The Germans sent out a scout, who was promptly shot by the Australians, triggering a fierce firefight.

Private Percy Prime, 23, worked his .303 bolt with the cool efficiency of a farmer from South Australia's wheat country, which he was.[39] 'What bombs we had were flung into the sunken road,' Prime said. The bombs ran out and soon the men were running short of rifle clips as well. Bidstrup's dwindling force was raked by a machine-gun deeper in the town; Anzac veteran Sergeant Henry Steuve, 22, was cut down by its fire. 'It was getting light, and when we could see we found that there were only about 20 of us left on our own,' Prime said. 'The rest of the battalion had somewhere or somehow disappeared.' Enemy bombers surged out of the bunker and attacked the Australian flanks. Fourteen of the remaining 20 Australians were killed or wounded, including Private George Watt, 30, a tyre repairer from Norwood in Adelaide, killed 'outright' by a grenade fragment.

The unwounded six, being out of ammunition and with no hope of escape, surrendered. 'The enemy … pretty well wiped D Company out,' said Private Percy Rehn, 28, another Anzac veteran who was taken prisoner with Bennett and Prime.[40] No surrender for Lieutenant Bidstrup. Cut off from the pack, he was shot multiple times. His corpse was ringed with dead Germans; his revolver empty, lying at his side.[41]

Lieutenant Wilf Bidstrup (AWM P09291.125).

The official Australian historian Charles Bean wrote that Bidstrup's Webley revolver was found with 'six empty chambers'. The Webley only has six chambers. Lieutenant Jose's Webley was found with five empty chambers. Yes, the deadly crossfire at the foot of the Noreuil valley accounted for the dashing young dux of St Peter's College. Jose's 1914 enlistment papers put him at 64kg; after enduring diarrhoea on Gallipoli, jaundice on Mudros and a frigid 1916/17 winter on the Somme, he cannot have weighed much more than that in April 1917. Yet Jose used the cannon (at 1.1kg unloaded, the Webley was a house-brick of a handgun) to deadly effect. 'Fighting like a tiger', Jose fell near Bidstrup, deep in the valley.[42]

The L'Hirondelle, as it 'flows' out of Noreuil (Andrew Faulkner).

Jose was born to lead and so he died, at the head of C Company's first wave. That Bidstrup and Jose were killed near one another showed that the left (D) and centre (C) companies' flanks were touching as they descended resolutely into the storm. Like D Company, Captain Harold Armitage's C Company also suffered heavily from machine-gun fire and faltered at thickets of wire deep in the valley. Shouting, 'Come on, Australians!',

Armitage rushed ahead of his men and led them through the wire.[43] Crossing the railway embankment and arriving at the L'Hirondelle River, D and C companies formed a rough line, hopped over the brook and followed the barrage flashes into the village. Fording a river sounds heroic, but barely a metre from bank to bank, the L'Hirondelle (translation: The Swallow) was no Amazon, so one river crossing did not a victory make.

From the high ground on the right, B Company's Private Gilbert Jacob saw a thrilling and indelible sight. Shell flashes momentarily illuminated men advancing through the 'field of ruined walls' below. 'It is hard to tell now from a dream … they were D Company and C, Armitage's men. For a moment I saw them by a bright flash, but the image is still clear and never to be forgotten.'[44] Will Longstaff never made it to Noreuil; if he had, this might have been the battle's *Menin Gate at Midnight* moment.

Like D Company on the left, C Company left parties to destroy strongpoints: bombers peeled off to deal with a post in the Noreuil-Lagnicourt road. With high barricades in a deep cutting about two-thirds of the way down the hill, this post appeared impregnable. Sergeant James Wilson, in charge of the company's last wave, sent his bombers in.

A six-man section sized up the forbidding redoubt. Under covering fire, Private Charles Washington, a 26-year-old farmer from unforgiving country north of Elliston in SA's far west, dashed up to hurl his Mills bomb. He was riddled with machine-gun fire and 'killed right out'.[45] The ground was too exposed to risk another flanking attack, so two privates hatched a plan. In the Australian vernacular, they would go at the bunker 'up the guts'.

As a native Dane, Joergen Jensen probably wasn't completely across the full canon of Australian vernacular, just as his Copenhagen birthplace transgressed the Anzac ideal. But Jensen *was* an Anzac: he served on the Gallipoli peninsula and was a certified larrikin – he was severely punished by the army for twice being AWOL. Under his forearm tattoos were muscles hardened by hauling rope on a River Murray paddle steamer and labouring in the industrial town of Port Pirie in SA's Mid-North.

Like his mate Jensen, Private Bill O'Connor also railed against authority. A free-spirited stockman from Burke and Wills country in the top left corner of NSW, O'Connor sprung from the pages of a Banjo Paterson ballad. He was a crack shot; as Jensen loaded up with bombs, O'Connor drew a bead on the German machine-gun team peeking over the barricade.

Crack! O'Connor shot the machine-gunner as Jensen leapt into the sunken road to go straight at the high barricade, brandishing a bomb in each hand. Crack! Crack! Crack! O'Connor worked the bolt as his mate hurtled forward. Jensen threw a grenade and, as it exploded, clambered up the steep cutting bank and onto the parapet. Drawing the pin of a third grenade with his teeth, he held both bombs high and (presumably after spitting out the pin) yelled at the wounded and dazed enemy below: 'Surrender, you bastards. You're surrounded by Australians!'[46]

A badly wounded Sergeant Andrew Johanson lay in the dugout with other Australians captured by the German garrison early in the battle. The Swede Johanson knew the Dane Jensen well. 'Don't throw it, Jensen,' Johanson said quietly. Jensen obeyed his sergeant and the Germans obeyed Jensen. Jensen might not have dared so mightily had he known 45 enemy manned the post he had charged in Australia's own Captain Winters-at-the-Crossroads stunt.

Germans in a trench some distance away had been shooting at a Stokes mortar team further up the hill – so much that the mortars had failed to knock out the post seized by Jensen. So, in a stroke almost as audacious as his grenade bluff, Jensen sent a prisoner to tell them to surrender. It worked. As the unarmed Germans walked towards Jensen and his small party, Australians oblivious to their surrender opened fire. Jensen leapt on the barricade and frantically waved his helmet to make his comrades stop. They stopped. Lightly wounded diggers escorted the prisoners up the hill, freeing Jensen and his mates to try to catch up with the rest of the company in the village.[47]

'Surrender, you bastards.' Joergen Jensen (AWM D00020).

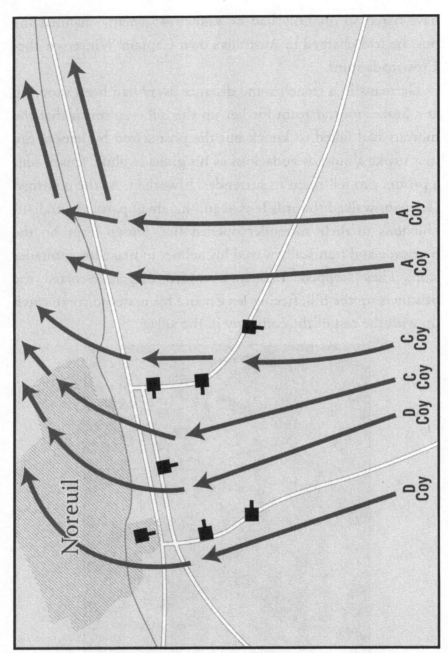

Machine-guns enfiladed D and C companies when they reached the valley floor.

Leaving Lieutenant John Edwards' mopping-up men to clean out houses, sheds and bunkers, Captain Armitage pressed on into the fields beyond Noreuil. Wheeling right as per his orders, he came under a 'dangerous fusillade'. His left flank still touched Churchill-Smith's right but he was too busy and too harried to realise that a gap had opened between his C Company and Captain Todd's A Company on the right. Armitage's men raced across the field, plunged into the unfinished German trench and dug for their lives to escape the hail of lead and iron.

The men were magnificent. As they rushed up to the half-finished trench, a bullet punched through Private Fred Woolfitt's right hand. But Woolfitt carried on. He could no longer fire his Lewis gun with his right hand so he dug with his left. And dug. And dug. When he could no longer dig, he took over a dangerous observation post. He did a job. He helped his mates. He carried on.[48]

After half an hour digging in under heavy fire, Lewis gunners Lance Corporal Percy Foster and Private Tom Bland were 'just settled in the trench' when 'a big piece of shell hit [Foster] in his face … killing him right out'. Foster was an Anzac original who was wounded at Gallipoli.[49] The company's Lewis gunners and their loaders and ammunition carriers suffered heavily – soon 31 of the 38 had been killed or wounded. 'But we still had all four guns,' Corporal Will Spurling said.[50]

The gathering light aided the enemy's artillery spotters on the spurs folding north-east towards Bullecourt. It was also snowing; a fact barely mentioned in the accounts written by the men in the front line – they were more concerned with shellbursts, snipers, machine-guns, dressing their mates' wounds, digging and the counterattack they knew would soon come. However, the snow was a problem for the stretcher-bearers: dead and wounded were quickly covered with white crusts, creating mounds 'just like newly formed graves' in the fields, Private Ernest March said. Each mound had to be checked to see if it contained the dead or the living. 'When we got back we had to go through all that again as the bodies we looked at before were covered with snow again.'[51]

There were far more wounded than there were stretcher-bearers, so volunteers were sought from the reserve B Company. Private William Potts, 28, stepped forward to help March. Once more into the breach went March's four-man team. A German marksman in a crater had no compunction shooting at stretcher-bearers – shot through the head, Potts was killed instantly, another volunteer was hit in the shoulder and a round glanced off March's Rising Sun badge on his collar. March and the other unwounded bearer loaded the surviving volunteer on their stretcher and scampered to the harbour of a sunken road. There they found ex-50th Battalion Captain Charlie Long, now in charge of the mortar battery. When March told the captain about the enemy rifleman, Long replied: 'I'll get him.' They all watched the Stokes bomb soar in a high arc, tumbling end-over-end onto the German's crater. 'That's the stuff to give the bastards,' March said while pumping Long's hand.[52]

Up at the front, C Company bearer Private Frank Lee[53] could not keep up with the casualties. No matter how hard they worked, and how many volunteered to help, the bearers could not get to every man. Lance Corporal Edward Budgen lay alone and apparently forgotten after being peppered with shrapnel as C Company fought its way into the village. Budgen lay in no-man's land behind the front line, a void between the front and rear. The main force had surged past the village but there was no line of communication to the jumping-off point. Like Gallipoli, the foremost troops had gone too far – and like Gallipoli, it was all part of the plan.

The diggers kept digging and shooting and watching their front. Armitage grew increasingly concerned about fire from across the river valley where the 52nd Battalion was supposed to be. And where was A Company? What was all that gunfire to his right rear? At 7am, as planned, the plane flew over the line and the Australians fired their flares, as planned, signalling all was well when it quite clearly was not. Armitage scribbled a message to be conveyed to Lieutenant-Colonel Salisbury by a no-doubt terrified pigeon (carried into battle by signaller Private James Downey). 'No touch with right. Enemy enfilading us from cutting on road from Lagnicourt. Enemy MG still active from railway cutting. Armitage, Churchill-Smith, Waine alright. Consolidation favourable.'[54]

Casualties unspeakable. Yes, he, Churchill-Smith and Waine were alright, but Armitage didn't tell Salisbury that Hoggarth, Bidstrup and Jose were dead. Nevertheless, Armitage rightly stressed the crucial point – the yawning gap on the right. Yet, before we address the mystery of the missing A Company, we must retrace our steps to the village, to tell the story of Lieutenant Edwards and the mopping-up men.

Private Joergen Jensen's section raced to catch up with the rest of C Company. They came upon small and isolated parties of mopping-up men crouching in the ruins and trading shots with Germans. Lots of Germans. The enemy seemed to be multiplying. Germans called their dugouts *caninchenlochen*, 'rabbit holes' – well, figures in field grey poured out of Noreuil's cellars like a plague of Australian rabbits. The audacious Jensen seized yet another prisoner, again using his impressive powers of persuasion to induce the German to divulge the location of an enemy strongpoint. However, there were too many strongpoints and too many Germans even for the mighty Jensen – it quickly became clear the town had to be retaken, if indeed it had been taken in the first place.[55]

Oliver Winter was in the village too. The baby-faced Anzac born and bred at the mouth of the River Murray was displaying a quality often ascribed to Australian bush soldiers – initiative. With so many officers and NCOs hit, Private Winter took charge of the men around him. While leading them through the ruins, Winter's rifle was shot out of his hands. He was slightly wounded and his rifle was wrecked: he clicked his bayonet out of its socket and set about hunting Germans with 17 inches of cold steel; the industrial war regressed 2000 years as Winter brandished his bayonet like a Roman with a short sword.[56]

Scattered throughout the broken houses, splintered trees and cratered streets, men like Winter were persevering and pressing on: D Company's moppers-up in the left half of the village and C Company's in the right, as per the plan. But you have heard about plans not surviving contact with the enemy? This plan had a quick death and was unmourned.

Many of D Company's moppers-up had been mown down at the south-western corner of the village; others were captured, as we have seen. C Company assigned 33 men to mop up its half of the village, but even if all 33 had made it to the town unscathed – which they had not – it was too small a force to prevail. Emboldened Germans emerged from the ruins to overwhelm the vastly outnumbered Australians.

When Lieutenant John Edwards marshalled his C Company bombers he counted only eight men. Picking their way through the rubble, Edwards' small force lobbed grenades through windows to silence machine-gun nests, and ratted out dugouts and cellars. Soon Edwards' command was reduced to two. 'I then came to the conclusion that there were too many Germans in the village for these two bombers and myself to cope with,' Edwards noted blackly. His two faced 200 or more of the enemy; the moppers-up were being mopped up.

The D Company men captured early in the battle were herded into a building. As soon as the Germans were sure they had gained the upper hand in the town, the prisoners were prodded at bayonet-point through Noreuil towards the German lines. Other Australians were collected on the way; shot once in the leg and three times in the arm, Private Fred Douglas had been written off. 'I saw Douglas lying dead in the sunken road,' a comrade said.[57] The very-much-alive Douglas was borne out of the village by his captured mates, a party that included Sergeant Walter Wood and Privates Patrick Bennett, Percy Prime, Percy Rehn, Albert Barratt, Walter Green and Norman Churchman.[58]

Pressing eastwards through the village, the Germans rolled up what was left of the C Company bombers, gathering more prisoners as they went. Private Reuben Starr, 31, an orchardist from South Australia's Riverland, was found with bullet holes above his left knee. A digger hoisted Starr onto his shoulders and the column of POWs marched on. Somehow, Jensen, Winter and Bill O'Connor escaped the German trap. Others made it halfway across the field towards the main body of D Company before being forced to the ground by machine-gun fire. Captain Churchill-Smith popped his head over the parados to shout encouragement. Keep coming! Only one man made it to the sanctuary of the D Company trench.[59]

Back on the eastern edge of the village, Lieutenant Edwards took stock of his resources. Dispatching one of his two remaining men back in the direction of headquarters with a message explaining the situation, he sent the other man forward to ask Captain Armitage for help. As Edwards waited, alone, the Germans surged out of the ruins, pushing their prisoners to the front of the column flowing down the valley towards where A Company was supposed to be. Human shields!

Edwards knew the Australian objective lay along the eastern road. If he could race the Germans down the valley, he could warn A Company. The whole of A Company depended on him. Not just A Company, because if the enemy turned the 50th's right flank, C and D companies would also be imperilled. As he scampered across the field, a machine-gun traversed in his direction and opened fire. Edwards kept going but was hit in the arm. He kept going. As did the Germans with their human shields, coming straight down the road behind him. He paused to bandage his arm in a crater, sharing this temporary harbour with a dead Australian sergeant. Where was A Company? Behind him the Germans tramped inexorably down the valley track.

Now it was only a short dash into the arms of his comrades. Rising again, Edwards sprinted across the open to drop into the sunken road. It was filled with Germans. Right where A Company was supposed to be.[60]

4

The lost company

Since the time of Sparta, the right of the line has been the position of honour. In classical times, the Spartans fought in phalanxes. The hoplites (infantrymen) bore their shield on the left arm and hacked and thrust with sword and spear with their right. Each shield protected two men – the bearer and the man on his left. The man on the far right was vulnerable. So the best man in the phalanx was placed on the right of the line.

Ergo, a military tradition had its genesis in a practical application. The honour of being on the right of the line survived to World War I (and beyond – in 1942 the 9th Australian Division was proud of its place on the right of Montgomery's 8th Army at Alamein).

At Noreuil, tradition, theory and practicality converged. For Captain David Todd's A Company on the right flank was set the hardest task. It had to plunge into the valley, stop and wait for the other two companies to pivot on its axis, then wheel right and fight its way to the objective road. It had to do all this under fire.

Whether A Company was the best in the battalion is unclear, but it had the senior commander. Of the battalion's higher-ranking officers, only Lieutenant-Colonel Salisbury and Major Loutit had more combat experience than Todd. Stepping ashore as a platoon commander in the first wave at Anzac, Todd was promoted to captain and led a company during his more than six months at Gallipoli. A dapper, diminutive soldier, Todd wore a Charlie Chaplin moustache and was a walking example of not underestimating the size of the dog in the fight: at five feet six and a quarter inches, he squeaked past the five feet six minimum when he joined up in 1914. At Noreuil, A Company was leavened with Anzacs and not lacking for leaders: platoon commanders Lieutenant Max Gore and Lieutenant Pat Auld had both won Military Crosses at Mouquet Farm.[1]

In an acknowledgement of A Company's mighty task, Salisbury thickened up its ranks with B Company's 7 Platoon under Lieutenant Alexander Mills. Mills was commissioned after being awarded the Distinguished Conduct Medal as a sergeant for bravery and leadership under heavy shellfire at Mouquet Farm.[2] Unlike the left and centre waves, A Company did not have to divert men into specialised bombing and mopping-up parties – trench mortars would deal with a machine-gun nest on its front. Two Vickers machine-guns were sent out to the far right flank. Todd's force did not want for firepower.

Starting on time and unmolested, A Company moved off at a 'leisurely pace'. Indeed, soldiers described the Stokes mortar bombs blowing up the strongpoint as the only sound disturbing the dawn calm. On the extreme right, Lieutenant Gore's 3 Platoon passed the smoking machine-gun nest. Poking his head over the parapet, Gore saw a figure in the murk. It was a bearded German with his hands raised. Gore shot him, justifying his action by recalling an incident at Mouquet Farm when he sent a prisoner to the rear under the guard of a single digger – and both were never seen again. 'I decided I wasn't having any [prisoners].'[3]

The benign start gave way to a cacophony. Up arced the enemy's SOS flares, momentarily bathing 200 Australians in a shimmering green. Tracers zipped and cracked, field guns barked from the black horizon, and men fell. Lance Corporal Ernie Goodes, 24, a veteran of Anzac, died quickly and quietly after taking a chunk of shrapnel in the abdomen. Noreuil was gathering a bitter harvest of Gallipoli men.[4]

It nearly gathered Lieutenant Auld, who was knocked out of the fight with a flesh wound to the upper thigh. Another Gallipoli man, 2nd Lieutenant Bernard Holloway, commanding the 13th Machine Gun Company's two Vickers guns, was shot in the foot (the Central Powers were attacking Holloway from top to toe – he was shot in the face at Gallipoli). Lieutenant Mills took a bullet in the arm soon after the hop-off, so, just a few minutes into the battle, Todd's complement of officers numbered two – himself and Gore.

So the men looked to their sergeants and corporals. Those who were left. Corporal Harold Harper was one of the first B Company men to be hit, killed instantly by machine-gun fire. The German who killed him homed in on the target – several of Harper's Lewis gun section were cut down. Lance Corporal Cornelius Shea was killed outright by shrapnel. Private Glen Jacob stepped over his mate and pushed deeper into the cauldron of fire.[5]

There was no time to stop and identify the dead, let alone bear them to the rear. When Private Clarrie Taylor was shot in the hip he remained where he lay. 'They wanted me to get up and go with them, but I could not walk so they left me.'[6]

Gore was having trouble getting his men to go with him too. After picking through a thicket of barbed wire, he dropped to his stomach and signalled for his platoon to follow. What happened next blows a hole in several leading myths – such as Australia's alleged universal and exclusive ethos of mateship and the notion that every digger was brave and noble.

Gore was shot. From behind. By an Australian.

Given the short range, and the fact the sun had now risen, it was unlikely that the man who shot Gore was *that* poor a rifleman. It might have been a stray round from further up the hill, but a later incident adds weight to the unpleasant probability that Gore was shot deliberately. As they advanced, a man lowered his rifle at his platoon commander and said: 'What sort of trap are you leading us into now, Gore?' So it appears Gore was fragged. The bullet passed through his thigh, missing bone and artery, enabling Gore to limp on, metaphorically as well as literally. 'I had always thought that a bullet would be like a red-hot poker ... instead, it was just a heavy blow followed by an immediate numbness.'[7]

A gap opened between the centre and right attacking waves. Maintaining touch was crucial but the separation was understandable in the chaos of a hard battle. Private Gilbert Jacob's line of B Company men, for example, drifted, corrected, and drifted again in the half-light and shellfire and smoke. Orders came from both sides but Jacob heard only the commands, he could not discern the words. Finding himself alone on a fireswept field, he lay down to shoot at a trench. 'I kept up a hot fire … and decided to give them a bomb.' He pulled the pin, ran at the enemy, and heaved the grenade with such effort that his helmet fell and rolled away. He chased his tin hat as the bomb burst just short of the enemy parapet. Losing his way, he fell in with a Vickers team, dressed a digger's wounded foot, then crept down the hill to trade shots with a large post 'doing deadly work' 50 yards away. 'I made one grey helmet spin high up in the air. It would have made a good souvenir, but I don't trouble much about souvenirs.'[8]

The right flank. Todd's force had to quickly pick its way through the barbed wire, advance to the valley floor, then wheel right to the objective (near the chalky cutting in the centre of the frame) (AWM E00506).

Despite its difficulties, Todd's force made it to the foot of the valley in good order. The platoons reorganised, turned right, and paused, as per the plan, to allow C and D companies to pivot on A Company's axis. The advance resumed down the valley with Gore's platoon on the right, straddling the Noreuil-Queant road. Accounts that boast of the men wheeling as if on parade do not say that this parade ground was anything but flat, had just been seized from the enemy, and was under fire.

The gap between C and A companies was closed when the men paused to reorganise before the battalion made its right turn. Indeed, A Company men reported the 'never-to-be-forgotten and wonderful sight in that grey dawn' of C Company advancing behind Captain Armitage across the slope on their left.[9] All was well as A Company started its 1000-yard advance to the Lagnicourt-Bullecourt road.

Almost immediately, as many as four machine-guns rattled into action from where the objective road ran up towards Lagnicourt. Gore took no pleasure from being right about the position of the machine-gun nest his patrol had found two nights earlier – this was the very same post. What had Todd told Gore the day before? 'The CO of the 52nd Battalion said that the machine-gun could not possibly be where you said there was one, because that is where his left flank rests.' Lieutenant-Colonel Pope's mythical machine-guns unfortunately fired real bullets. They set to work killing Australians.[10]

The guns started firing at long range but the further A Company advanced, the closer the diggers came to being enfiladed by their deadly fire. Just over halfway to the objective, the Noreuil-Queant road forked. The main body of A Company under Todd took the left branch and Gore the right. The further Gore's platoon went, the more men fell. Another German post lower on the facing slope added to the fusillade. Lance Corporal John Taylor, a 19-year-old clerk from Port Adelaide, was shot through the head and died instantly.[11] As the fire increased, Gore drew his flanking sections into the cover of the sunken road. 'We advanced in single file, crouching as we did so behind a bank varying in height from two to three feet,' Gore wrote. As they went, the bank tapered lower, and lower. Soon they were on all-fours. Then they were on their stomachs. Bullets cracked liked stockwhips overhead. Private Doug Coulthard had just finished dressing Sergeant Jack Mehaffey's wounded leg when Mehaffey was hit again, in the back. 'Doug, I'm settled,' Mehaffey said. And he was. 'He was very popular with everybody and was a good soldier,' Private James Medhurst said.[12]

The fire intensified. 'The crack of bullets was like a thousand deal fires in our ears,' a No 1 Platoon man recalled.[13] Machine-guns 'seemed to be everywhere … we seemed to be under fire from all sides', Private John Murphy said.[14] Gore ignored the throbbing in his leg to slither to the head of the platoon's line, encouraging his men as he went. He told them the 52nd Battalion would soon stream down and knock out the machine-gun nest on the hill, as per the plan. Presently, the head of the column inched its way into the crossroads where the Noreuil-Queant road met the Lagnicourt-Bullecourt road. The objective! Still there was no sign of Pope. Gore was seized with dread: 'A quarter of an hour went by, and then half an hour. Surely some ghastly mistake had not occurred in the staff work? Perhaps the 52nd Battalion had copped it in the neck from the same strongpoint? I searched my mind for a reason.'

Todd was asking the same questions as his column fought along the left branch of the road, becoming further adrift of Gore's platoon as he went; so that when he neared the objective some 100 metres of exposed field lay between the company's twin thrusts. Gore was worried about the gap too; he called for a volunteer to break cover and climb the steep bank on their left to seek the rest of the company. Up went Private Sam Searing, down came the machine-gun fire and down came Searing – falling when the ground beneath his feet was blown away by bullets. 'Not a soul in sight,' Searing told Gore.[15]

Todd's men were there alright, scattered in penny packets of three and four men in whatever cover they could find. Some were in the long triangle between the two diverging roads and some were in the southernmost part of the long and shallow trench stretching up and over the northern ridge – the one being occupied at about the same time by D and C companies out of sight over the curve of the hill. The main body of A Company was hunkering in the upper fork of the sunken road, where Todd made his HQ in a small dugout. The Lewis teams tried to silence the enemy's guns and the riflemen kept up a steady fire – but ammunition of all types was running low.[16]

The killing field: A German machine-gunner's view of the deadly triangle (the fallow paddock, centre frame). The car is where the roads to Bullecourt and Queant intersect (Andrew Faulkner).

Gore's casualties mounted. 'The enemy's fire was terrific,' Gore wrote. 'All we could do was lie on the flat of our stomachs and await the 52nd.' Still there was no sign of the 52nd Battalion, so

Gore had to be content with the arrival of a Lewis gun team under one of the bravest and toughest men in the 50th – Sergeant Bill James. After silencing one enemy gun with a quick burst, James sprung up to fire at another and was shot in the head. 'Look after me,' James said, before dying.[17] 'Certain death, and he knew it,' a comrade wrote.[18]

Sergeant Bill James (seated) (AWM P09291.090).

A Company had a strong contingent of men from the South-East region of SA. Sergeant Mehaffey was from Naracoorte. So were the Boston brothers; the ones who joined up on the same day and had consecutive regimental numbers. The unceasing fire cut down the elder Boston, Angus, 28. Helping him was suicide but Corporal Tom Boston, 25, had to help his older brother. He was shot at Angus's side. Both died.[19]

Corporal Tom Boston (AWM P09291.309).

Private Angus Boston (AWM P09291.310).

'You could almost feel the bullets whistling around you,' 2 Platoon's senior corporal Keith Tamblyn, 24, said. 'We couldn't do anything. If we moved we were shot.'[20] Todd's men had slightly more cover than Gore's exposed platoon – its branch of the road had a higher bank – but they were raked with fire from the same posts across the valley and faced frontal attacks from the objective road. Increasingly bold Germans were now close enough to hurl 'potato masher' grenades into the sunken road. The enemy sensed the weak point in the Australian line, so fed more men into the valley. Todd sent a signaller, Private Sid Ringberg, to seek help from Armitage but Ringberg was hit, his thigh fractured by a bullet. He started crawling to C Company's trench, unaware that C Company was fully occupied with its own troubles.[21] The battalion's centre and right thrusts had lost touch. A yawning gap opened in the Australian line.

'Todd's company arrived entirely alone.' This uncharacteristically short and blunt sentence in Charles Bean's *Official History* rams home the point. With enemy to its front and overlooking it from the right, A Company's position was precarious. Low on ammunition, greatly diminished by casualties, and with the 52nd Battalion still missing in action, it suddenly became a whole lot worse for Todd's beleaguered force.

For at that point the Germans started streaming out of Noreuil.

Todd rushed two Lewis guns to his rear to meet this new threat, but they could not be brought to bear without killing the prisoners at the head of the German column. 'If we had fired, our mates would have received our bullets,' 2 Platoon's Private Carmichael Anderson said.[22] The enemy seized the moment to stream out of its front line in the Lagnicourt-Bullecourt road. Out of ammunition, ideas and escape routes, Todd's force was overwhelmed. What was left of it. The survivors were taken at bayonet-point to the German support trenches. As they were led away, the spotter plane lumbered over to be greeted with 'success' flares from Armitage and Churchill-Smith. Some success – Todd's war ended at 7am.

The L'Hirondelle Valley and Queant Rd from the top corner of the Noreuil triangle. The enfilading machine-gun was in the objective road leading up the opposite slope (Andrew Faulkner).

Lieutenant Mills's 7 Platoon suffered badly throughout the action and many of the survivors taken prisoner were wounded, including Ernest Powell (shot in both legs), Glen Jacob (head wound), Roland Carter (shot in the left shoulder) and Frank Swanston (shot in the face). The prisoners joined the gaggle of D and C company men captured in the village and were taken under guard to the German front line.

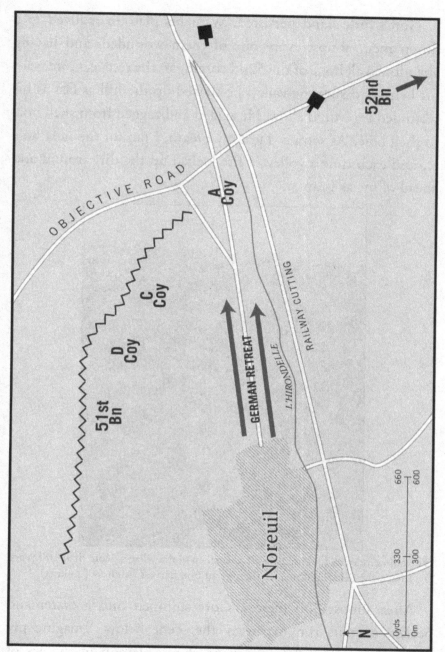

'Todd's company arrived entirely alone' – Charles Bean.

Gore's little band persisted. With his platoon reduced to a dozen men, almost every one of them wounded, and having abandoned all hope of the 52nd coming to the rescue, Gore went for help. Crossing the valley, he started up the hill as fast as his wounded leg would allow. He zigged and zagged from shell hole to shell hole. 'As soon as I got my breath, I ran for the next hole … and each time a volley of fire kicked up the dirt around and ahead of me as I ran …'

The objective road, looking back up the valley to the village. More than 100 years later, the fields continue to disgorge an iron harvest (Andrew Faulkner).

After almost 300 metres, Gore slumped into a crater and peeked over its rim to survey the scene below. 'Imagine my dismay when I saw the remnant of my platoon in the act of surrendering. I turned and looked despairingly up the hill in the direction whence we had hoped in vain for support … there was not a soul in sight, friend or foe.' Then, a stone's throw away, to the east, Gore saw one of his platoon surrendering to a German rifleman. 'Slowly, I climbed out of the shell hole and walked down whence I came and joined the rest.'[23] With Gore's surrender, A Company was struck from the battle map – it ceased to exist at 7.30am.

The Germans sorted their haul of prisoners. Five badly wounded men would remain until a wagon could be brought up to bear them to the rear. The five included Sergeant Walter Stanford, with an ankle wound that forced the later amputation of his left foot, Lance Corporal Henry Franklin, shot in the right thigh, and probably Private Sam Searing – Gore's volunteer lookout in the sunken road had been shot in the thigh later in the battle.

Gallipoli veteran Sergeant Henry Haythorne had been shot in both arms but could walk so was ushered into Gore's group of unwounded and walking wounded. Sergeant Stanford said Gore and the rest of his platoon were then 'marched off to Berlin'. The sad band comprised Gore, Haythorne, Corporal Tamblyn, Lance Corporals Stan Barnard and Hurtle Blake and Privates John Murphy, Haddon Bowen, Vivian Brown, Willie Clifford, James Medhurst, Carmichael Anderson and Albert Last. Brown (severe concussion), Clifford (groin), Anderson (neck) and Last (arm) were wounded.[24]

One of Todd's runners had slipped through the Noreuil noose. Private Arthur Hargrave arrived at the rear to pant the dreadful news – A Company was no more. And, moments after Todd's party was led away, C Company mopper-up Lieutenant John Edwards dived into his crater containing the dead Australian sergeant. It was the brave Lewis gunner, Sergeant James. Before they were taken prisoner, James's mates rolled him into the crater and used his corpse to hide his Lewis gun from the enemy.[25]

Germans flooded into the rent in the line to wedge themselves on either side of the river. The machine-guns that had wrecked Todd's force lifted their sights to the C and D company trench trailing away across the opposite slope. At about 7.30am, the enemy artillery started pounding the Australian line with high explosive and shrapnel. Under cover of this fire, the enemy started bombing up the Australian trench. Armitage and Churchill-Smith were outflanked, overlooked, outnumbered and outgunned. The Battle of Noreuil had turned in Germany's favour.

High on the southern ridge, not far from where A Company of the 50th Battalion began its descent into hell, the Vickers gunners of the 13th Machine Gun Company peered through the smoke in search of targets of opportunity. There, trailing down the valley, the machine-gunners saw a long line of retreating Germans and opened fire. 'Party of 150 enemy dispersed,' the Company's war diary recorded. 'Casualties inflicted unknown.'[26]

Charles Bean reckoned he knew. He estimated the machine-guns accounted for as many as 20 … Australians. Yes, as if Captain David Todd's men had not suffered enough, they were shot by their own countrymen while being led away by their German captors. 'Between 10 and 20 were shot down by the Australian machine-guns,' Bean declared. The men were hit 'just beyond the objective road'.[27]

Private Patrick Bennett, the D Company mopper-up captured early in the battle, had survived the slaughter on the extreme left flank and the perilous journey through the village – the last leg as a human shield. Now he was supposed to be safe behind the enemy's lines, his war over, he was being shot at by his own kin. 'While being taken back with a number of other prisoners our own machine-guns opened fire, killing eight of us. I took cover in a shell hole with Captain Todd, Sergeant (Lewis) Norman and Private Barrett (Albert Barratt), and we remained there until dark, when we attempted to regain our lines but were again recaptured.'[28]

Thank goodness for Private Bennett's testimony, because all Todd and Gore wrote in their joint report of the incident was this: 'On being marched back, our own machine-guns played havoc with us.' Private Albert Marks was also with Todd's group but his account also posed more questions than answers: 'After capture I was wounded.'[29]

A Vickers crew shoots at enemy aircraft over Noreuil. An Australian Vickers crew is credited with downing Manfred von Richthofen (The Red Baron) on the Somme in April, 1918 (AWM E00458).

We know men were killed in the 'friendly fire' fiasco – most likely eight men, given how the detail in Bennett's account gives it credence – but we don't know their names. Perhaps that is a good thing, given how the truth could only have exacerbated their families' pain. This might be why soldiers such as Private Tom Robinson declined to identify the dead: 'One man who I knew well was shot by our own guns,' Robinson said after the war.[30]

Perhaps we know one name. Because Private Bill Wheeler thought a dead mate deserved more than an anonymous death. 'We were marched to the rear and on our way Private J [John] Bath was killed.'[31]

At last, a name. A clue. Private John Bath, 37, was a fisherman on the Murray when he joined up in March 1916. He had tried to enlist earlier but was rejected on account of having defective kidneys. Much of his war was waged with illness – he was in and out of hospital with rheumatism, myalgia and mumps. By the time of the attack at Noreuil he appeared to be in good health – he had been back with the battalion for more than six weeks. Fit and healthy just in time to be killed by Australian machine-gun bullets.

The official records shed little light on how Bath was killed. His Red Cross file is prosaic: 'Killed in Action 2/4/17, previously reported missing.' Other than Private Wheeler's brief mention, there are no witness accounts of his death. The paucity of information raises the possibility that Bath might not have been killed by the Australian machine-guns – he might have been murdered after being taken prisoner.

How do we know this? Private Stan Coombs was part of the trench mortar team that knocked out the enemy strongpoints early in the battle. Like his commanding officer, Captain Charlie Long, Coombs had transferred to the 13th Light Trench Mortar Company from the 50th Battalion. He retained a close association with his old unit. When interviewed by the Red Cross three months after Noreuil, Coombs said: 'After they were taken and were in a German trench, orders were given by the Germans to the Australians "officers to the right, men to the left", and that after this order had been obeyed, the Germans turned a MG on the men killing several of them.'

Coombs's story is chilling but, emanating from 'two Tommies' who escaped, it is also third-hand.[32] As is Private Roland Riggs's account: 'One man escaped ... and reported that the Germans had turned their MGs on them.'[33] Third-hand accounts are unreliable. Yet there is no more credible source than Bean, who jotted the following in his notebook from an interview with an escaped 50th Battalion prisoner who was captured after being wounded early in the battle. 'He had been with Captain Todd's party. They were lined up by the Germans in the Sunken Road (the Lagnicourt-Bullecourt road). Captain Todd could talk a little German and was spoken to by a German officer. The German said something and Todd said "right turn" and moved the men along a bit. The officer said something else and Todd said "left turn", which brought them with their backs to the Germans. The Germans then suddenly opened on them with rifles. The line broke and ran for shell holes. Todd and another and this man were in one shell hole together. The Germans signed to them that they must come in. The wounded man asked them to stay with him – they would be safe, he thought – but they gave up.'[34]

So, where does the truth lie? We will likely never know. We do know that soldiers have been accidentally killed by their comrades since Stonewall Jackson was mortally wounded by a sentry after routing the North at Chancellorsville. Smoky, loud, often dark and usually terrifying, battlefields are confusing places. Add a dash of human frailty and accidents happen. It was not even the first time Todd and his fellows had been shot at by their own men – at the Anzac landing panicky troops disobeyed orders to hold their fire until daybreak. 'I told them again and again not to open their magazines,' a 9th Battalion sergeant said as he lay dying from a .303 wound on Plugge's Plateau.[35]

The anonymous machine-gunner who broke up the 'German' column was recommended for a decoration. It appears the recommendation was quietly allowed to lapse.[36] As for the allegations of a massacre, if it occurred it is puzzling that Todd did not mention it in his post-war report. Perhaps he just wanted to get home rather than front boards of inquiry. And, as we have seen, the Australians had no right to be holier than thou. Australians committed illegal killings: Turks were shot as they surrendered at Anzac and Gore's first act of his final battle was gunning down an unarmed German.[37]

For his last act as a fighting man, Gore contemplated killing a group of German artillery officers with the grenades he still had in his pockets after handing over his revolver to a German sergeant (who gave Gore a swig of cognac from a flask). 'I convinced myself that it would be wrong on two counts: Firstly, because my surrender had been accepted, and not refused as had been the case with the bearded German earlier in the morning. Secondly ... all the other men with me would pay for it with their lives as well.' Thirdly, and perhaps most importantly, he was too bloody scared to pull the pins and throw the bombs. He called over a guard, who 'gave a nervous laugh as he accepted them'.[38]

Private Gilbert Jacob was carrying belts of Vickers ammunition to the firing line when he came upon a wounded Australian near the river. The man told Jacob he had been taken prisoner with 12 others. 'As they were being hurried away, he heard a revolver shot from behind, and fell with a bullet through his leg. They left him there to perish.' After binding the man's wound, Jacob dragged him to a small hut out of the bitingly cold wind, retrieved his belts of machine-gun bullets, and resumed his journey to the front.[39]

How the 50th's prisoners of war died is important. But we don't even know their names. All we have is Private John Bath. He was listed as missing after the battle, which was changed to killed in action six weeks later. In February 1920, his mother Mary wrote to the authorities from her home in Renmark asking after his 'kit and personal effects' – she had received nothing and had heard nothing since being told he was dead two-and-a-half years earlier. She did not even know where he was buried. The army replied by saying it was searching the old battlefields for the missing men. Of his kit, there was no trace. No letters. No pipe. No shaving gear. There was nothing left of her son, not even a marked grave.[40]

5

A baton in every knapsack

Siegfried Sassoon's Sherston trilogy is a triptych of the Western Front's barbarity, inhumanity and stupidity; yet, Sassoon wanders from the bleak path to digress about bees fussing in blackberry patches, blackbirds singing in the undergrowth and similar idylls. He even birdwatches under fire: during an artillery duel at the Somme, Sassoon writes of larks that 'flutter above the trench with querulous cries, weak on the wing'.[1]

Turtledoves were on the wing at Noreuil on 2 April 1917. No querulous cries, only a whirring as they arced above D and C companies of the 50th Australian Infantry Battalion. The distinctive sound heralded death – because the 'turtledoves', as they had been nicknamed, were mortar bombs that fluttered like pigeons on the wing. Fired from a spigot mortar, the 1.8kg pineapple-shaped projectiles sprayed shrapnel that killed or wounded any living thing within a 15-metre radius. Invented by a Hungarian priest, the Priesterwerfer – officially

Granatenwerfer 16 – challenged British assertions that God was on their side.[2]

A Granatenwerfer mortar on display at Le Tommy café in Pozieres (Andrew Faulkner).

The German mortarmen set their sights to the absolute minimum – 50 metres – because that was all that separated the opposing lines. The pineapple bombs competed for air space with field artillery shells shrieking in from the distant east and stick grenades lobbed from the inner south. The Australians' shallow trench offered some protection to small arms fire but wasn't deep enough to protect them from artillery and mortars. Then, with A Company wiped from the map, the Germans poured into the Noreuil-Queant valley and started bombing up the Australian trench. While they did this, their comrades in the Lagnicourt-Bullecourt road blazed away with their rifles, chattered away with their machine-guns, and launched localised attacks. To suggest that Captains Jim Churchill-Smith and Harold Armitage were hard-pressed is like saying General Custer was in a spot of bother at Little Bighorn.

On the left of the 50th's front, Churchill-Smith's D Company was weakened by casualties – he lost the whole of 13 Platoon and two officers at the village – but with the 51st Battalion on its left and C Company its right, at least both flanks were secure. From his position above the valley, Churchill-Smith saw Captain Todd's force being cut down and then captured. An increasingly cocky enemy hoped D and C companies would soon suffer the same fate – Germans in the objective, Lagnicourt-Bullecourt, road climbed onto their parapet to signal Churchill-Smith to surrender. He told his men to shoot the arrogant Bosche back into their own trench. 'But I don't think our men are very good at sniping,' Churchill-Smith said. 'For they continued to sit up and beckon us, bold as brass.'[3]

With its section of trench angling closer to the German line as it trailed down the hill, Armitage's C Company was in a diabolical position. Armitage himself was wounded, but joined his boys on the parapet to add his service revolver to their dwindling firepower.[4] His 7am pigeon message reported that he was being enfiladed from the opposite hill and had no touch with Todd, but 'consolidation' was 'favourable'. When A Company's destruction left his right flank in the air, Germans launched determined attacks up his trench. Armitage sent his best NCO, Sergeant James Wilson, to push them back. Wilson was tough, experienced and respected: as a private, the Broken Hill train driver was in the first wave at Anzac. 'Take charge and hold on,' Armitage told his sergeant.[5]

Corporal Arthur Verrier, 21, was holding on. He was doing more than that; Verrier's section had tried desperately to bridge the gap between it and A Company. It gained ground, but too late to save Todd and his men. Here, at the epicentre of the battle, when the fight was in the balance, Verrier's little force refused to yield – even after its corporal was shot in the face.

Corporal Arthur Verrier (State Records of SA GRG26/5/4).

Arriving at a crucial time, Sergeant Wilson supervised as the men barricaded the trench. Still the Germans came. A fierce, close quarters bomb fight raged ... four enemy rushes were beaten back by Verrier's men, now reinforced by Lance Corporal Harold Pritchard's section.[6] Pritchard had taken over when Corporal Hedley Leverington, a 25-year-old grocer's assistant from Payneham, was killed. Corporal Frank Hudson, 21, had stepped up to replace Sergeant Peebles, who was killed by a shell before the battle.[7] All over the battlefield, lance corporals were filling the roles of corporals, corporals were replacing sergeants, and sergeants were leading platoons. Old hands from the Landing such as Sergeant Royce Spinkston gave the men heart in this dark hour.[8] If the Anzacs can take it, so can we. Inspired by their leaders, the men of the 50th drew on their training, experience, honour, discipline, fitness, courage and character to excel under the most murderous fire.

The 51st Battalion sent down extra Lewis guns and gunners to boost the firepower at the barricade. Or rather restore the firepower, as most of C Company's machine-gunners had been killed or wounded. Private Albert Lehmann, 20, was the last man of his gun team standing, yet inspired all around him by carrying on alone. It was deadly work: to fire, the gunners had to expose themselves to an enemy closing on two sides. Corporal Will Spurling spotted a forest of bayonets in the objective trench, less than 50 metres away. The enemy was massing for a frontal counterattack.

'They came at us shoulder to shoulder … I lifted my Lewis gun to the parapet and pulled the trigger. They dropped like hay before a binder from the fire from my gun. I stopped about 200 men and, talk about a heap of corpses, it was an awful sight. What I didn't get fled and they were shot down by rifle fire.' Spurling reckoned it would be all over for C Company if the Germans came again, as the Australian trench was 'full of dead and dying'. His battle was soon over in any case. A bullet creased his scalp and another thudded into his shoulder, pushing him back into the trench – where he was hit by shrapnel. Shrapnel from a drop-short shell. The thrice-wounded Spurling then *walked* to an aid post kilometres to the rear.[9]

Corporal Will Spurling (kneeling, right) in Morphettville camp, 1915
(Max Slee – VWMA).

Sergeant Roy Clark was digging in with his C Company platoon when Armitage hurried past to see for himself how Wilson and his men were faring on the right. '[Armitage] cheered the men with his quiet words as they dug in for dear life,' Clark said.[10] After surveying the scene, Armitage wrote another message for Lieutenant-Colonel Salisbury and handed it to a runner. Armitage reported that his left was secure, but the objective road was strongly held and the machine-gun fire from the opposite hill was raking his line. 'Position on right is precarious as he is in fair strength in gully and enfilades from right. Casualties increasing – casualties among Lewis gunners very severe. Two men per gun left. We are holding well and consolidation is proceeding favourably.' The message was marked 8.45am.[11]

A few minutes later Armitage was shot in the head. 'Watch the right flank,' he said to Sergeant Wilson, and then died.[12] Word spread along the line, eventually reaching Sergeant Clark's platoon. 'The depression was noticeable in the gloomy expression on every man's face,' Clark wrote in a letter to Armitage's father.[13] A depressed and decapitated C Company faced its ominous fate.

With Captain Armitage and Lieutenant Jose dead, and Lieutenant Edwards captured, command of the company fell to Sergeant Wilson. Obeying Armitage's final order, Wilson returned to the barricade, where he instructed the men to fall back about 30 metres. Arming his men with all the Mills bombs he could muster, and posting Lewis gunners on both flanks, Wilson waited for the next attack. When it came, the Germans were greeted by a 'shower of bombs' while the Lewis gunners hosed the top of the barricade. 'Not a German got over it,' Charles Bean wrote.[14]

The win at the barricade, coupled with Spurling's heroics with his Lewis gun, had bought the men time. Nevertheless, they could not hope to hold out on their own. Were their messages getting through? Why wasn't Salisbury sending help? And, most of all, the men of D and C companies – like their A Company mates before them – wondered when the 52nd Battalion would silence the infernal machine-guns dealing death from the opposite hill.

* * *

In the fields outside Vaulx-Vraucourt, one of those Pas-de-Calais towns which owes its double-barrelled name to a long-ago rural conurbation, the 50th Battalion's headquarters staff awaited news from the fight raging 3km to the north-east. Lieutenant-Colonel Salisbury, his second-in-command Major Loutit, adjutant Captain Fowler, and the rest of the HQ staff had to rely on runners, pigeons and a forward observation post for news. As we have seen, Salisbury had no hard information upon which to direct the men in at least the first hour of the fight. The battle was in the hands of his company commanders.[15]

A taciturn man, Salisbury was not one to be familiar with his men. He was, however, prepared to trust them – to delegate authority. Battalion signals officer and acting intelligence officer Lieutenant Herbert Carlton would be Salisbury's eyes and ears for the opening stages of the battle. Setting up an observation post and signals station on the southern ridge, Carlton came under artillery fire soon after the rifle companies attacked. Carlton was hardened to battle, having served more than six months on Anzac as an NCO with the 4th Light Horse. So he was undaunted as he closely watched the men's progress in the valley, feeding information to Salisbury and his staff.[16]

Carlton was the first to bring news that all was not well. From his own observation, and a message from the 51st Battalion, he gleaned that the village had not been cleared by the mopping-up parties. This was relayed to Battalion HQ before 7am, presenting Salisbury with a quandary. The three remaining B Company platoons comprised his reserve, a precious resource not to be precipitously squandered at the first sign of trouble. Keeping one platoon in hand, he sent the other two under Captain Harry Seager into the village. However, after receiving Armitage's pigeon message reporting trouble on the right, he played his last card – sending Lieutenant Esson Rule's platoon to find Captain Todd's missing A Company. A blacksmith from

Burra in civilian life who had risen through the ranks after landing at Gallipoli as a corporal, the tough, lean Rule, 22, was just the man for the rescue mission.[17]

Seager's force set off first. Plunging into the valley, it shook out into artillery formation but took casualties as it advanced through the curtain of shellfire draped across the upper slopes. Sergeant John Yeatman, 27, an Anzac veteran from Auburn in the Clare Valley, was knocked senseless by an explosion but dusted himself off and kept going, rallying his platoon as he went.[18] Arriving at the village, Seager's men set upon, and quickly overwhelmed, the only enemy they could find – small detachments of Germans guarding a few captured Australians. Other than that the village was deserted, the main body of Germans having withdrawn to the east with their prisoners. Seager set a course for the rattle of small arms down the valley.

Rule, meanwhile, found no sign of A Company when he arrived at the valley floor. There were, however, no shortage of Germans – his platoon was immediately embroiled in a fierce firefight. Rule was wounded in the foot and, like Todd and Gore before him, could not silence the machine-guns in the Lagnicourt-Bullecourt road and from the scrubby trees further down the valley. Craving news, Salisbury sent Loutit to investigate.[19]

Salisbury was fortunate to have a fighting soldier as his second-in-command. Because Loutit was more at home on the field of battle than in a chalet or command dugout. Short – at 5 feet 4 inches, goodness knows how he sidestepped the 5 feet 6 inch enlistment limit – compact, and with an innate military bearing, Loutit was renowned in the AIF for making it further up Gallipoli's confounding hills than any Australian on 25 April.[20]

Mentioned in despatches at Anzac, Loutit enthused that sniping Turks was 'better than shooting rabbits'. Now, aged just 23, the major was a combat veteran of the highest order. As he set off for the front, Webley at the ready, he was presumably attended by a retinue of headquarters privates. However, none of the accounts say he was accompanied – it would not surprise if he joined the battle on his own. He set off to find Rule, his old D Company comrade from the Landing at Anzac Cove.

Collecting a Vickers gun and its team and organising an ammunition carrying party on the way, Loutit arrived to find Rule wounded and his platoon beleaguered. As Loutit surveyed the scene, Rule was hit again – fatally. Loutit took charge. Seeing Germans marshalling in the left branch of the forked road to mount a fifth attack up Armitage's trench, he considered his options. He could wait for Seager's two platoons, which were on the way after finding the village deserted. But C Company was in grave danger, so he chose to attack with Rule's depleted platoon. Rather than charging headlong into the enemy's flank, Loutit instead coolly and quietly led the men along the right branch of the road, the route taken by Gore. The manoeuvre took the party *behind* the Germans. With hindsight, Loutit's reasoning appears straightforward: unsuspecting enemy combatants standing side-on were juicy targets – but unsuspecting enemy combatants standing with their backs to their foes were irresistible targets. Hindsight is all very well, but taking the men down a road strewn with A Company dead – and still overlooked by enemy machine-guns – was an audacious stroke by Loutit, who gambled on the Germans' fixation with destroying C Company. All went well at first; Loutit's men were undetected as they crept down the sunken road and clambered to the top of the bank.

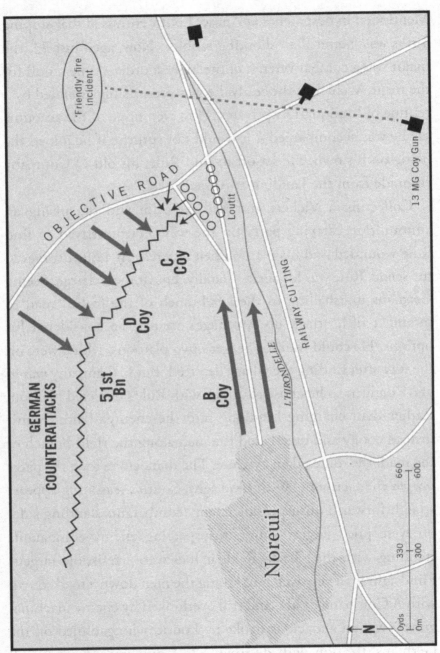

'Friendly' fire incident

13 MG Coy Gun

OBJECTIVE ROAD

Loutit

C Coy

D Coy

51st Bn

GERMAN COUNTERATTACKS

B Coy

L'HIRONDELLE

RAILWAY CUTTING

Noreuil

660
600

330
300

Oyds
0m

N

Loutit's bold stroke, and the 'friendly fire' incident.

Each man was allocated a target. On Loutit's command, a volley of .303 bullets thudded into the Germans' backs. Dead and wounded Germans slid down the bank, out of sight. Coupled with Sergeant Wilson's tactical withdrawal at the barricade, Loutit's masterstroke eased the pressure on C Company – there were no more attempts to bomb up the Australian trench.[21]

Loutit's bank (right). The opposite, low, bank gave A Company scant cover as it advanced down the valley (Andrew Faulkner).

However, now they had been seen by the Germans up the valley and on the right slope. The enemy's machine-gunners lowered their sights to the road where they had scythed through A Company a few hours earlier. Leaving a Lewis team at the Noreuil-Queant-Lagnicourt-Bullecourt crossroads, Loutit shifted his men back to the crater at the fork in the road. By the

104

time Seager arrived with his two platoons, the heavy enemy fire had also forced the Lewis team back to the main body at the crater.[22]

Still there was no sign of the 52nd Battalion on the right, so the yawning gap either side of the valley remained. The 50th's orders – seize the Lagnicourt-Bullecourt road – were unchanged, so Seager attacked with his two relatively fresh platoons. Once more into the breach went the Hungry Half Hundred, what was left of it.

The rattle of German machine-guns was subsumed by their field guns and 5.9-inch howitzers – B Company advanced into the deadliest fire yet encountered by the Australians in the battle. Seager's men didn't waver. Concussed in the advance down the hill, Sergeant Yeatman remained at the head of his platoon despite being wounded a second time in the valley. Corporal Halcro Main, 32, a Glasgow bank worker who migrated to Adelaide in 1911, was hit twice yet kept encouraging his section until hit a third time.[23] Once again, the battalion's NCOs were the taut strings that held the company together.[24]

Nevertheless, the quality and quantity of leaders is immaterial in a broad daylight attack across observed ground against a skilled enemy. Seager's men were forced back just short of the objective road. Private John 'Skeet' Mullins, 25, from North Unley, was riddled with machine-gun bullets trying to rescue wounded comrades.[25]

Something caught Lance Corporal Clem Grant's eye in the left branch of the sunken road. It was an officer's webbing and equipment – closer inspection revealed it was Captain Todd's webbing and equipment. Grant was holding Todd's revolver when a bullet punched through his lung.[26]

Seager rallied for another attack but it was also repelled. B Company switched from attack to defence. A Vickers, probably the one collected by Loutit, was brought down to cover the valley: Seager detailed infantry soldiers to assist its solitary gunner – the rest of his team had been killed or wounded.[27]

By noon the battle was seven hours old. Both sides paused to take a breath. Loutit didn't believe in taking breaths; his decisive action in the valley had turned the battle, yet to furnish Salisbury with a full report, as ordered, he needed to keep moving. Entering C Company's trench, he traversed the front line, organising and rallying the men, before leaving the trench via the 51st's positions on the crest of the northern ridge.[28] From there he descended into the village, crossed the river and hurried to an advanced signals station set up by Lieutenant Carlton at the sunken road post seized by Jensen. Loutit called Salisbury via a newly laid telephone line, but the CO recalled him to battalion HQ to report in person.[29] Loutit covered as much ground at Noreuil as he did in reaching the Third Ridge on 25 April 1915.

Seager and his men watched their front, casting an anxious eye at the machine-gun post on the hill. Presently they saw heads bobbing over the lip of the sunken road – Germans heading down for ammunition. Sergeant Fred Watson, 22, of Kent Town, ordered his men to open fire. Such was the quality of Australian marksmanship, only one of the Germans made it to his lines – and he was shot on the return trip back up the hill. Its ammunition exhausted, the machine-gun nest, at last, fell silent.[30]

Swords, pikes and muskets at the ready, Captain Harry Seager's antecedents spring from the pages of *Deeds That Won the Empire*. Seagers sailed with Drake against the Spanish Armada and charged with the Light Brigade at Balaklava. A Seager knight lies with medieval warrior kings in York Minster. Harry Seager's father Clarendon was a captain in the 8th King's Royal Irish Hussars before migrating to Australia. If Harry Seager ever contemplated straying from the martial path, his full name reminded him he was born to soldier – and Harold William Hastings Seager, aka 'Daredevil Harry' for his exploits at Gallipoli, was doing his ancestors proud at Noreuil on 2 April 1917.[31]

Captain Harry Seager (AWM P00030.001).

After leading his men in two failed attempts to seize the Lagnicourt-Bullecourt road, Seager reconnoitred the length of the 50th Battalion's front. Arriving back in the valley, he messaged Salisbury, saying he would 'have a shot' at seizing the far end of the triangle of roads if given artillery support and a fresh company on his right flank. Salisbury had no fresh companies, and it was plain the still missing in action 52nd Battalion could not be relied on to do what it already should have done. Salisbury declined Seager's request.[32]

Salisbury was content for Seager's men to cover the gap in the line with their machine-guns. For although there were signs the Germans were conceding the battle – after slackening before noon, their artillery fire ceased at 1.45pm – the threat to the Australians' hard-won gains remained. Sure enough, about 5pm grey figures were seen massing in front of the 50th Battalion. Surviving officers and NCOs scrambled for their SOS flares and the counterattack was quickly broken by an emergency barrage. Then, at 8.10pm, waves of infantry flowing over the eastern hills were also hit hard with a rain of shells. Delaying actions? The Germans were hotly contesting the open ground beneath the Hindenburg Line's ramparts.[33]

Night fell and in a thickening snowfall, D and C companies trickled out of the front line, handing over their trench to a company of the reserve battalion, the 49th. Seager's B Company remained in place and active on the right, Sergeant Fred Watson leading a patrol up to link with the 52nd Battalion. Two posts filled the gap on the right at last. Reconnoitring for a planned dawn attack, Seager led a patrol up the northern, or left, branch of the forked road at 2.30am. All was quiet so he kept going – and found the Lagnicourt-Bullecourt road empty.

He brought men up to the trench and the following day the 49th and 51st also found the Germans opposite their section of trench had gone. The whole line moved into the objective road.

On the night of 3–4 April, Private Alex Young, 19, from North Adelaide, led a patrol that sallied more than a kilometre into no-man's land. Young's daring, skill and dedication enabled the whole line to push forward another 1.5km – the final jumping-off position for the upcoming First Battle of Bullecourt.[34] In this sector, at least, the *Taking of the Outpost Villages*, as Bean called his chapter of the *Official History*, was over.

* * *

The men were warned to beware of German boobytraps in the newly won trenches. Shovels, stoves, telephone lines ... ordinary objects were rigged with tripwires and detonators and fuses.[35] There were other surprises too – Australian voices. Sergeant Walter Stanford, Lance Corporal Henry Franklin and two or three other badly wounded A Company men were found in a dugout near the crossroads at the foot of the valley. When they marched Gore's party away, the Germans had promised to return with a wagon – it never came.[36]

A patrol near the Lagnicourt-Bullecourt road heard a very Australian-sounding German voice: 'Mercy, Kamerad.' It was a wounded A Company man, who, having escaped the POW massacre, covered himself with snow and lay doggo for two days and nights. All done in, he surrendered when he heard the 'German' patrol. The digger who found him replied: 'Who the hell are you?'[37]

Back at battalion HQ, the 50th tallied its battle booty: 76 prisoners, two machine-guns, two trench mortars, four Granatenwerfer mortars, many rifles, most of which were brand new, revolvers and 'well-oiled' and 'bayonet-like' daggers 'for storming purposes'. The loss of four bugles and three bicycles presumably did not significantly damage the German war effort.[38]

If recording captured bicycles and bugles sounds like a line from *Blackadder*, then the 4th Division report – tapped up in Bapaume, 10km to the rear – might have been dictated by General Melchett: 'Attack carried out on Noreuil. This attack was completely successful.' At 9.40am on the morning of the battle, with A Company recently annihilated and the rest of the battalion fighting for survival, the division received message of congratulations from General Birdwood. What ho![39]

Compare and contrast the missives from the distant brass with the private soldier's harsh reality. Private Gilbert Jacob had covered a lot of ground after attacking with the right wave. Up and down the hill he went, shooting, bombing, dressing wounded men, carrying ammunition and getting lost. Collected by Loutit, he was led to C Company's trench, where he was wounded yet remained at the front until the battalion was relieved. 'I was limping home in the dark behind all the rest, tired, wet, and covered from head to foot in mud.'[40]

The bedraggled remnant of Seager's company rejoined the battalion at its bivouac near Vaulx-Vraucourt. Lightly wounded men who had remained with the company reported to the battalion's regimental medical officer, Captain Harold Powell, 30, of Malvern, at the aid post near battalion headquarters. The more seriously wounded had been evacuated via a wagon station in the L'Hirondelle Valley west of Noreuil to the 4th Field Ambulance's dressing station in a distillery behind Vaulx-Vraucourt. From there they were taken by ambulance to the main dressing station in Bapaume and thence by train to hospitals at places such as Rouen. The lucky ones sustained a wound not too serious to be life-threatening, but bad enough to be sent to 'Blighty'. It was not uncommon to be snug in a London hospital bed within days of being wounded. The charnel-house battles at Fromelles and Pozieres had created an industrial-scale efficiency mirroring the mechanical methods that did the maiming.[41]

Corporal Will Spurling's experience was instructive. Wounded in C Company's section of trench, Spurling walked out of the line to an aid post kilometres to the rear. Passing through several dressing stations, he was in a hospital in the port city of Boulogne by 5 April. A bullet was removed from his shoulder the following day, and he was soon on a hospital ship to Dover and then a train to a London hospital. 'All the way over from France the people were very good and could never do enough for one,' Spurling wrote in his diary.[42]

Many men were missing. Jensen and O'Connor, the intrepid C Company men who seized the deadly German post in the central sunken road, were added to the long tally of missing until … they emerged from the smoke the day after the battle. Side by side, as usual.[43] C Company CSM Alfred Bridley gathered them into the fold as he tried to fashion Armitage's survivors into a fighting force.

As the shattered battalion assembled outside Vaulx, Anzac veteran Private Harold Willmott, 28, and a few mates volunteered to collect the dead after dark – the enemy's artillery made it too dangerous during the day. Out they went, wondering which of their comrades lay under each little mound of snow. The dead were gathered and buried next to the sunken road that led down to the south-west corner of the village. It was a convenient and apt location – this was where Bidstrup's 13 Platoon was wiped out early in the battle. 'We made a little cemetery … Fritz shelled us several times while we were digging the graves,' Willmott said.[44]

Willmott and his mates had a hard time accommodating all the dead in their chosen rectangle of French field as, according to Charles Bean, 'five officers and over 90 men' of the 50th had been killed. Ninety-five men of the battalion lie in the cemetery. All the unit's dead in one cemetery? War is seldom so neat. And there was nothing neat about Noreuil.

As the men trickled back, the company HQs started the grim accounting – except A Company HQ, as it had no company to count. Captain Dick Wilton returned from a training school to news five of his fellow officers were dead and three were missing – Wilton was greeted by a burial party presenting him with Sergeant Hedley 'Ned' Joyce's personal effects.[45] Welcome back, sir, sorry sir, but poor Joyce and a few others have gone west.[46]

It was soon clear the death toll was north of 'five officers and over 90 men'.[47] Yet, divisional headquarters said the attack was 'completely successful' and General Birdwood conveyed his congratulations. All the airbrushing, soft-soaping and back-slapping by chalet-skulking, claret-quaffing warriors cannot bring men back from the dead. Men owed the truth were instead eulogised with lies by those who sent them to their graves. Consider how Brigade Major Roy Morell, in an upbeat after-action report flowing with superlatives, wrote that the brigade's estimated casualties were 351.[48] That's 351 killed, wounded and captured for the whole brigade of four infantry battalions and all their supporting arms. This libelled the dead – Bean reported the 50th Battalion alone had 360 casualties, which was too low in itself, as we are about to see.

6

The reckoning

'The Battalion suffered very heavy casualties amongst Officers,' Lieutenant-Colonel Salisbury wrote after the battle. He might have written that the battalion suffered very heavy casualties amongst everyone. Recording that 96 men of the 50th had been killed and four had died of their wounds, the sting was in the tail of Salisbury's after-action report: 'Of the missing, 1 Officer and 28 men are believed killed.'[1]

So, if Salisbury was right about the 'believed killed', 129 were dead. On the other hand, he put the number of prisoners ceded to the Germans as 62, which was a significant underestimate. The battalion moved on to other fronts and fresh battles, leaving its Noreuil casualties unreconciled. Officially, the dead numbered 100. Yet by closely examining the Australian War Memorial's Roll of Honour, the National Archives' collection of personal service records, the Commonwealth War Graves' records, the battalion's Field

Returns and the Red Cross's interviews with surviving soldiers, we can divine a death toll.

One hundred and forty-one men of the 50th Battalion were killed in action or died of wounds sustained at Noreuil. Of those, four were killed by shells or while on patrol in the days before the battle, 122 died on 2/3 April, and three died of their wounds or from shelling in the week after the battle. Eleven more died of wounds between 9 April and 17 June. Others surely succumbed to their Noreuil wounds in the months and years that followed, but it is harder to attribute their deaths to Noreuil, so they are not included in the 141. The last man whose demise can be directly sheeted to Noreuil is Corporal Will Spurling, the C Company machine-gunner who mowed down an enemy counterattack then walked out of the line with a head wound, a German bullet in his shoulder and British shrapnel in his back. Spurling died in an army hospital in Weymouth on the Channel coast on 16 August. Officially, the cause of death was septicaemia – blood poisoning from a scratch – but he died with shrapnel still in his back and hope in his heart; his last diary entry read: 'We can see miles out to sea here ...'[2]

About 190 men of the 50th were wounded and almost 90 were captured at Noreuil.[3] According to Charles Bean, the battalion sent 750–800 over the top on 2 April.[4] So, if 410–430 men were killed, wounded, captured or missing, that equated to a 52–56 per cent casualty rate – meaning the 50th was not so much decimated as dimidiated. The percentage matched the slaughter at Fromelles the previous summer, the exemplar of Australian loss and waste.[5]

The Bostons of Naracoorte, killed side-by-side in the valley, were not the only brother casualties. Private Ernie Norman was killed and his brother, Sergeant Lewis Norman, was taken prisoner. The Shadgett family of Parkside mourned the dead Alan and worried about the captured Ken. With almost all the 50th's complement coming from South Australia, population 440,000 in 1914[6], familial links ran through the ranks: cousins Private Mick Smith and Private Joseph Woodgate, both of Echunga in the Adelaide Hills, were dead; and Private Joseph James Earls, No 3804, of Callington, KIA at Noreuil, joined his cousin, Private Joseph Clement Earls, No 3803, also of Callington, on the Roll of Honour. Joseph Clement had died the previous August from wounds sustained at Mouquet Farm.

The five Norman brothers of Yahl, South Australia. Lewis (second left) was captured at Noreuil and Ernest (standing, centre) was killed there (AWM P05517.001).

Noreuil joined Mouquet Farm as a dreaded word in the Harvey family. Private Ernest Harvey, 27, of the 50th Battalion, was buried where he fell, killed by a shell between Pozieres and Mouquet Farm on 16 August 1916. Eight months later James and Martha Harvey received a second telegram – Private Hurtle Harvey, 20, of A Company, 50th Battalion, had been killed by a shell at Noreuil. Both boys listed their occupations as farmers – was that the end of the line for the Harvey dairy farmers of Prospect Hill, rolling, high-rainfall hills 50km south-east of Adelaide?[7]

Of the battalion's 141 fatalities, 25 men were Anzacs, including 12 original Anzacs. A platoon of Anzacs dead. All that knowledge accumulated in two years of fighting – gone. Everything they had to teach those who followed – gone. Their powers of inspiration on the field – gone. The battalion could have done with another 25 old hands in the fights to come at Ypres and back at the Somme. All for a ruined village, several acres of farmland and a mention in Field Marshal Sir Douglas Haig's despatch.[8]

Private John Hunt was wounded at the Landing but survived Gallipoli. He was wounded at Mouquet Farm but survived the Somme. Noreuil was a battle too far for the 23-year-old labourer from Dandenong in Victoria, but no account survives of the circumstances of his death, other than he belonged to A Company. Nor do we know how migrant Finnish labourer and original Anzac Private Karl Ljung, 24, died at Noreuil. Nor Private Nick Herring, 20, the Anzac who told his officer to 'go and get fucked' in Egypt. Nor Private Clifford Goode, who landed at Anzac with Armitage and fought and died under Armitage in C Company. Nor Private Thomas Murrin, the 34-year-old miner who was sent back to the trenches after being buried by a shellburst at Mouquet Farm. We do know how Lance Corporal Ralph Mann, 29, died – of wounds from a high explosive shell. Mann was hard to kill: he was shot in the left thigh and right arm at Gallipoli and suffered wounds to both hands at Mouquet Farm.[9]

Continuing in the 'men as materiel' vein for a moment, the quality of men lost can be gauged by examining the dead's ranks: six were officers – all company or platoon commanders, nine were sergeants, eight were corporals and 17 were lance corporals. The nine sergeants included six Gallipoli veterans: Bill James, the defiant Lewis gunner killed at the malevolent fork in the Noreuil-Queant road; Henry Steuve, gunned down with his D Company platoon on the left; Sydney Wills, 'hit in several places' in the race to the village; Joseph Peebles, killed on the southern ridge before the attack[10], Port Adelaide labourer Charles Hendry, probably in 13 Platoon's attack on the bunker on the left; and, the man whose lyrical account of the Landing at Anzac Cove graces the start of this book: 'I never gave them time to train a rifle on me,' Henry Cheney wrote of the first day at Anzac. Mercury himself could not have side-stepped the tracers zipping across the Noreuil valley.

In *Lost Boys of Anzac*, historian Dr Peter Stanley hunts the tangled hills and steep gullies for the men of the first wave killed on 25 April 1915. Determining that many had no known grave, Stanley calculated the first wave death toll to be 101 – 40 fewer than the 50th Battalion lost at Noreuil. Now, almost two years later, Cheney joined his comrades in the ranks of the forever young. For, like so many of the lost boys of the Landing, Cheney disappeared. We know he belonged to C Company, but there is no Red Cross file explaining his fate and he has no known grave. There is a further complication – he is both 'Known unto God' and listed as buried somewhere in the Noreuil cemetery. It appears his cross was destroyed by a shell later in the war and the exact plot was never recorded. Cheney is Noreuil's unknown soldier.

He is, however, not the only one who is Known unto God. Twenty others killed in the attack have no known grave. We know how and where some were killed: Lance Corporal Ernie Goodes, for instance, by shrapnel early in A Company's advance; Sergeant John Mehaffey, shot twice as Gore's men slithered along the valley road; and Lance Corporal Jack Brakenridge, killed instantly by a machine-gun bullet near the German cemetery – but we know not where they lie.

Yet didn't Brakenridge's brother, Sergeant Hamilton Brakenridge, tell the Red Cross he was present when Jack was buried? When the Red Cross wrote to Hamilton many months after the battle, it was clear that Jack's burial details were lost in the fog of war. Hamilton wrote back to say his brother was buried with 'many others including officers of the same battalion … there was a cross put up for all the brave fellows that fell that day and a little cemetery made'.[11] So perhaps Jack lies with his mates in the Noreuil cemetery.

Corporal James Murray might lie with them. More than a century ago a clerk inked 'Buried at Mil. Cem. Noreuil' on his file but officially Murray is Known unto God. Murray and Private Sydney Mace are lost in another way – they are Lost Diggers of Vignacourt; their photos are among a trove of 4000 lithographs and glass-plate negatives discovered in an attic of the French village Vignacourt in 2011. Murray and Mace appear in a group shot alongside a battalion-mate who later deserted and another awarded a Military Medal but who died of wounds sustained at Fricourt in November 1916. Three dead men and a deserter …[12]

(Back row, left-right) Private Arthur Hewitt, Private Sydney Mace (KIA, Noreuil), and Private William Hodgens MM (died of wounds, 9 December, 1916). Corporal James Murray (KIA, Noreuil) is seated (AWM P10608.001).

Fragments of information survive to help us know something, anything, about the Noreuil dead. As we have seen, being a company runner was a fraught occupation on 2 April. A dead runner was found with Captain Todd's undelivered message raising the alarm about A Company's desperate plight. Captain Churchill-Smith wrote that two runners were shot at his side; one of these was likely Private Walter Holman, 30, a farmer from Balaklava north of Adelaide, because he is listed as a D Company man in the Field Returns and his mother Mary wrote he was a runner in a Roll of Honour circular returned to the authorities. But we know not where he lies.

One of the more beguiling men of the battalion also is Known unto God. A station hand, a Gallipoli man, and apparently a larrikin – he was stripped of his corporal stripes for disobeying an officer – this lost digger of Noreuil was an archetypal Anzac. Archetypal except for his uncommon name: it seems Private Prince Charles Edward Begley's parents were royalists.[13]

Privates John Joseph Dwiar, 27, and John Francis O'Rielly, 21, were likely less inclined to the monarchy. Dwiar and 'Jack' O'Rielly, who also answered to Paddy and had a strong Irish brogue, were collected by the same burial party and interred together in the new cemetery. Multiple witnesses accounts indicate the pair was collected as quickly and cleanly as they died – both shot through the head. 'Poor old Jack was knocked clean out,' Private Allan Wasley said. Being retrieved from the field and quickly buried did not, however, rule out administrative error – both men were initially posted as missing.[14]

Private Clarrie Fischer, 21, a labourer from Two Wells, north of Adelaide, was among the volunteers who combed the cratered fields and village rubble for their dead friends. Working mostly at night, they gathered their mates' bodies amid desultory enemy shelling, piercing wind, and 5°C temperatures. Lance Corporal Harry Simmonds and Private Alfred Marsh joined Fischer and Harry Willmott in digging the graves while ducking the shellbursts.[15] The burials were supervised by 2nd Lieutenant Edward Price, a newly arrived reinforcement who was either part of the 'left out of battle' group or was attached to battalion headquarters during the attack.[16] The grisly work continued for at least four nights: on 5 April the gravediggers were driven to cover by artillery fire; on 6 April another 40 men were brought in for burial.[17]

Men who fought and died together were collected and buried together. Ned Joyce, Harold Hughes, Alfred Tucker and Gethen Turpin were retrieved from the A Company sector on the right, and buried by men of their own company. '[Tucker] was taken out at night and buried at Battalion headquarters,' Private John Kloss told the Red Cross. 'There was a small cemetery there, [or] rather a cluster of graves.'[18]

Private Harold Hughes (AWM H05570).

It appears the Protestants, at least, were given Christian burials, for Anglican Brigade Chaplain Donald Blackwood conducted the Methodist Hughes's funeral.[19] It follows that Blackwood buried the Methodist Sergeant Joyce as well. Joyce was a 'real true solid Christian [who] had a most distinct influence on the fellows',

Private Arthur Riley said. 'Many is the chap who would have gone to places that were no good to him but for Joyce. He was a very jolly chap with a bright word always ready for everybody.'[20]

It is probable that at least some of the Catholics received the last rites from the tireless and exceedingly brave Irishman, the Brigade's Catholic Chaplain Michael Bergin. 'We non-Catholics deeply appreciated his beneficence and his concern on our account ... [he] deservedly had the respect, admiration, and affection of all,' Pat Auld wrote.[21]

Even with all the witnesses to Joyce's death and burial, including Captain Dick Wilton, who was given Joyce's effects after returning from an officers' school, Joyce was initially listed as missing. His death was later confirmed by A Company CSM Rupert Francis, who was likely in the 'left out of battle' group with C Company CSM Bridley. After landing as a private at Anzac, Francis had risen through the ranks to be promoted in the field to Warrant Officer Class 2 on the Somme in the winter. With Todd and Gore missing, Auld in hospital, and most of A Company dead, wounded or captured, Francis was a CSM without a company to direct or officers to obey. He busied himself by investigating and recording when, where and how his men were killed.

Scores of promotions were rushed through to upfill for the casualties. Salisbury directed Wilton to take over what was left of A Company, while 2nd Lieutenant Price was sent to D Company and Lieutenant Joe Waine took over Armitage's C Company.[22] Gallipoli hero Joe Weatherill DCM was promoted to Warrant Officer Class 1 and appointed Temporary Regimental Sergeant-Major – 'temporary' was to mean eight months in Weatherill's case. Private soldiers only had to emerge from Noreuil unscathed to be in the running for promotion: the rabble-rousing Anzac Herbert Bice – whose list of stripped ranks totalled lance-sergeant, temporary sergeant, corporal and lance corporal – was reunited with a single stripe.[23]

Technically the 50th was in reserve but it was *hors de combat*. Many of the wounded remained with, or quickly returned to, the battalion. But in the hospitals back on the Somme, over on the Ancre, and way, way back at Rouen, on the Seine, men of the 50th died of their Noreuil wounds: Private William Batt, 21, on 8 April, gunshot wound, head; Private Andrew Gay, 35, 9 April, shell wound, shoulder; Private Douglas Moore, 22, 16 April, shell wound, knee; Lance Corporal Dudley Evans, 21, 19 April, bullet wound, right thigh, gangrenous. 'Patient collapsed and gradually sank,' the officer commanding No 6 General Hospital, Rouen, told the Red Cross when it inquired about Evans. 'Died in spite of all treatment.'[24] Some lingered long enough to die in England. Shot in the head and knee, Private Douglas Johnston, 24, died on 5 May. Ten days later a note was left with the Red Cross: 'We hope that it will be somewhat of a comfort to his mother to know how three or four old family friends saw a good deal of him and almost to the end when to us all he seemed so bright and so likely to recover.' Johnston was buried in a Cambridge cemetery: A corner of a foreign field that is forever Australia.[25]

The average age of the battalion's Noreuil dead was 26: the age of Corporal Bewick Vincent, the man whose playful words in a letter to wife Sylverea and 'my dear little Willie' on the eve of battle were all he wrote. On 21 April, he was struck off the battalion roll because he had been 'in hospital over three months'. He never made it to hospital – he was killed on 2 April, but we know nothing of the circumstances of his death.[26]

The mode (most commonly occurring) age of the Noreuil dead was 22.[27] Yes, they were mostly young men, but boy soldier cliches are not supported by the data. Only eight of the 141 were teenagers: seven were 19 and one was 18 – Private Bert Osborne died in captivity a week after the battle. Given his baby-faced pre-embarkation photo, and the fact he gave his enlistment age as exactly 18 years, at the time of his death Osborne was probably younger than his official 18 years and nine months.[28]

Inconsistencies in the official records show others were cavalier with their stated ages at enlistment: Private Charles McIvor was positively profligate with the truth in claiming to be 37 years and 10 months when he presented at Keswick base on 15 July 1915. The army's age limit was 38 – McIvor must have thought 37 and 11 months was too obvious a lie, so 37 and 10 it was. The truth was revealed in death: when McIvor's daughter Mary received a request to fill out a Roll of Honour circular for her father, she divulged he was 50.

Private William Watson was an old soldier whose numbers also told a story – his service numbers were 1 and 1a. The honour of being No 1 presumably resulted from Watson being appointed Regimental Sergeant Major of the 4th Light Horse Regiment soon after its formation. The Dublin-born Watson had fought with the 9th Lancers in the Boer War and the Light Horse at Gallipoli. He was reduced to corporal and then private for being drunk on duty, forging a leave pass and escaping arrest. His misdemeanours are well-documented, yet we know nothing of his death, aged 38, fighting in Armitage's C Company.

Anzac veteran Private Thomas Russell, 33, was born in Edinburgh and served with the Black Watch in India. It appears Russell was a free spirit – he was punished for being AWOL five times and once for impersonating an NCO. His record says he was killed by machine-gun fire, but how could the army be that specific when no further account survives of his death and he is Known unto God? He was with A Company, so perhaps he vanished in the smoke and smother as Todd's force was rounded up and cut down by 'friendly fire' or murdered by their captors.[29]

Private Roderick McLeod (AWM P09291.376).

Nor do we know how Private Roderick McLeod, 39, died at Noreuil – but the AWM nominal rolls tell us he fought in the Boer War; the National Archives show he was taken prisoner by the Boers; and his square-jawed and full-chested AWM portrait exudes strength and dependability. At least older men such as McLeod had time to live something of a life. Born in Port Lincoln, McLeod was a horse driver when he enlisted for the

South African War, and later worked across the Eyre Peninsula and the Riverland as a clerk, storekeeper, paymaster, surveyor and mounted policeman.

The dead men's occupations suggest that the 50th was a blue collar battalion. Almost a third (45) were labourers. Thirty-two were tradesmen/factory workers, 18 were office workers/shop assistants, and 18 were farmers/primary producers. Railway workers – especially locomotive firemen – were well represented. Herbert Kernick was out on the Nullarbor laying tracks for the transcontinental railway when he downed tools and travelled to Adelaide to enlist.[30] The Noreuil dead included men whose jobs would eventually also disappear: Watson was a commercial traveller, Lance Corporal Horace Richardson was a horse driver, and Private John Fanning was a locomotive engine cleaner. Surprisingly few worked in the public service, and the service sector so prevalent today was almost absent in the numbers – the dead included one barman and one cook. There were precisely zero consultants, people and culture professionals, or occupational health and safety officers. The most incongruous jobs belonged to Lieutenant Alf Sheard and Private Frank Lillecrapp – draper and draper's assistant respectively.

The 'boys from the bush' trope is also unsupported by the data. The city/country divide was about even – 65 of those killed were from Adelaide and 62 were from rural South Australia (SA) or regional towns such as Port Pirie. The other 14 were from Broken Hill (eight), elsewhere in NSW (three), Victoria (two) and Queensland (one).[31]

According to his friend Harry Seager, Armitage had a 'presentiment' of his death as they waited on the start line for the barrage to begin. The post-sentiment was an outpouring from private soldiers to the highest brass – in a letter to Armitage's father Henry, Lieutenant-General William Birdwood wrote that 'his loss ... is a great one to the AIF'. More poignant was the letter from Armitage's men: 'It is with sorrowful hearts we pay this last tribute to our departed Captain, who was not only our Commanding Officer, but also our great Friend and trusty Advisor. We all feel we can never have another 'Chief' like him, and we want you please to realise how hard it was for all of us when we saw him fall.' The letter was signed by three officers, 17 NCOs and 85 men – 'all that were left' of Armitage's C Company. At least 36 men of the company were dead or would die of their wounds and about 50 were wounded: Gallipoli veteran Lance Corporal Allan Brown lost his left leg; Private Patrick Tippins' index finger was amputated from his smashed left hand; Anzac veteran Private Frank Duthie was shot in the ankle, and the battalion's supreme bushman, Ted Lamming, was shot in the arm but was back with his mates inside three weeks.[32]

However, for many survivors, Noreuil was their last fight. The following is a selection of C Company men returned to Australia, and the wounds that ended their war: Private George Bottomley (gunshot wound, head); Private Tom Guscott (gunshot wound, left forearm); Private Peter Clarn (shell wound, buttock); Private Charles Grigg (gunshot wound, back); Private Alec Mills (gunshot wound, shoulder), and; Corporal Victor Weate (gunshot wound, arm).

Men's loyalties were first to their section, then their platoon, company and battalion. Comprising about 200 men, the company was too large for each soldier to know every other by name. So a measure of Armitage's standing is found in B Company Private Gilbert Jacob's tribute to 'our best soldier' – the OC of another company: 'More than a soldier, he was a gentleman … he was not only respected, but also loved by all his men, and all the men of his battalion.'[33]

Before Mouquet Farm, and after seeing his old company of the 10th suffer 50 per cent casualties at Pozieres, Armitage tried to soften the blow for his family if he was killed. 'Anyhow, I'll go into action with the calm reassurance that I have done my duty to my men and my country. If I happen to fall, rest content with the knowledge that I have played the game, and done my job thoroughly, which is more than some folk in 'khaki' can conscientiously affirm.'[34]

Lieutenants Sheard, Hoggarth and Bidstrup were dead at the rock stars' age of 27. Storming ashore with the first wave at Anzac, being the first Australian officer to set foot on Mouquet Farm, and leading D Company's assault at Noreuil, Hoggarth was a remarkable soldier. Rising from Gallipoli private to commissioned rank, he epitomised the ideal of the egalitarian AIF. His nerve was intact despite being seriously wounded at Gallipoli and Mouquet Farm. He led his men right to the very end, urging them to press on after he was shot in the stomach. Such a man might have been better employed than in a frontal attack against emplaced machine-guns.

Wilf Bidstrup's potential was identified early: after enlisting in May 1915, he was sent to an NCO school and then the officers' college at Duntroon, in Canberra. He is immortalised by Bean as the man found with an empty revolver and ringed with dead Germans. Six months later the Red Cross found an eyewitness to Bidstrup's death. 'He was killed under my eyes,'

Private Bill England said. 'Not instantly, but he died of wounds shortly afterwards.'[35]

Wilf Jose had just turned 22. Jose's death engenders a sorrowful sense of potential lost. You can see it his portrait: determined eyes glower from his cherubic face. Did we lose a Test cricket captain at Noreuil? A World War II general? Or a great civil engineer to rebuild Adelaide after the Great Depression?

With five years in the cadets and a year in the 81st Infantry before presenting at Keswick at the outbreak of hostilities, Tom Rule spent a large portion of his 22 years in khaki and under canvas. Made corporal immediately after enlisting, he was promoted to sergeant on Gallipoli, where he served for the duration bar one week in a Lemnos hospital with influenza. Commissioned soon after his transfer to the 50th in February 1916, he was recommended for a Military Cross for, with Armitage, rallying the men and extracting them from a deadly corner at Mouquet Farm. Curiously, neither Rule or Armitage received medals for their leadership at Mouquet Farm, a snub that rankled Armitage.[36] At Noreuil, Rule continued to lead his men after he was shot, before he was hit a second time and died – another victim of the deadly crossfire playing on the valley floor.

Churchill-Smith felt the loss of his fellow officers deeply. As the war continued into 1918, he made a list of the battalion's dead, wounded and captured officers in his diary. Below his entry for Noreuil, he wrote: 'The Officers were absolutely the best the Battalion had and ever will have, and as I read the names I cannot help thinking what a great loss the Battalion, and the Australian Imperial Force, have had.'[37]

Yes, the toll of officers was horrendous. But death has no truck with rank or station. It employs a strictly non-discriminatory policy. Raw reinforcements and veteran hard cases were reaped in equal measure and without prejudice. Private Oswald Griffen, 22, a storeman from Riverton in SA's Mid-North, had been with the battalion only a fortnight. Posted as missing on 6 April, Griffen was listed as dead on 29 May. We know nothing of the circumstances of his death. We do know, from his portrait, that the blue-eyed Griffen had movie star looks and in death was reunited with a brother, Lieutenant Reginald Griffen, killed at Fromelles the previous July.

Private Oswald Griffen (AWM P09291.052).

Griffen was not the only newcomer to die. At least 14 of the Noreuil dead – one in 10 of the fatal casualties – had arrived on 18–20 March, joining the battalion as it rested and refitted at Buire, south-west of Albert, on the Ancre, before it departed for the front on 21 March. They were: Private Henry Dougal, 34, Private John Dwiar, 27, Private John Fitzpatrick, 21, Private Harold Hollis, 26, Private Herbert Kernick, 37, Private Frank Kingsley, 23, Private Andries Norman, 29, Private John O'Rielly, 21, Private Richard Tavender, 19, Private Hugh Thompson, 20, Private Ernest Truan, 23, Private Herbert Wall, 19, and Private William Walsh, 37.[38] Little wonder then that there are often scant or no details of their deaths – their fellow soldiers probably didn't even have time to learn and remember the new chums' names.

After a spell in hospital recovering from a scalded foot, Private Percy 'Brusher' Beauchamp, 21, a labourer from Goodwood, rejoined the battalion in the frontline on 30 March. He was killed in D Company's attack on the left flank. 'I myself recovered his paybook and personal effects the following day,' Sergeant Harold Rawnsley said. Rawnsley said Beauchamp was buried in the Noreuil cemetery – 'the graves were registered, each one being identified' – but his plot was destroyed by shellfire later in the war.[39]

Incredibly, Private Joseph Woodgate arrived from hospital on the *day of the battle*. Just in time to be killed. Comrades told the Red Cross he was buried 'just outside Noreuil with many other Australians', or 'in a trench with one big cross', or 'I am almost sure that' Woodgate is 'buried in the Military Cemetery at Noreuil'. He was there, but like Beauchamp, his grave was destroyed by shellfire.[40]

Back on the road to Vaulx, the 48th Battalion was slogging its way to the front, its sluggish progress documented by one of the leading characters of the AIF, Lance Corporal George Mitchell, an original 10th Battalion Anzac. Mitchell's prose painted a lyrical *Guernica*: 'Snow-whitened horses' heads hang dejectedly … eighteen-pounders baying across snowy fields … a snow-crusted signpost, Vaulx, 3 kilometres.' And then: 'Noreuil. A line of dead 50th Battalion men. Many old mates of the original 10th among them. How long, oh Lord, how long?'[41] Mitchell had landed with Cheney, Peebles and Steuve at Gallipoli.

Given the cost, Noreuil was the definitive pyrrhic victory. And in the bitterest twist, its purpose was to provide a jumping-off point to assault Bullecourt on 11 April – a fiasco second only to Fromelles in the hallows of Australian mourning. So the 50th's 'success' at Noreuil was all about enabling abject failure and wholesale slaughter. But how did it go so wrong?

✻ ✻ ✻

After the war, Captain Max Gore described the Noreuil battle plan as 'one of the most grandiose and stupid ever drawn up'.[42] Gore conceded that Brigadier William Glasgow was a 'very competent officer', but asserted that the brigadier's retinue of NCOs and junior officers had been promoted beyond their stations. 'What else could be expected but a debacle like Noreuil?'[43]

Shot by one of his own men and taken prisoner, Gore had every right to be bitter. But did not every man of the 50th who survived the battle – having been wounded or captured or spattered with their close friends' blood and/or brains – have such a right? Sergeant Roy Clark did not hold back when he described Noreuil as 'the most disastrous stunt that our battalion had taken part in'.[44] He was right – the battalion suffered more casualties at Noreuil than in any other action. However, the British and Australian brass considered it a great victory while proffering mealy-mouthed excuses for the heavy cost.

Exhibit A is in Brigade Major Roy Morell's after-action report. The spin appears early in the narrative, when the 5.15am hop-off time was described as 'a most suitable hour'. The supporting artillery barrage was 'carefully made out and thoroughly executed'. The enemy strongposts guarding the village were 'enveloped and silenced by rifle grenades and bombs'. And the gap that opened between C and A companies was in part because of 'the peculiar formation of the ground' – mother nature conspired to destroy A Company, apparently. (Although, according to brigade HQ, A Company was not destroyed – only 'a portion' of Captain Todd's force was captured.) In closing, 'contact to aeroplanes by flares gave admirable results'. Yes, the aeroplanes knew exactly where C and D companies were being bombed, machine-gunned, sniped, rushed and shelled, not that brigade made any effort to staunch the slaughter.[45]

While containing enough facts to escape categorisation as a whitewash, the brigade report was certainly a greywash. Addressing its misnomers in turn, the 'most suitable hour' was not especially suitable for the men mowed down by the tracers criss-crossing the valley. As for the 'thoroughly executed' barrage, that might have been the case, but the supporting shellfire was inadequate for the job at hand. After the battle, everyone bar the brigade staff felt the barrage was too thin: Lieutenant-Colonel Salisbury wrote that it was 'unfortunately, not thick enough'; Captain Seager described it as 'a bit ragged'; Corporal Keith Tamblyn said the barrage comprised 'half a dozen shells … if we'd had an artillery bombardment it might have been different'; even the loyal-to-a-fault Captain Churchill-Smith said the barrage was 'not heavy enough'.[46] This was no fault of the gunners – it appeared the brigade's staff had underestimated the enemy's strength.

The 'peculiar formation of the ground' should not have been so peculiar to an Australian force that had been overlooking the battlefield for days, had sent many patrols into the valley, and which had the benefit of aircraft photos of the terrain. Indeed, the brigade report boasted that 'careful reconnaissance had been made by all concerned'.[47]

Salisbury's after-action report was more austere than Morell's flawed account. Nevertheless, Salisbury also neglected to mention the unsubdued enemy post on the left flank wiping out Lieutenant Bidstrup's platoon, and he also referred to 'the peculiar formation of the ground' causing trouble on the right (the identical wording suggests Morell cut and pasted Salisbury's words without the brigade staff seeing the ground for themselves). Salisbury's report also reveals the Australians committed a mistake made at Gallipoli, a mistake as old as war itself – they underestimated their enemy.

'There is evidence in the village to show that the enemy had no intention to give it up for the present,' Salisbury wrote. The I Anzac Corps diary includes testimony from a German prisoner that 'Noreuil was to be held until the 12/13th April'. So if the battle planners assumed the sight of Australian bayonets on the horizon would send the Germans scuttling back to the safety of the Hindenburg Line, they were sorely mistaken.

This assumption that the Germans would withdraw as soon as they were seriously challenged showed the Allied generals were behind the game – they were fighting the last battle, the Battle of the Somme. Because the Germans had recast their tactics since the 1916 campaigns. Under their new doctrine, an 'outpost zone' was arrayed to 'contain enemy raids and patrols, to provide warning of major attacks, and to disrupt those attacks'. Aggressive defence was ordered: 'The defender must not surrender the initiative to the attacker.'[48]

The new tactics dictated new ways of deploying defensive forces. Machine-gun posts were ideally placed on reverse slopes for concealment and surprise – just like the one that wrecked A Company of the 50th Battalion. Rather than continuous lines of trenches, squads of defenders would occupy strongpoints made of wood or rubble, built for all-round defence – just like the redoubts in Noreuil's sunken roads. They were sited to enfilade the enemy – they did just that to D and C companies in the valley. 'The strongpoints would remain fighting even if cut off by the enemy advance.' Which was exactly what happened on the 50th's left flank, and in the village itself. 'The defence was aptly called elastic for it was to resist, bend and snap back.' Todd's company was snapped up when the Germans bit back hard at the crossroads. So it can be argued that the British and Australian tacticians were soundly defeated by their German counterparts at Noreuil, leaving the diggers to clean up the generals' mess.[49]

As well as underestimating the Germans' tactical nous, intentions and resolve, the Australian planners misjudged the quality and quantity of their opposition. This was self-evident in the insufficient number of D and C company men allocated to mop up the village. The Germans had deployed a battalion-strength force from the 26th Reserve Division to defend Noreuil: a company guarded the southern approach, another company was strung around the western and northern edges of the town, a third company was in close support, and the defenders were reinforced by an attached platoon from another regiment and elements of two other regiments. Seven extra machine-guns were sent to the Noreuil front before the battle. The 26th Reserve Division had fought in the Battle of the Frontiers, the Race to the Sea, and the Battle of the Somme. It was rated as first class by the British.[50]

Furthermore, the change in German doctrine was complemented by a concerted improvement in the quality of its army since the Somme. '[In April 1917 the Allies] faced a German army that in only seven months, despite severe economic and manpower constraints, was organised, trained, equipped and led according to [the] new defensive principles,' the authors of a US Combat Studies Institute paper wrote.[51]

Bean highlighted the Germans' healthy morale in his official history, noting that the Allied battle planners could not assume an encircled enemy force would surrender. 'The spirit of the German troops, especially after the short rest afforded by the withdrawal (from the Somme), was in many units equal to that of their keenest opponents ... it was quite unsafe to assume that any detachment of them which found their opponents in its rear would lose its head and throw up the fight.'[52] As Bean noted, the Germans that emerged from Noreuil's cellars to attack Captain Todd's rear did anything but lose their heads and throw up the fight.

We should not be hasty in sheeting too much blame to the complicated plan, because the 50th, for the most part, did as it was asked. The leading companies set off on time, swept through the village, and successfully executed the right wheel – in Churchill-Smith's words: 'Our battalion changed direction right to line up and advance with the 51st – it was done wonderfully well and just like on parade.'[53]

Nevertheless, Todd's A Company might have taken issue with Churchill-Smith's assessment. After the war, a member of Gore's platoon – possibly Gore himself – wrote: 'To our consternation C Company kept bearing about quarter-left, until the line had an open centre as well as an open flank.'[54] However, the gap between Armitage's and Todd's companies was probably due more to the murderous fire hosing the valley than C Company losing its way or the 'peculiar formation of the ground'.

Parts of the plan were poorly executed. The 2nd Gordon Highlanders, supposed to seize the hamlet of Longatte on the 13th Brigade's left flank, instead formed up behind the 51st Battalion, ultimately advancing with the Australians. The Gordons' experience in a failed attack on two villages to the north, Croisilles and Ecoust-Saint-Mein[55], on 29 March should have forewarned the British command that the Germans were not inclined to be easily dislodged from the outpost villages. The British response to the 29 March reverse was instructive – they sacked their local divisional commander. 'It is probable that the repulse was not due to lack of energy, but to failure of the higher staff to recognise the difficulty,' Bean observed of the 29 March battle.[56]

More attention should have been paid to the machine-gun post in the sunken road on the right, the one that ultimately held the key to the whole Noreuil battle. Glasgow biographer

Peter Edgar summarised it well when he wrote: 'The position of the machine-gun below the 52nd had been discovered by patrols but somehow the need to target it, for example by the mortars, had been overlooked. This was an oversight at both brigade and battalion level.'[57] And divisional level: the author of the 4th Division's summary of operations for the first week of April was apparently unaware of the irony in him writing the 'results of the patrolling [at Noreuil] proved very accurate'.[58]

After studying the battle forensically, Edgar declared it had been 'completely successful' despite being 'marred by errors'. Glasgow's plan proved 'too ambitious' – it might have been better to send a battalion across each of the ridges to converge and clasp the village in a vice-like trap, leaving the surrounded enemy to be dealt with in detail. Perhaps Glasgow learned an important lesson at Noreuil, for he was one of the architects of such a plan a year later at one of the greatest victories in Australian history.[59]

All the above amounts to a hill of beans against the one monumental blunder, one catastrophic failure, that you, astute reader, have been anxious to see addressed since Max Gore anxiously scanned the hillcrest for help way back in Chapter 4 – the 52nd Battalion's absence from the field. Why had Lieutenant-Colonel Pope left Todd's A Company to its awful fate? According to the brigade diary, the 52nd was supposed to advance down the road from Lagnicourt to overlook the crossroads in the valley.[60] The brigade gave the 52nd a map reference from where it would link with the 50th Battalion. However, the brigade's after-action report stated that the 52nd had 'pushed forward' – yet to a map reference well short of the position in its orders.[61] Incredibly, the 52nd claimed it had reached the position ordered – well past the German machine-gun nest that destroyed A Company, cut up B Company, enfiladed C and D companies, and very likely killed Captain Armitage. The 52nd then defamed its sister unit by writing after the battle: 'Right of 50th Battalion did not get in touch with our left.'[62] This slur was repeated by Brigade Major Morell: '[The 50th] could not get in touch with the 52nd.'

Thank goodness for the disinterested judgment of the independent observer, for Bean settled the matter: 'Pope had believed and reported that his flank had been advanced to the position intended. During the afternoon, however, his intelligence officer, Lieutenant JH Julin, reported its precise position, several hundred yards short of the battalion's objective. It was near the top of the spur, screened from sight of the valley, whereas it should have been near the bottom of the spur.'[63]

Salisbury (second from the left) and Pope (right) with their fellow 13th Brigade battalion commanders (AWM E00641).

Either Pope and his senior officers (other than Julin, clearly) were incapable of reading a map, or they were covering for their attacking companies' failure to make the required progress down the hill. The latter seems unlikely, for the 52nd was a first-rate battalion. Whatever the reason, the responsibility for the 52nd's failure rested with its CO. Pope had only been back in France three weeks, so perhaps his off-handed dismissal of Gore's pre-battle report about the machine-gun in the sunken road was a ham-fisted attempt at asserting his authority. After a desperately hard Gallipoli, Pope had broken down – and suffered the indignity of being sacked in the field – when, through no fault of his own, his brigade was shattered at Fromelles. So, given the tide of the 2 April battle was decided by a single unsubdued machine-gun post, we might say the Fromelles fiasco begat the Noreuil tragedy.

7

Glory and black days

'I might as well have a look at it, just the same as anybody else,' Joergen Jensen told the Overway Hotel[1] publican when he joined up in early 1915.[2] From that moment Jensen had a look at a lot of places – Anzac Cove, for starters, but mostly the inside of tents and orderly rooms at disciplinary hearings: Serapeum, absent from tattoo, forfeit two days' pay; Chichester, absent without leave, forfeit two days' pay; Wareham, absent without leave, 12 days detention, forfeit 24 days' pay ... Jensen reckoned life was too short to bother with frivolous regulations.[3]

He had a look at Buckingham Palace too. Not as a sightseer, as a guest – the day the King pinned a Victoria Cross (VC) on his chest. Corporal[4] Jensen, 26, was the battalion's – and brigade's – first VC winner. His audacious stunt at the sunken road barricade earned him immortality. Lieutenant-Colonel Salisbury wrote up the VC recommendation on 10 April, it was duly endorsed by Brigadier Glasgow, and announced on 11

June. When the news broke in Adelaide, via London cable, the *Register* dispatched a reporter to the Overway, Jensen's pub of choice when in Adelaide. Publican James Stephenson said the hero was a quiet and unassuming Danish sailor. 'You would not think the fellow had much go in him at all. There was no talk about him.'[5]

The absence of Jensen interviews from the public record, and the scant details about his life, confirm Stephenson was speaking the truth. Jensen was a quiet man but also a hard man and harder drinker, and no doubt warned off more than a few unfortunate reporters sent to secure an exclusive for their masthead. After the Buckingham Palace investiture he returned to his barracks in Wiltshire, where he reverted to the mean: Codford, absent without leave, severely reprimanded, forfeit five days' pay.[6]

Jensen's VC crowned a cavalcade of silver and ribbon presented to members of the battalion for Noreuil: a Distinguished Service Order, three Distinguished Conduct Medals, two Military Crosses and 13 Military Medals. The Packsaddle stockman Private Bill O'Connor won a DCM for his supporting role in his mate Jensen's VC stunt. Sergeant James Wilson's DCM was reward for taking over C Company when its officers were all dead or captured. The third DCM went to Corporal Arthur Verrier, who 'showed conspicuous gallantry and devotion to duty' when leading his section after being shot in the face as the battle hung in the balance.

Issued to NCOs and enlisted men for acts of gallantry in the field, the DCM was a high honour, second only to the Victoria Cross. By rights, a fourth DCM should have gone to Private Oliver Winter, the fresh-faced farmer from the mouth of the

Murray, who – wounded and armed only with his bayonet – led a hunting party of moppers-up through the village. Winter instead received a Military Medal, an enlisted men's medal ranking below the DCM. Winter's C Company comrade Lance Corporal Harold Pritchard earned his MM for his leadership in the bomb fight at the barricade, while Fred Woolfitt and Bert Lehmann were recognised for their Lewis gun work. In recommending Lehmann for the MM, Salisbury wrote: 'Although every other member of the gun crew was a casualty, he continued to work his gun with great coolness and determination. This set an inspiring example to his comrades and played a big part in holding the line.' Private Frank Lee, C Company's sole surviving stretcher-bearer, received an MM for 'unceasingly' tending to the wounded in 'the hottest corner of the fight'. Lee bore men from the field for close to 20 hours straight, 'his untiring efforts undoubtedly saving many lives'.

If his MM citation is taken literally, mortarman Stan Coombs should have got the VC. Private Coombs captured a machine-gun and five prisoners 'single-handed and unarmed'. He must have been a smooth talker, the young labourer from the Riverland. Presumably the captured Germans were stunned by a round from Coombs's mortar.

Sergeant John Yeatman, the twice-wounded Anzac who played an inspirational role in the counterattack, was one of four B Company men to be awarded MMs. Thrice-wounded Corporal Halcro Main didn't last long enough to receive his medal – he died of his wounds on 12 April. Sergeant Fred Watson and Private Alex Young were decorated for doing what the whole of 52nd Battalion could not – closing the gap on the right.

Private James Downey received an MM but his heroic pigeons received nothing. Yet Downey did much more than carry a box of birds through the German fusillade: dumping their cage in the trench, he went back into the storm to rescue a wounded man. The battalion's signallers were justifiably well represented in the awards list: Private Stan Bishop was still bringing messages from the front line on 4 April, two days after the attack. In recommending him for an MM, Salisbury wrote that Bishop's journeys were all made under fire. 'He was always cheerful and cool, and displayed exceeding [sic]great courage. He was thoroughly reliable and deserving of high praise.'[7]

Private Carl Mengersen also ran the gauntlet numerous times. His route to the frontline was 'swept with heavy shrapnel, high explosive and machine-gun fire'. Mengersen also guided reinforcements to the fire trench and was 'cool, fearless, swift and absolutely reliable'. Little wonder three signallers received MMs – their OC, Lieutenant Bert Carlton, was an ideal role model: 'For 48 hours he did strenuous duty without any rest whatever.' Carlton received a Military Cross, effectively the Military Medal for officers. Few men could cope with such stresses; one of Carlton's signallers, Anzac veteran George Barrett, still only 20, was evacuated with influenza and trench feet, and repatriated to Australia in early 1918. Noreuil was his last fight.

Harry Seager received an MC for attacking 'with the utmost skill and determination' while setting 'a fine example of courage and coolness throughout'. And WOII Allan Crace, the quartermaster who 'continued his work in his usual excellent style' while his ration dump was shelled throughout the battle, was mentioned in despatches after being recommended for a Meritorious Service Medal.

The Noreuil battle was fought soon after a change to the eligibility criteria for the Distinguished Service Order. From January 1917, following complaints from fighting soldiers that non-combatants such as staff officers were being awarded the prestigious medal, a directive was issued that it only be given for combat operations. Loutit's experience was a case study in the change: on 4 June 1917, he received a DSO for his Gallipoli service, his work as adjutant during the 50th's formation, and his contribution as Salisbury's second-in-command since October 1916. Two weeks later he was awarded a bar to his DSO for his extraordinary bravery and leadership at Noreuil. 'Probably within the whole British Army during the Great War no DSO and Bar were won by the same officer within such a remarkably short time,' Cecil Lock wrote in *The Fighting 10th*.

Salisbury received the French Chevalier of the Legion of Honour, Fifth Class, for his leadership of the battalion during and after Mouquet Farm and particularly at Noreuil, where the operation's success, according to the French citation, was 'largely due' to his 'thorough preparation and excellent handling of the battalion'.[8]

The battalion's VC, all three of the DCMs and six of the Military Medals went to members of C Company, a fact proudly added to the foot of the survivors' condolence letter to Captain Armitage's father, Henry. Armitage was acknowledged two months after his death – on 1 June, he and Sergeant Bill James, the Lewis gunner killed at the crossroads, were Mentioned in Despatches for their heroism at Mouquet Farm – the paperwork was lodged a month before Noreuil. 'The loss of his services would be a distinct disadvantage to his battalion', Salisbury wrote of the 'energetic and thoroughly reliable' Armitage a month before he was killed at Noreuil.[9]

Honours are subjectively bestowed and inconsistently awarded. If no-one sees a man's act of gallantry he receives no award. If the act is seen by a man who is later killed, the hero receives no award. If an officer does not see it, then it likely won't be recognised – and officers were in short supply at Noreuil because they were mostly dead or wounded. Armitage was piqued at not getting an MC for Mouquet Farm and disparaged the awards system as flawed. 'The men know who can fight and who can lead, and that is quite sufficient for me.'[10]

On occasions, recognition of gallantry descended into high farce: after Mouquet Farm, the men were paraded in the Somme town of Albert for General Birdwood to distribute medals. As usual, Max Gore was untroubled about exposing army incompetence. 'Imagine the chagrin of the rest of the brigade when the only battalion that had not been in the action, because it had been in reserve, received 75 per cent of all the decorations,' Gore wrote.[11]

Plenty saw Gore's dogged persistence under the most extreme hardship in the Noreuil valley, but almost all of those not killed or wounded were captured. Their accounts of the battle would have to wait until after the war. Of course, we have no such encumbrance – to Gore and his fellow prisoners the narrative now turns.

* * *

'We have recently captured two or three villages,' an anonymous German wrote in an unsent letter found in Noreuil after the battle. 'And the Black Australians give themselves up as soon as they feel our mailed fist.' Where to start? The 'recently captured' outpost villages – Noreuil, Lagnicourt, Longatte et al – had been in German hands since 1914. And clearly the letter-writer had a) not seen an Australian and b) been misinformed as to their predominant skin colour. Bean copied the letter excerpt into his notebook, complete with a rejoinder: 'They retreated voluntarily for about a fortnight and now were opposing a number of black Australians whose faces went quite white whenever they felt the German mailed fist. They were giving themselves up in large numbers.'[12]

The 113 Germans seized at Noreuil was indeed a large number. However, so was the number ceded to the Germans – as many as 100 men of the 50th were captured on 2 April. Perhaps 10 were killed soon after being captured – either by 'friendly fire' or vengeful Germans – leaving 85 to enter the official records as POWs.[13] There was a scintilla of truth in the German letter: one 'black Australian', Private Roland Carter, 25, a Ngarrindjeri man from Raukkan on Lake Alexandrina, was captured in the valley. Suffering a bullet wound to the left shoulder, Carter was hospitalised in Valenciennes, a large French town 25km north-east of Cambrai, and eventually was detained in the Halbmondlager – the Crescent Moon Camp – in Germany.[14]

Carter's colour had dictated his destination, because the Crescent Moon Camp housed Muslim prisoners from the colonial French and British armies and the Russian Empire. Carter was black, so the Germans lumped him in with Senegalese French and British Punjabis. German anthropologists visited to study the assorted ethnic groups, and Carter shared Ngarrindjeri medical treatments with the German doctors. 'I am in very good health,' Carter wrote in early 1918. 'I am having a good time here and if all goes well shall be going to the Moving Pictures tomorrow. We go to church every other Sunday and I like it very much.'[15]

Private Roland Carter (AWM 2017.727.1.3).

Carter's experience was not representative of his 50th comrades, who were routinely overworked, relentlessly starved and regularly beaten. Private Fred Mawby, to choose an extreme example, died in Paderborn, Germany, on 18 January 1918, officially from 'inflammation of the brain', but only because he was 'worked practically to death' according to a fellow prisoner. Mawby was 22.[16]

For the reinforcements pitched into the Noreuil battle days or weeks after arriving at the front, it was out of the fire and into the pan. One day of terror and death and destruction gave way to the slow burn of 18 months of hunger, mistreatment and humiliation. It was a long campaign, the war behind the wire.

But to return to events immediately after their capture: Captains Todd and Gore were interrogated separately, giving little to their captors as there was little to give – on many topics the German officers knew more about the 13th Brigade than Todd and Gore. Afterwards Gore limped off in a column of fellow prisoners; a German orderly chased him up the road, stopped, saluted smartly, and presented Gore with his watch, which he had taken off while washing his face. Then, a 'fatherly looking' German presented Gore with a walking stick. 'Bitte,' the German said. 'Danke Schoen,' replied Gore, the words sidestepping the large lump in his throat.[17]

About a third of the 50th's Noreuil POWs were wounded. Private Tom Gillespie carried his badly wounded mate Private Bert Osborne 3 miles to a German aid post. Thence Osborne was transported to Valenciennes hospital where his leg was amputated. He died on 9 April. 'I was with him when he died,' Private Edward McMullen told the Red Cross. '[Osborne] was conscious … said he was done for. He died about 8 o'clock in morning. Was taken out of the Ward by a French man and two Russians in a rough coffin. I have not seen his grave.'[18] Private Bill Langford was embittered by young Osborne's death, stating after the war: 'At Valenciennes Hospital Osborne died of wounds owing to bad medical treatment.'[19]

Hit in both shins, Private Ernest Powell lay in the open while the bullets cracked and his comrades fell around him. After the surrender, Powell's mate Private Roy Houston carried him out; Powell's wounds were dressed and he was packed into an ambulance for the long and bumpy drive to Valenciennes. There he received good care and eight weeks later was taken to an excellent hospital on the Baltic coast, where a Russian doctor amputated his left leg below the knee. Powell was repatriated via a prisoner exchange at Aachen at the end of 1917.[20]

Badly wounded by shrapnel in his left thigh in C Company's charge down the hill, 40-something Anzac veteran Lance Corporal Edward Budgen had somehow ended up at the other – German-held – end of the valley.[21] German surgeons were pulling shrapnel out of Budgen well into 1918. The tough old Anzac reported in August 1918 that his wounds had almost healed.[22]

Sergeants and Anzac veterans Henry Haythorne and Ernest Fishburn also went into the bag suffering wounds from the fight in the valley. Both were admitted to the Valenciennes hospital. A 'big Red Cross Hun' carried Private Norm Holthouse into a dugout, cut his clothes off, and bandaged the shrapnel hole in his left side. 'I was nearly dead from loss of blood,' Holthouse said. He hung on long enough to endure the ambulance ride to Valenciennes, where he was ordered to strip, bathe and submit to an X-ray. 'The doctor ... said he must operate, but I refused.'[23]

He did a lot of refusing, did Holthouse. A high-spirited individual, he did a lot of escaping too. The first time he was on the run for seven days before being bailed up by a German civilian brandishing a double-barrelled shotgun. The second time he was out three days, and the third he was 10 metres into his journey when a guard walked out of the bushes and greeted him with: 'Halt, English schweindhund.' The 'English' was the most offensive part of the invective, as Holthouse believed he had been betrayed by a Tommy prisoner.

Bayoneted for refusing an order, imprisoned in darkness for days, made to stand at attention for 10 hours straight, Holthouse worked on a farm, slaved in salt and coal mines, cut and carted wood, sweated in a Krupp foundry, and was hospitalised with Spanish influenza. He woke one morning to find the men in the beds either side of him were dead. The corpses remained in the beds for two days. Starvation rations, hard labour and illness reduced the strapping country boy to 46kg. But Holthouse survived to be repatriated to England on Boxing Day, 1918.[24]

The Germans mostly provided good medical care but there were exceptions. Set upon by German bombers, all eight of Private Albert Molloy's party were wounded. Grenade fragments in Molloy's right arm remained untreated for almost a month, during which time an old Mouquet Farm foot wound 'broke out' and was also unattended.[25] Private Frank Swanston went into captivity with the left side of his mouth blown away by a bullet. His wounds remained undressed until he arrived at a village 10km behind the lines. The Valenciennes hospital praised by some of the prisoners was condemned by Swanston. 'There was practically no medical treatment,' he said after the war. 'My jaw had been broken and was not set.' Swanston arrived back in England with his left teeth either missing or reduced to decaying stubs. Part of his cheek had to be surgically separated from his jaw.[26] Private Reuben Starr had a different experience. His leg wound was dressed immediately and he was treated well during his 11 days in the Valenciennes hospital.[27]

'I still suffer with me head a little, mostly when the weather changes,' Private Glen Jacob wrote from his camp in Soltau,

Germany, in September 1918. A glancing bullet had riddled his scalp with shards of steel helmet. One of his five brothers in uniform wrote to the Red Cross four days after the battle inquiring about Glen's fate. Given the glacial progress of communications, how did Ross Jacob know his brother was missing? Well, lieutenant-colonels had some privileges, and Ross was CO of the 10th Battalion. As well as agonising over a missing brother, he was mourning many comrades – Ross was the 50th's original second-in-command. Lieutenant-Colonel Jacob wrote: 'Till 7/5/17 at Hotel Russell, Russell Square. Asks for immediate news.' He was told his brother was a POW on 6 June.[28]

Private Fred Douglas was badly shot up when he entered captivity. When he had recovered sufficiently from multiple wounds – one in his leg and three in an arm – he was savagely beaten by guards. 'The general treatment was harsh, the hours long and the work hard, and we depended entirely on Red Cross parcels for food.'[29] The sentence is an apt summary of the men's experience in captivity.

After capture, the officers and enlisted men were separated and the latter were marched through a string of villages, where they were quartered in a succession of cellars, lofts and houses ringed with barbed wire – anything that could serve as a temporary prison. Eventually they were jammed into rail-cars for the half-day ride to Lille, about 50km north of Noreuil. The human cargo was unloaded, lined up on the platform – where a diminutive German, more Himmelstoss than Hochstetter, stood on a box to warn that anyone trying to escape would be shot – and paraded through the city's streets as a living war trophy.[30] Whenever a defiant French man or woman dashed out with food for the Australians they were set upon by Germans. 'When a man did manage to get anything, it was promptly taken away from him and he received a smack with the butt of a rifle or a kick,' Private John Murphy said. 'The men were famished and took a lot of risks to get biscuits and were pretty badly handled in consequence.'[31] Also badly handled was the little French girl jabbed with a rifle butt for trying to give the prisoners cigarettes. A guard pocketed the cigarettes and his comrades laughed.[32]

Once they had been marched 'pretty well through every part of the town', the men arrived at their destination – the Black Hole of Lille, official name Fort MacDonald. They descended into dungeons, 120 men per dungeon. The absence of any bedding was immaterial as there was barely room to lie down. It was cold – there was no heating – dark – nor lighting – and smelly: the toilet was a wine barrel in a corner. 'We were given a bucket to empty it with every morning, but they did not give us sufficient time to properly empty it,' Murphy said. 'Consequently it became very foul.'[33]

Dungeon rations were a loaf of black bread per nine men, per day and weak, watery soup for dinner. The men mouldered in the stifling darkness, allowed out for five minutes of fresh air in a week. 'The conditions in this abominable prison were indescribable,' Private Tom Rampton said. 'Miserable as bandicoots,' was how Corporal Keith Tamblyn summarised the mood at Lille.[34] Privates Bill Wheeler, Willie Clifford, Patrick Bennett, Haddon Bowen and James Walsh were among those who long remembered their week in the Black Hole of Lille.[35]

The brutal treatment was not typical of the Allied POWs' experience. The men had the misfortune of being captured at an unfortunate time: they were being deliberately mistreated to persuade the British to stop using German forced labour to haul ammunition and build fortifications behind the lines – which was expressly forbidden according to the Hague Conventions of 1899 and 1907.[36] These conventions decreed that prisoners must be treated humanely, which plainly was not the case at the Black Hole of Lille. 'We were told we were being treated like this as a retaliation for the way the British were treating the German prisoners,' Murphy said.

The Germans made no secret of their transgression. Quite the opposite – they wanted the British to know their prisoners were being badly treated. In 'A Declaration to the British Government' issued to the POWs at Fort MacDonald, the Germans encouraged the Australians to write 'to their relatives or friends of influence in England' stating that they would continue to be mistreated until the British pulled German prisoners back at least 30km from the front line. Until then prisoners of the Germans would be denied normal rations, accommodation and bedding. And they would be 'worked beside the German guns under British shellfire'.[37] So the 50th Battalion men were sent back to the front to dig machine-gun pits for the enemy.[38]

Detraining at Douai, they were lined up for a route march towards the distant crump of guns on the Arras front. En route they were made to wait at every estaminet, bar and café while their Prussian guards downed beer and wine. The prisoners were given no water. Stragglers were beaten by drunk guards. 'Most of us were more dead than alive when we reached our destination,' Murphy said.

They had not eaten since leaving Lille and there was nothing to be had at their new camp because the bakehouse and QM store were smoking ruins – the camp was within range of the British artillery. Murphy was appointed cook for

200 men – goodness knows why – he was a carriage builder by trade (although he was Captain Gore's batman). He did the best he could with the ingredients provided: dried mangel-wurzel, the ubiquitous black bread, and horse meat cut from victims of the aforementioned British shelling.[39] Sometimes cook Murphy received a horse leg – complete with shoe. Sometimes it was a horse's 'lights' – its lungs. It all went into the soup. At another camp a cow's head, horned, emerged from the steaming soup cauldron.[40] 'It was not very nice food,' Murphy said. 'But we had to eat it to keep body and soul together.'[41]

Murphy's job was as unpalatable as the food he was forced to cook but at least his kitchen was a bit further back from the British guns. Vivian Brown, Patrick Bennett, James Masters, Percy Prime, Bill Lucas, Bill Wheeler and James Walsh worked amid shellbursts for months. They were never out of danger: their billet, a damaged church, became progressively more damaged by the shelling – part of the ceiling came crashing down while they slept.[42] Willie Clifford recorded the names of six diggers killed when a 15-inch shell hit an ammunition dump in early May.[43] The men were made to keep working through the barrage while their guards retreated to their dugouts.[44]

The cruelty had its intended effect: the British acceded to demands to pull German POWs out of the battle zone. Germany responded by gradually doing the same on its side of the scar of trenches zig-zagging through northern France. In late November the 50th Battalion POWs were shunted through a series of camps before many of them arrived at a 40,000-plus prisoner compound at Schneidemuhl in Prussia[45], where some remained until the Armistice. Others were separated from the group when the starvation rations, poor sanitation and hard labour contributed to various ailments that required hospitalisation. Murphy, for example, contracted a fever that providentially led to him being chosen for a prisoner exchange in Holland – he arrived in England in September 1918 and was immediately hospitalised suffering from neurasthenia.[46]

From their assorted camps in Germany, many 50th Battalion men went arbeitskommando[47], or as the diggers called it, 'on commando'. Translated, arbeitskommando means 'work detail' or 'labour detail'. These mobile gangs worked in mines and factories, built railways, felled trees and laboured on farms. Private Bert Marks was sent down a coal mine. 'The work was very hard. I was the only Englishman. The rest being Russian and Italian who were treated very badly.'[48] The men's experiences 'on commando' varied greatly – Vivian Brown wrote: 'My treatment here was very good and I was well fed and allowed plenty of freedom.'[49]

Private Tom Robinson's gang of timber cutters boldly tackled the problem of their poor rations by depriving their 70-year-old guard of his bayonet and single bullet and going on strike. 'He got the wind up and left to see a boss who came back with him. We got more food.'[50] Of course, not all the guards were decrepit and compliant pensioners. Private Malcolm Brown was kicked and knocked senseless, suffering permanent damage to his eyes, although there were extenuating circumstances – he had thumped the French interpreter and two guards who rebuked him for refusing to salute.[51]

And, of course, not all the guards were vicious martinets. Keith Tamblyn encountered a German sergeant whose placid demeanour Tamblyn attributed to his country background. 'He wasn't one of the big city blokes ... you couldn't have wished for a finer fellow anywhere.' When the sergeant went on leave, the POWs made him a hamper from their Red Cross parcels. He wept. 'My family will wonder where I got it from,' he told his Australian friends.[52]

The privileges of commissioned rank applied in captivity; Captains Todd and Gore and Lieutenant Edwards were not required to work so were sent to camps in Germany. However, shoulder pips were no match for starvation rations, inadequate clothing and general brutality. Reunited at Holzminden in central Germany, the three 50th Battalion officers suffered harsh treatment under camp commandant Captain Niemeyer.

Todd, Gore and Edwards at Krefeld prisoner of war camp in May, 1917. They are seated together in the second row. Todd is fifth from right, Gore (with pipe) is fourth from right, and Edwards is third from right (AWM P08451.002).

Gore described Niemeyer as a 'petty tyrant' who had apparently lived in the US for a time, because he affected an 'extravagant American accent superimposed on his guttural German one'. Niemeyer was cruel but could be easily baited and was prone to 'turn from vermillion to purple' when jeered by the parading prisoners. This greatly amused the POWs, whose hysterics climaxed when a flustered commandant on one occasion spluttered: 'I guess you think I know nothing. I know damn all.'[53]

Niemeyer might have been Blimp-like but he was no Colonel Klink. Given the commandant's practice of jailing his own sentries for refusing to fire on escaping prisoners, it is not surprising that an Australian pilot was shot after he was captured outside the wire. Lieutenant Alec Couston, ex-10th and 50th Battalion and an original Anzac, transferred to the Australian Flying Corps in 1917. His Sopwith Camel was downed by Albatross Scouts over Lille in February 1918. Apparently Couston didn't believe the rumours the war was about to end – in October he was shot in the arm escaping from Holzminden. As he lay wounded, he was shot again at point blank range, the bullet passing through his jaw and out via his mouth. He had corrective surgery in Australia after the war.[54]

Lieutenant Edwards had an eventful captivity. Hospitalised in Valenciennes, he saw three English privates die of starvation. An interpreter told him it was payback for British mistreatment of German POWs. When his wound had healed he was taken to Karlsruhe in the German Rhineland, where he was locked in a small hotel room, starved and denied exercise. He was later interned at Strohen, where the drinking water was drawn from stagnant pools, the sanitary arrangements were poor, and the diet of carrots, turnips and potatoes was life-sustaining but monotonous. This was no life for the dasher who ran through the Noreuil storm to warn his mates of their impending doom.

Edwards escaped in October but was quickly recaptured. He was sent to Holzminden, where the conditions were better, but escaped again anyway. He was recaptured within 24 hours. He was shifted to a camp deeper in Germany, in the Harz mountains. The British major-general in charge of the POWs posted an order prohibiting escapes. Edwards escaped and was quickly recaptured again. He claimed to be betrayed by an English prisoner. Gore speculated that Edwards's training as a journalist made him a master of observation: 'He escaped at least three times by the sole method of observing loopholes in the methods used to contain us.'[55] Gore also escaped and he nearly made it too – he was recaptured at the Dutch border.[56]

The POWs' accounts are replete with their hunger. The hungrier they were, the more they wrote about mangel-wurzels and thin soup and sawdust in the bread. Britain's naval blockade meant the whole of Germany was short of food, and the POWs were at the end of the (black) bread line. Pictures of the worst cases could be mistaken for photos of the next generation of Australian POWs in South-East Asian hellholes. However, help was at hand.

In June 1917, the authorities in London received a list of Australian POWs via Switzerland, dispelling familial fretting about men posted as missing since Noreuil. The Australian Red Cross Prisoner of War Department in London immediately sent thousands of food and clothing parcels to where it believed the bulk of the Australians were interned, at Limburg in the Rhineland. As we have seen, most of the enlisted men were in work gangs behind the frontline, so did not receive Red Cross parcels until later in 1917.

Seven enlisted men of the battalion testified that they 'depended entirely on Red Cross parcels for food' while 'on commando' in Germany.[57] 'I got my Red Cross parcels and they saved me from starvation,' Private Albert Marks said. Private James Masters was 'entirely dependent on Red Cross parcels for food and clothing, our clothing being taken from us on some occasions'. Carriage builder-cum cook Murphy received his first parcels in November – almost six months after they had been sent from England. 'They were a godsend and I was almost afraid to touch the contents,' Murphy said. And from Lance Corporal Tom Reynolds: 'I could not wish for better parcels than those sent to us by the Red Cross.'[58] So what did the parcels contain?

Historian Aaron Pegram described them as a 'veritable pantry' compared with the German food. Each individual package had three tins of meat, beef dripping, cheese, biscuits, oats, jam, condensed milk, tea and sugar. Wounded men also received milk powder, beef tea and infant formula.[59] The Red Cross even arranged for the prisoners' bread to be baked in Switzerland and Denmark, so it was fresh when it arrived in the camps.[60] 'By 1918, they were among the best-fed people in Germany.'[61]

Six food parcels per month, per man, were sent, with the Red Cross claiming a 98 per cent successful delivery rate. The men also received 160 cigarettes a month, more than a kilogram of tobacco and plenty of soap. Additional consignments included clothes, toiletries, sewing kits, toothbrushes and playing cards.[62]

It appears Private Bill Lucas's parcels fell into the 2 per cent that failed to find their intended mark. Lucas was working as an orderly in a Mons hospital when the Australians' parcels were pilfered by a decorated English soldier, who Lucas named in his official statement made after the Armistice. Treachery was not confined to soldiers of the old country – Gore wrote about a young officer from the colonies (not Australia, Gore said) who was convicted of stealing food by a court of fellow officers and tossed into a cesspool in front of a parade of the camp's complement. 'Poor fellow; he was just weak and hungry, but weren't we all?' There was no more stealing, Gore said.[63]

In another wan echo from the camps, Private Julius Henning sent a sad – but mysterious – note home on a postcard from Dulmen dated 29 May 1917. 'Got no other friends.' That was it; his only message in 19 months of captivity.[64]

The men were dotted across Germany, Poland, France and Belgium when the Armistice was signed on 11 November 1918. Most were quickly and efficiently repatriated via Denmark and various Baltic ports, but some men, fearing German retribution, did not wait for friendly authorities to reach their camps. Willie Clifford, for example, snuck out of his camp in Liege and walked to the Allied lines at Kortrijk, east of Ypres. He said the journey was 50km, but Kortrijk is almost 200km from Liege as the crow flies.[65]

When the war ended, not all the men were sweating in salt mines or going stir crazy in barbed wire cages. Those billeted to farms to assuage Germany's chronic labour shortage had comparatively benign times in the second half of 1918. Tom Robinson's farm was run by a widow whose son was crippled by the war. 'When the Armistice was signed I was very ill and Mrs Spicher looked after me. She paid a doctor out of her own money. She was one of the good, old souls.' At the end of November, Robinson farewelled his German friends. 'Mrs Spicher asked me to stay and she would give me the farm and her daughter and anything that I wanted – but I said goodbye and left.'[66]

8

Gentle sobbing in the south

Mrs Mary James, widow, of Gaffney Lane, Railway Town, Broken Hill, received her son's personal effects on 1 February 1918: the package contained Sergeant William James's wallet, cards, photos, a notebook, a 'book of views', testament and a letter. Such highly personal items were a comfort to the bereaved families. In Mary's case, however, they had the opposite effect ... because they were not her son's. 'The things sent must belong to another James,' Mary wrote back to the army's Base Records Office in Melbourne.

They did belong to another James. Another Bill James. Another Sergeant Bill James of the 50th Battalion, even – William Harold James, not William John James. In an impressive display of amateur detective work, Mrs Mary James of Broken Hill, New South Wales, contacted Mrs Eleanor James of Coromandel Valley, South Australia, whereupon the latter wrote to Base Records claiming her dead son's effects: 'We are both certain that the package belonged to Sergeant WH James,' Mrs Eleanor James wrote.

William Harold James had been reported killed four days after the battle. But there was a further, fortunate, twist. Seven months later, Eleanor broke the happy news to the army that he was alive and interned in Limburg, Germany. How did she know? She had received a letter from him. She had also been told by the Red Cross. 'I have been notified unofficially by Military Authorities that he is a prisoner of war ... I should be very glad if you could fix up his papers as his pay was stopped on 24 June 1917.' She received her son's effects, via Broken Hill, on 22 April 1918. Hers was a rare case of a soldier son coming back from the dead. Meanwhile, Mary James received Bill's effects – letters, papers, photos and cards – in July ... July 1920.

Back from the dead: Sergeant William Harold James sent this postcard to fellow POW Sergeant William Groves. The reverse read: 'From Jamesy, as a remembrance of captivity together in Gustrow, Germany. 28/11/18.' (AWM P09591.047).

We should not be too harsh in judging the army for mistaking William Harold for William John James. Granted, there were no excuses considering its administrative resources: starting with a staff of three in 1915, by 1917 the Base Records Office in Melbourne had assumed dimensions of a good-sized government department. More than 300 administrative workers processed the information generated by the more than 300,000 Australians in uniform.[1] It is understandable that some of the Noreuil men were missed or mixed up given their battle was immediately followed by First and Second Bullecourt in April/May 1917, in which the AIF sustained more than 10,000 casualties. Subsumed by mountains of paper, Base Records clerks and typists under Major James Lean were bound to make mistakes.[2]

The clergy was pressed into service to break the news to the bereaved families.[3] In Wilf Jose's case, this presented Base Records with a problem (or a degree of superfluity?) – the rector of his parish was The Reverend George Jose, his father.[4] Presumably the telegram was sent instead to the nearest Church of England minister. Whatever Base Records chosen course of action, the Joses were among the first families to be notified: Wilf's death notice appeared in Adelaide evening paper *The Journal* on 12 April.[5]

As Base Records diligently distributed the dreadful news to parishes across South Australia and beyond, a mournful book of verse by an Adelaide teacher was receiving glowing notices and winning literary prizes. *Songs of a Campaign* was the debut anthology of poems by repatriated Anzac Leon Gellert. Gellert had landed at Gallipoli with Jose's A Company – one of his poems was devoted to Jose's platoon commander, who was mortally wounded at the Landing. But the most poignant of Gellert's poems, as Base Records' telegraph tapped like a snare drum at a funeral march, was *Anzac Cove*, which contained lines that might have been written about the place in France where, a few weeks earlier, his friends had died: *There's a torn and silent valley ... there's an unpaid waiting debt ... there's a sound of gentle sobbing in the South.*

The debt was being paid as ministers Anglican, Catholic, Presbyterian, Methodist, Congregational and the rest trod solemn paths to the doors of the dead men's families. In Naracoorte, 360km south-east of Adelaide, the town's Presbyterian pastor, the Reverend RW McLean, received two telegrams on Anzac Day, 23 days after the battle. The brothers Boston, Tom and Angus, were dead. McLean visited the boys' parents, Thomas and Hannah, and young Tom's widow, Cecilia. 'Captain-Chaplain' McLean was all-in with the war effort; as head of the local recruiting committee, he was there at the beginning and the end of the local soldiers' wars.[6] His messages delivered, McLean attended the town's Anzac Day service in the Agricultural Hall. He said a prayer for the Bostons and the band played 'O God Our Help in Ages Past' and 'Dead March in Saul'.[7]

'The news ... cast quite a gloom over the place,' the *Narracoorte Herald* wrote of the deaths of the Boston brothers.[8] The pall enveloping Naracoorte thickened. In the morning, Church of Christ Pastor WG Oram delivered the news to Howard Stark's parents. A week later official word arrived that Sergeant Mehaffey was missing. At least two men saw Mehaffey killed in the valley road but no-one knew what had happened to his body. He is missing still.

The Fosters of Lucindale were told their son, original Anzac Percy, was dead. Other 50th men were listed as missing or wounded. The *Narracoorte Herald* scanned the names, dates and units of those killed and broke the news of the Noreuil battle on Tuesday, 8 May: 'It would appear therefore that the 50th Battalion had a severe engagement that day [2 April].'[9]

The 50th's 'severe engagement' reached into homes and touched hearths throughout the South-East region of South Australia. At Glencoe, 25km north-west of Mt Gambier, the Medhursts received word James was missing. He was still listed as such in late May, prompting his mother to write to the Red Cross seeking information: 'Kindly try and find him if he has been killed or taken a prisoner or what his fate might be … trusting to hear from you as early as possible.' The Red Cross replied on 5 July – Medhurst had been taken prisoner: 'We trust the knowledge that he is at least alive will comfort you a little.'[10]

It appears the death toll in the state's South-East region motivated Major Pendlebury of Keswick Barracks to travel 430km from Adelaide to personally visit the bereaved. He called on the Norman family of Yahl, a crossroads just out of Mt Gambier, to tell them Ernie was missing. Later that same day the Normans were told that Ernie's brother Lewis was also missing. Eventually they learned that Lewis was a POW, and Ernie was dead.

A year earlier, Ernie Norman had been farewelled in a farm shed festooned with Union Jacks and French tricolours. A full program of speeches and patriotic airs feted three local soldiers: Ernie, Dick Button and Alex Pasfield, who were presented with wristwatches and soldiers' companions.[11] The brave boys responded, all assembled sang 'God Save the King', and supper was served. Like Norman, Button was killed at Noreuil. Methodist minister PH Chennell delivered the news to Button's family and the Yahl Red Cross Society closed its fortnightly meeting early out of respect for the dead soldier. The third man farewelled in the Yahl barn, Alex Pasfield, was killed at Broodseinde in Belgium in October. [12]

On 28 April, the day that Chennell visited Edward and Mary Button, Major Pendlebury wrote to the bereaved couple: 'I am directed to convey to you the deep regret and sympathy of Their Majesties the King and Queen, the Commonwealth Government, and the District Commandant, in your sad loss you and the army have sustained by the death of your son, the late No 1890 Private RJ Button, 50th Battalion, Australian Imperial Force, who was Killed in Action on 2nd April 1917.' [13]

The word Noreuil made its first appearance in South Australian newspapers on 26 March in a Charles Bean article dated 20 March. 'We could see the Germans quite clearly retiring in extended order over the far hills beyond Noreuil,' Bean wrote. [14] This account supports the Australian commanders' mistaken belief that Noreuil would be ceded without much of a fight.

The battle's first mention in print came from a surprising source – the enemy. And on a surprising date – the day after the fight. According to a 'wireless official German message', 300 'British' prisoners had been seized at Noreuil, 'four miles south-east of Croisilles, between Arras and Bapaume (Australian readers were learning new names)'. Of the 300 prisoners, only 60 made it to the German lines – the rest were killed by 'English' machine-gun fire, the enemy claimed. So the Germans knew about the friendly fire incident and squeezed every last drop of propaganda out of the tragedy. Fortunately for the families of the Noreuil dead, their dreadful telegrams would not arrive for weeks. So unless they kept scrapbooks of war clippings, or had particularly good memories, they were spared the angst of thinking their beloved had been accidentally killed by an Australian Vickers gun.[15]

The Western Front stalemate was born of the opponents trading bullet for bullet, shell for shell, wasteful charge over deadly ground for futile counter-attack over the same killing field. And so it was in the propaganda war: Field Marshal Haig's dispatch, published in *The Advertiser* on the same day as the German 300 prisoners claim (4 April), boasted of capturing a string of villages – including Noreuil – without mentioning the enemy's staged withdrawal to the Hindenburg Line. The Germans 'suffered heavy casualties' but Haig said nothing of his own losses. Peel back the layers of obfuscation and puffery and the 50th Battalion's 'success' appears in his dispatch: Haig reports 182 enemy prisoners were taken along a 10-mile front – as we have seen, most of these were seized at Noreuil.[16] There are no outright lies in Haig's dispatch; rather fragments presented as the whole truth.[17]

The lies came later. In a 'report from British headquarters' dated 9 April, and published in the *Chronicle* on 14 April, the British fired a salvo of mistruths in response to the German '300 prisoners' lie. 'The German claim to have captured 300 at Noreuil is a falsehood. Our total casualties in the district did not reach 300, and the missing are under 60, though we buried over 500 Germans.'[18] Balderdash. On 6 April the 13th Brigade reported it had sustained 704 casualties at Noreuil, which was a significant underestimate. As for burying 'over 500 Germans', there are scant, if any, surviving Australian accounts of German burials after the battle – the army had enough trouble counting its own dead.

Consider the case of Private William Wheeler, confirmed by Lance Corporal Herbert Rumbelow in June as killed at Noreuil. 'A Company went over and got wiped out,' Rumbelow told the Red Cross from his hospital bed in Boulogne. 'About half a mile past Noreuil ... we saw Wheeler lying dead on the road side, within 100 yds of the objective. Two or three of us recognised Wheeler.' Private Harry Dohnt also 'recognised' Wheeler, whom he 'knew very well'. Wheeler was 'near dead' in the sunken road beyond Noreuil, in the same place as described by Rumbelow. 'He moved slightly when I was passing him,' Dohnt told the Red Cross. Whoever the poor man was, it wasn't Wheeler, who was an unwounded prisoner.

Similarly, a private had 'seen' Sergeant Walter Wood killed as C Company attacked the village. The eyewitness and a few others took over Wood's Lewis gun. Another survivor said Wood was buried 'to the right of the Cemetery where he fell'. Wood was confirmed a POW on 2 June. The fog of war was especially thick in the Noreuil valley in the half-light of the 2 April dawn.[19]

It was easier to account for the dead away from the mayhem of the battlefield. When Private Andries Norman died from his chest and leg wounds in a casualty clearing station near Pozieres, 25km behind the front, the administrative machinery whirred into action and his widowed mother was one of the first of the Noreuil next of kin to receive a telegram, on Friday the 13th of April.[20]

From that point the telegrams flowed and the obituary columns filled. The Shadgetts of Parkside received their double blow – Ken was missing (and later found to be a POW) and Alan was dead. Alan's death notice was one of 13 in the *Express and Telegraph* on 2 May. All bar one of the 13 families stated their loved one had died in France, the exception being Captain Armitage, who was 'killed in action near Bapaume, France'. Few knew that the 50th's epic battle had been at a place called Noreuil.[21]

Soon the connection was made. On a 3 May page filled with portraits and pen-pics of the dead, an *Advertiser* journalist joined the dots in short articles about two close friends from the small Mid-North town of Saddleworth, Privates Edgar Maxwell and Bill Dullea. 'They were probably both killed on April 2 in the capture of the village of Noreuil, on the Bapaume to Cambrai road,' the un-named reporter wrote.[22] Mrs Mary Dullea was mourning another son, Corporal Michael Dullea, killed at Pozieres the previous August. She would lose a third son, Private Charlie Dullea, in the coming August.[23]

The 3 May *Advertiser* also ran brief obituaries for Lance Corporals Cornelius Shea and Harold Harper and Privates Clarence Ash, Henry Dougal, Jack Stewart, Lachlan 'Les' McQueen and Joe Earls. Private Tom Eglinton was listed as suffering from a severe leg wound; word was yet to arrive that Tom's youngest brother Laurence was killed at Noreuil.[24]

The weekly *Chronicle* was popular in South Australia's rural communities. So imagine how those communities were devastated by its 5 May edition, which carried three full pages of war obituaries, including 26 for men of the 50th. The paper reported that Burra's flags were at half-mast for Lieutenant Esson Rule.[25]

Then, like a crashing wave, the scale of the loss was laid bare in the *Southern Cross* of Friday, 11 May. Under the heading OUR FALLEN SOLDIERS – ANOTHER LONG LIST, the Catholic paper filled almost a column with the names of more than 100 dead soldiers, including 84 men of the 50th. Each had the date of their death in brackets after their names, almost exclusively 2 April in the case of the 50th men. The horrific list exposed Field Marshal Haig's 4 April communique as cant.[26]

It also, of course, cast communities into despair. The black shroud descended on Broken Hill in late April when news arrived that Lance Corporal Arthur Gilbert and Privates Jack Neddermeyer and Ernest Newton were dead. Sergeants Bill James, Henry Steuve and Joseph Peebles and Lance Sergeant Sydney Wills (Broken Hill was doing its bit for the war effort by keeping up a steady supply of NCOs) took the Silver City's toll to seven. The reaper then struck deeper into the desert, arriving at the tiny gold town of Milparinka in the far north-west corner of NSW to tell the Cox family that Joseph was dead.

The case of the two Sergeant Jameses illustrated how the Base Records Office was overwhelmed. However, some mistakes might have been avoided had more caution been exercised. Matilda Gurney, aunt and next of kin of Gallipoli veteran Horace Richardson, was told her nephew was wounded at Noreuil. 'In the absence of further reports,' Base Records wrote on 16 April, 'it is to be assumed that all wounds are progressing satisfactorily.' Richardson died on 20 April.[27]

In late April Mrs Elizabeth Griffen of Riverton in SA's Mid-North was farewelling one son while fretting for another. Private

John 'Jack' Griffen enlisted on 27 April after being rejected on medical grounds the previous October. Lieutenant Reg Griffen had been missing since the Battle of Fromelles in July 1916. On 3 May, Mrs Griffen was told a third son, Private Oswald Griffen, of the 50th Battalion, was missing. However, the authorities gave Oswald's number as 6863 instead of 2863 – had there been a mistake? she asked hopefully. There had, but only in the number: on 8 June, Private Griffen was pronounced killed in action on 2 April. In August an inquiry ruled that Reg had been killed at Fromelles. His remains were identified and reinterred in 2014. Jack Griffen was posted to the 43rd Battalion – was his subsequent transfer to the 50th in homage to his dead brother Oswald? Jack survived the war.[28]

Private Robert Haines slipped through the net. Possibly one of his comrades had reported seeing Haines binding his own arm early in the battle but had not seen him killed by a shellburst soon afterwards. Because on 24 April Haines's wife Mary was told he was slightly wounded. This was despite an officer apparently sending her a letter of condolence immediately after the battle. 'I hope you received it alright,' Haines's platoon-mate Lance Corporal Charles Donnelly wrote in an annotation to Haines's diary, which he posted to Mary. 'Bob was one of the bravest lads I have known. He is sorely missed by us all.' Haines was verified killed in action on 15 April – nine days later Mary was told he was slightly wounded and to assume he was 'progressing satisfactorily'. She received the truth, that her husband was long dead, on 17 August.[29]

The home front's hunger for information was addressed by an 'occasional correspondent' to Millicent's *South Eastern Times* on 15 May. Armed with newspaper clippings, a good map and a measure of common sense, the author deduced that the 50th had a hard time taking Noreuil on 2 and 3 April. The anonymous writer argued strongly against withholding the truth of the war from civilian Australia: 'For some reason or other no word comes through of the different battalions which are in action, though as the enemy meet them now face to face, there seems little cause for holding back such information.'[30]

Bereft mothers hung their hope on slivers of scuttlebutt and scraps of news. Sarah Graham of Brinkworth in SA's Mid-North heard from a 'friend serving in the same battalion' that her son, Private James Graham, might have been taken prisoner. 'His mates believed him to be a prisoner of war,' Mrs Graham told the Red Cross in July. The Red Cross instead confirmed Graham was dead – his grave had been identified by the army: previously Known unto God, Graham was buried in the Noreuil cemetery. Mrs Graham sent the Red Cross £1. In a final cruel turn, the authorities reversed their ruling on Private Graham's grave – he reverted to being Known unto God and is commemorated at the Villers-Bretonneux Memorial to the missing.[31]

In June, a desperate Mrs Louisa Turpin, of Dale St, Port Adelaide, wrote to the Red Cross asking if her son was a prisoner of war. Lance Corporal Gethen Turpin was officially killed in action but Mrs Turpin had received a letter from another son, Lance Corporal Richard (surely Dick) Turpin of the 10th Battalion, saying Gethen was missing. She had no reason to doubt the news, as Richard would have served with many of Gethen's comrades before the 10th men marched in to the new 50th Battalion. It was a false hope – although they hadn't seen him fall, several men told the Red Cross Turpin was buried in the Noreuil cemetery.[32]

When the missing men did not return from hospital, or when they did not turn up in POW camps, it was safe to assume they were dead. But the army needed a mechanism to confirm such determinations, so the missing men's names were brought before specially convened courts of inquiry, conducted by their own battalions. The courts usually comprised officers of the unit – Churchill-Smith was presiding officer for some of the 50th Battalion's courts. They were typically perfunctory affairs; the battalion was, after all, still fighting a war. One such inquiry ruled on 31 October 1917, that Corporal Ernest Goodes, of A Company, was killed in action on 2 April.[33]

One dead soldier's family did not lament his loss because he had no family. When he enlisted in June 1916, Private Bert Osborne gave his next of kin as 'Weston, Harry (Friend)'. In allowing Osborne to nominate Weston, the army's attestation officer had created a problem for Base Records – because a soldier's next of kin had to be a family member. A 'state child' who required the SA Children's Department's permission to enlist, Osborne was apparently given up by his mother as an infant and knew nothing of his father. He was living with Weston when he enlisted. The army searched for blood relations but, finding none, accepted Weston as Osborne's next of kin. Weston signed a bond declaring he would take care of Osborne's medals and effects – he duly received a tobacco pouch, gold shell ring, paper wallet, three playing cards and a letter.

Government secrecy, propaganda, the great distances involved and the sheer number of dead conspired against timely and accurate information being conveyed to the dead men's families. The detail they craved came, at last, from Charles Bean. Dated 6 April but published in Australia on 15 June, the official correspondent's 1665 words about the battle ('Copyright Reserved by the Crown') answered many of their questions. Perhaps they gained a scintilla of solace from an opening paragraph that extolled 'one of the most … gallant fights that has been fought by Australians in France'. Describing the battlefield in forensic detail, Bean dissected the complicated plan and explained the 50th's many difficulties in fulfilling its mission. Individuals were not named, but they are there, dying between the lines. Jose: 'There were five empty cartridge cases in his revolver.' Bidstrup: 'Their officer was killed after emptying every chamber of his revolver.' Hoggarth: 'A man whose history will connect always with another fierce fight at Mouquet Farm.' And Armitage: 'He died before he said another word.'[34]

Showing rather than telling, Bean illustrated how the enemy's machine-guns exacted such a toll, how the moppers-up were outnumbered and overwhelmed, and how A Company's survivors were cut off and rounded up. The reader is then walked through Loutit's battle-turning intervention step-by-step. And while far from happy, the ending is positive – Fritz fled and the battle was won. Bean's gritty, brick-upon-brick journalism gave the bereaved something less than succour, something more than not knowing. They might imagine their boy storming the guns, sticking a hulking Hun with his bayonet and dying with his cartridges spent. It gave them pride after the fall.

* * *

A family's grief was measured in the currency of everyday items touched by the Noreuil dead. Ordinary objects were sanctified. A hairbrush. Shaving gear. A photo of a last happy moment in a cheery estaminet. Perhaps a letter from the family, returned to Australia to close the circle. Horace and Alice Funnell, of Elizabeth St, Norwood, in Adelaide's inner east, received a more intimate item than most – a lock of son Arthur's hair.

Private Arthur Funnell (AWM P09291.280).

The Funnells also received more items than many families: when it docked at Melbourne in early 1918, HMAT *Marathon* disgorged Arthur's identity disc, photos, photo films, wallet, notebooks and the lock of his brown hair. Funnell was in D Company but of his death we know nothing. In 1923 the Imperial War Graves Commission exhumed an unknown soldier from the Noreuil battlefield. The man was wearing a wristwatch and had coins in his pockets. The items enabled the commission to determine it was Funnell, who was re-buried in the Noreuil Australian Cemetery, as the graveyard at the south-western corner of the village was now formally designated. The watch and coins were sent to his family. 'Doubtless you will value these momentos [*sic*] on account of their former intimate association with the late soldier,' the Base Records Office wrote to Horace Funnell. The letter is date stamped 6 May 1926, three years after the watch and coins were recovered. Were they sitting in a warehouse all that time? The watch suggested Funnell had a violent death. It was damaged. Smashed by shrapnel or a machine-gun bullet? If the hands stopped when he was hit no-one thought to record the time of death.[35]

A watch, presumably inscribed, is one thing, but a six-year-old letter quite another. In 1923, a letter 'considerably impaired through long exposure' was found on an exhumed body. The Imperial War Graves Commission was confident the letter belonged to a 50th Battalion man, but sent it to Australia – Hawker in the Flinders Ranges to be precise – for the next of kin's confirmation. Howard McFarlane inspected the frayed and mouldy parchment and replied immediately: 'I have traced that letter, which belongs to my late Brother.' Corporal Arnold McFarlane was reinterred and his brother chose the words on his headstone: 'A noble hero, true and brave, peacefully sleeps, in a soldier's grave.'[36]

In 1926 an exhumation unearthed a damaged prismatic compass and two identity discs, enabling the commission to identify, and prepare a headstone for, original Anzac Charles Hendry. The compass and disc were sent to his widow, Martha, who had apparently married again as she was now Martha Baldwin.[37]

But how and why had these men not been identified when they were buried? As usual, nothing is simple in war and, as we have seen, all was chaos at Noreuil. The dead were buried by their battalion-mates but their battalion-mates were in shock – they had just fought a battle in which every second man was killed, wounded or captured. And the burials proceeded under shellfire and within sight of the German lines. There were bound to be errors in identifying the dead and recording their names.

Despite these difficulties, most of the Noreuil Australian Cemetery burials were identified and all were marked with crosses. Four officers lie in graves trailing down the hill, towards the town, all in the shadow of the customary large stone cross. First is Wilf Bidstrup ('No life is lost, that's nobly spent, no hero's death premature – Mother'); then Bill Hoggarth, (no epitaph); then Harold Armitage ('A loving son, a devoted officer, a soldier, and a man'); and Esson Rule ('Sadly missed at home').

Bidstrup, Hoggarth, Armitage and Rule are buried in a rough line below the Noreuil Australian Cemetery cross (Andrew Faulkner).

The war wasn't done with the dead yet: many crosses – and presumably some graves – were subsequently destroyed by shellfire. So most of the battalion's Noreuil dead – at least 82 out of 141 – lie in unidentified graves in the cemetery. The 82 are commemorated on headstones lining the graveyard's eastern end. Each stone is of the same dimensions as the tens of thousands in France and Belgium, carrying the soldier's name and his family's dedication. The only difference is each is crowned with the words: *Known to be buried in this cemetery*. They are here, but we know not where.

The shells that obliterated sections of the cemetery spared the 50th's officers ... only enlisted men are represented in the 'Special Memorial' section, as it is labelled by the commission, for the men whose graves have been lost. Enlisted men such as Private Richard Tavender, 19, whose mother Fanny's correspondence with the Red Cross speaks for all the families' despair but also their forbearance. Fanny was one of the first mothers to be notified of a son's death, but then heard nothing for a year. She sought the help of the South Australian branch of the Red Cross. 'We have been waiting month after month,' she wrote from her home at Angaston, in the Barossa Valley. 'Of course, somebody might have written but owing to so many ships being sunk ... it may have gone down. In one of his letters he told me he had sent his private kit bag to a kit shop in London. Can you tell me if there is any chance of getting it?' Replying promptly, the Red Cross promised to do all it could. There is nothing more about Tavender's possessions in his National Archives or Red Cross files, so it appears his effects – like his grave – were lost. While she wrote, Fanny Tavender was grieving the loss of another teenager – Boy, 1st Class Frank Tavender, 16, who fractured his skull in a fall on HMAS *Sydney* in Scapa Flow on 26 January 1918. Being under 21, both boys required their parents' permission to enlist and now they were both dead.[38]

Henry Steuve was buried near where he was cut down by machine-gun fire at the south-western corner of the town. At least we think he was. Initially he was listed as lying in the Noreuil cemetery, but later investigations could not locate his grave so his name went on the Villers-Bretonneux memorial for the missing dead. His mother Louisa wore a photo of a slouch-hatted Henry in a circular brooch. It is now part of the Australian War Memorial's collection.[39]

William Batt's family had a kindly hospital matron to thank for the return of his effects. When Batt died of his wounds in Rouen on 8 April, the matron collected his watch, wallet and letters – all on his person when he was shot in the head somewhere on the Noreuil battlefield. Again, an object gives us a clue as to where and when he was killed: Batt had pocketed a clip of German bullets, so probably made it to the enemy lines, at least. His broken ring was also sent home by the matron – the bullets were not.[40]

Items carried into battle were not always recovered and repatriated. Often the dead were buried wearing their rings and watches and with a loved one's portrait tucked in a pocket. Wristwatches were especially sought after by the bereaved.[41] Patrick Sheehan's father wrote to Base Records in October 1917: 'My son had a watch I gave him ... any possibility of getting same.' It probably went to the grave with its owner.[42] Louise Stagg was told Percy was wearing his watch the night before he was killed at Noreuil. 'His wish was if anything should happen to him he did not care about anything else ... as long as his mother got that watch,' she wrote in April 1918. She did not get the watch.[43]

Whatever the families received was usually retrieved from the battalion's kit store. Consignments of effects ranged from single keepsakes – a photo in Lachlan McQueen's case – to the hundreds of items packed up and sent to Bill Hoggarth's father William Snr. Hoggarth's repatriated belongings included his slouch hat, a whistle and lanyard, an English-French phrasebook, three novels, slippers, a dressing gown, two trouser pressers, four fly nets and 22 collars. All that were missing were cleft sticks and a collapsible canoe.[44]

The items exposed the egalitarian Australian Imperial Force as a myth (although Hoggarth had risen from private to commissioned rank). Officers typically had huge caches of paraphernalia in enormous trunks lugged around by their batmen, who – assuming they weren't also killed – packed their officers' possessions to be sent home. Wilf Bidstrup's vast shipment of possessions included a copy of the most popular book of the day – CJ Dennis's *The Sentimental Bloke*. Alf Sheard's family received a Smith & Wesson revolver and Harold Armitage's father Henry was sent a veritable library of military text books, a first aid manual, prayer book and book of poems.

Enlisted men had comparatively few possessions and no batmen to shepherd them home. John Hogan's effects were typical: a wallet, photos, cards, small crucifix, sprig of heather and religious pictures. Henry Cheney's more than two years' service yielded only his identity disc, diary, wallet, photos and a letter.[45] Halcro Main's family received his Military Medal citation – hopefully not branded with the word 'Dead' like Base Records' file copy.

Officers had more effects but commissioned rank did not guarantee the speedy return of same. Wilf Jose's did not arrive home until December 1918. An old school chum and section-mate from the original 10th Battalion processed his will – Arthur Blackburn VC was working as a lawyer after being invalided from France in 1916. How the men's paths had diverged since 'all our SA chums' – Jose, Armitage, Moule, Fowler and all the others – celebrated Blackburn's Victoria Cross on Armitage's 'perfect day' at the Trocadero in London.[46]

Some families received nothing. William Ranclaud's mother Bridget wrote to Base Records in November 1917, March 1918 and February 1919, asking after his possessions. 'I have never received any of his belongings and am very anxious to know if I might hold out any hope of ever receiving them,' she wrote in the third letter. Five months later AIF Headquarters in London replied to the Department of Defence's inquiry on Bridget's behalf: 'The improbability of obtaining any definite information in this connection through further investigations at this juncture is obvious.'[47]

Bridget's patience is illustrative of a generation's stoicism. As was the Mullins family's example. After being notified on Anzac Day, 1917, of John's death, they heard nothing about his effects or burial for more than three months. It appears the family gathered around their Hughes St, North Unley, kitchen table for a council of war on 11 August. On her widowed mother Mary's behalf, John's sister Miss E Mullins wrote to the Red Cross and Base Records the same day. 'As no confirmation of this (25 April) report, or any further particulars, have been received, we should be glad if you could get any further information regarding this soldier,' Miss Mullins wrote. The

Red Cross searchers went to work and discovered John died 'trying to rescue some of our men' and 'his face was not touched'.[48]

Edith Tiver asked the Red Cross to find her son Frank's effects. 'I have never had one single article from him which would be very precious and dear to me no matter how small,' she wrote on 30 January 1918. 'I have waited so anxious for these things as my neighbours has had theirs months ago.' There is no record of her receiving anything.[49]

Dudley Evans left two batches of effects. The larger cache – diaries, a photo wallet, prayer book, rosary, testament and 'religious medallion' – was brought home by the HMAT *Euripides* in late 1917. It was fortunate for Dudley's father Richard, then, that of the two consignments, only the smaller went to the bottom of the Atlantic when the SS *Barunga* was sunk by a U-boat south-west of Cornwall on 15 July 1918.[50] So, the Evans family lost only a pair of pince nez and a coat hanger, not Dudley's precious religious belongings, as he was a devout servant of St George the Martyr Anglican Church, Goodwood. 'There has never been a boy of St George's more respected and loved as a devoted adherent of all that St George's stands for,' Father Percy Wise said.[51]

On 2 April (note the date) 1919, Dinah Kennewell of Gawler South inquired about her son Sydney's effects. 'I have not received any of his Belongings up to date,' she wrote two years to the day after Sydney was killed. Replying promptly, Base Records said nothing had been received at its office but 'large consignments' were 'coming to hand from overseas'. It appears the 'large consignments' did not include Kennewell's possessions – his file contains no further mentions of effects.[52]

The records are mostly free of family disputes over the dead men's belongings. The case of Bill Roberts is an awkward exception. His parcels were sent to his housekeeper. Who, it appeared, was more than his housekeeper: she was listed as his next of kin when he joined up in May 1916. Four months later, Roberts signed a sworn statement changing his next of kin to his mother Elizabeth, suggesting he was estranged from the 'housekeeper'. When Elizabeth heard the woman was claiming her son's possessions, she dashed off a letter to Base Records that might have been penned by Lady Bracknell or a Wodehouse aunt: 'Dear Sir, Would you kindly explain to me why My Son Pte WS Roberts's belongings … were sent to his Housekeeper …' *To his Housekeeper* was underlined. 'I am writing this as the Person had the impudence to write and say that if there was anything that we would like it would be sent down.' It appeared Roberts's former partner would not readily cede her stake in his affairs – she certainly claimed his medals – and before long the police were involved. Foot Constable Dansie of Renmark Police reported Roberts's former de facto was 'well known in this District' to be of 'very low repute' and often moved 'from Town to Town in the company of men of bad repute'. In the event, her claim for a war pension was rejected, and Roberts's mother received his effects, medals and a £2 per fortnight pension. Elizabeth died suddenly on 27 January 1922, aged 67.[53]

Australia's war pensions system was among the most generous in the world.[54] In the year ended 30 June 1918, more than 37,000 dependents of the dead received pensions.[55] The family of Port Augusta labourer Andrew Gay (died of wounds, 9 April) is a good example: within months of his death his widow Catherine was receiving £2 a fortnight and their three children between

10 and 20 shillings each a fortnight, held in trust by their mother. Gay, like many of the Noreuil dead, also had a life insurance policy, in his case with the National Mutual Life Association of Australasia.[56]

It appears Major Lean and his Base Records staff did their best to provide families with as much information as possible. The Johnston brewing family of Oakbank in the Adelaide Hills received a highly detailed account – albeit one overly festooned with capitals – of Doug Johnston's funeral at Cambridge in May 1917.[57] 'The Coffin (polished elm) was taken to the Cemetery in a Hearse. The Last Post was sounded. A large number of Australians were present at the Chapel and Cemetery. Three Mourning Coaches were there to convey the wounded Soldiers. Floral Wreaths were sent by Mrs Shannon, Miss Kelly and Miss Stephens. Mrs Shannon and Miss Kelly were present at the Funeral.' This account must have been of some comfort to Doug's mother Effie, although she deserved nothing less after being advised on 7 May he had been removed from the seriously ill list – when he had been dead two days.[58]

The Red Cross searchers gleaned precious information from their bedside interviews with comrades of the dead. In a letter to its South Australian Division, John Manthorpe's mother Edith lauded the Red Cross's 'labour of love'. 'The relatives of fallen and wounded soldiers are deeply grateful to your branch of the Red Cross Society,' Edith wrote. 'You have eased much of the burden this cruel war has brought to us all.' Edith had a different view of Base Records. In a February 1918, letter personally addressed to Major Lean, she wrote: 'We are not at all satisfied with the package of so called "kit and effects" of our late son ... nothing of any value has been forwarded, simply a few post cards, a photo wallet, a newspaper cutting, a business letter and an identity disc – just what might be in a pocket. What has become of his other belongings? No soldier takes all into an attack, especially one such as Noreuil.' By early 1918 Noreuil had achieved notoriety befitting its magnitude.

What had happened to John's watch and other valuables? Edith asked. Major Lean (or more likely, one of his staff) replied in his usual imperturbable manner: 'In many cases several packets of effects have arrived at different dates ... anything further coming to hand will be promptly forwarded.' If anything did come to hand, its return was not recorded in Manthorpe's file.[59]

Other families were less strident about the return of inanimate objects – they were more concerned about what had happened to their flesh and blood. In September 1917, Mrs Mabel George of Kent Town sought the help of the Bank of Adelaide's Leadenhall St, London, office to trace her wounded and missing son Ednie. The Red Cross told the bank that Ednie was dead. In a variation of the false hope trope, in February 1918, Mabel wrote to Base Records retelling a rumour about Ednie's 'papers' being retrieved on the battlefield by an officer before the officer was taken prisoner. 'Could you tell us the name of [the] Officer?' Mabel wrote. 'Could you tell us his whereabouts as we would like to hear something about our boy as no one has written and there is nothing only "Killed in Action 2nd April 1917".' Her letter found its way to AIF headquarters in Horseferry Rd, where a clerical captain was unable to suppress his frustration in his reply to Base Records back in Melbourne: 'May she be advised, please, that no trace can be found of the officer she refers to ... the information provided in her letter is very vague.'[60]

Ednie's National Archives file contains a note that compounds the sadness. On 16 July 1915, his father David wrote a note for his 18-year-old son: 'Ednie Harold George is desirous of joining the Colours with our consent he is going to enlist.' At 19, Ednie died a hardened veteran of Mouquet Farm and Flers. In December 1919, a boy was born in Eastwood, just a few kilometres from David and Mabel's Kent Town address: Peter Ednie George, surely a nephew, served with the 2nd AIF in World War II.[61]

Mrs Mary Bath, of Renmark, had a similar experience to the Georges. After being told her son John had been killed, she quietly and patiently waited for further word ... for almost three years. In February 1920, the 'uneducated old widow'[62] approached the former secretary of the Renmark recruiting committee, Howard Evans, who wrote to Base Records on her behalf. 'Mrs Bath has heard nothing of her son with the exception of the announcement of his death,' Mr Evans wrote. Mary had exposed a flaw in the system: when there was no news to pass on, no news was passed on. Information generated action. There was no facility for telling the next of kin, in a sympathetic way, that there had been no developments. Base Records replied to Mary immediately, saying there was nothing to add to Private Bath being killed in France on 2 April 1917. 'However, an intensive search is now being made of all old battlefields with a view to locating unregistered graves.' That was promising, but the latest on John's effects was not: 'In view of the length of time which has now elapsed it would appear that nothing had been recovered from his person.' Eventually John was determined to be in one of the 82 damaged and unmarked graves in Noreuil Australian Cemetery. As we have seen, Bath died after being taken prisoner, probably killed by friendly fire or perhaps an illegal act. His body must have been collected and returned to the cemetery next to the village.[63]

Poor Mary, abandoned wife, widow and bereaved mother. 'I am next of kin as far as I can find out,' she replied to Base Records when asked late in 1921 if John's father was living. 'His father having left home some years ago and I have been unable to find his whereabouts since, but heard he was dead some time ago.' Mary, like all the rest of the Noreuil next of kin, heard a lot more from the authorities in the early 1920s as they distributed memorial scrolls and plaques and the trio of service medals; the 1914–15 Star, British War Medal and Victory Medal, collectively and colloquially known as Pip, Squeak, and Wilfred after a *Daily Mirror* (UK) comic strip.

The Noreuil battlefield in mid-May, 1917. The left sunken road runs through the centre of the picture, past the Noreuil Australian Cemetery (AWM E00504).

Apportioning of medals was accompanied by institutionalised sexism: a father was deemed a 'nearer blood relation' than a slain soldier's mother. And so mothers such as Ellen Mahoney of

Gawler suffered the indignity of being asked by the army if their husbands were still alive. Ellen's wild and strapping son Henry – 5 foot 11 inches, 13 stone and disciplined three times for being drunk and absent – is officially missing, although he is likely in the Noreuil cemetery with his comrades.[64]

Consider the bereft Edward and Bridget Dwiar of James St, Prospect. Despite at least three of Private John Dwiar's comrades telling the Red Cross they saw him killed – either by a shell or shot through the head – the Dwiars refused to give him up as dead. 'We have heard rumours here that he is in England having returned after being a prisoner in Germany,' Edward wrote to Base Records on 23 April 1919. The Dwiars' hopes were fuelled by the lack of official news since John's death and the absence of any of his belongings. Of course, it was false hope. But imagine the family's distress during the months when John was missing and his younger brother Bill's fate was unknown. Shot in the leg at Noreuil, Bill was evacuated to a hospital in East Sussex, where he was found by the indefatigable Red Cross searchers. 'I suppose you also got word of our Eldest Son being killed,' Bridget told the Red Cross in her thank-you letter for finding Bill. 'It is very hard and sad but we must be thankful for there are so many more lost and Dead Boys.'[65]

The longing lingered in a new decade. In November 1922, George and Louise Stagg replied to a Base Records' newspaper advertisement seeking them after they had shifted house. 'We shall be pleased to hear from you in reference of any news or anything about our loved son who is peacefully sleeping in France,' the Staggs wrote.[66]

Percy Stagg was 'sleeping' somewhere in the Noreuil cemetery, one of the 82 men of the battalion in unidentified, shell-damaged graves, and one of the 96 men of the 50th in the small, rectangular plot on the edge of the sunken road at the south-west corner of the village. How many mothers visited their sons' graves is unknown; perhaps none did. Without the means to visit the old world from the new, they were left to scrawl forlorn notes on official requests for information. 'Will you kindly send me a photo of my late son's grave,' wrote Percy Foster's mother May. 'I will willingly pay expenses.'[67]

Close examination of the 96 men in Noreuil cemetery tosses up an intriguing mystery: Private William Marshall, 50th Australian Infantry Battalion, was killed in action more than a year after Noreuil in a battle 45km to the south-west, across the Somme and far away. How did he get here? Did he leave instructions, if killed, to be buried with his friends at Noreuil? Did his mates bear his corpse to Noreuil? If so, it speaks of Noreuil's place in the memories of the battalion's complement and also its unwarranted anonymity in the Australian consciousness. There is a certain irony to asking to be buried in an unknown place way off the main remembrance route – because Marshall was killed at the epicentre of Australian commemoration on the Western Front. He was killed in action in the 50th's night attack at Villers-Bretonneux, on Anzac Day, 1918.

9

You saved France

A row of trees points the way to the ruined town, which is bathed in a spectral light. The town is framed by larger trees, like McCubbin's bracketing of a distant Melbourne in *The Pioneer*. In the foreground, diggers go at the Germans with bayonet and rifle butt as a searchlight plays on a plane bombing the town. In the middle distance, beyond the trees, a figure is backlit with a Christ-child–like orb of yellow – a fragment of Will Longstaff's trademark spiritualism in a painting that is all about light. Completed in 1919, many years before *Menin Gate at Midnight*, Longstaff's *Night Attack by 13th Brigade on Villers-Bretonneux* lauds the living, whereas his more famous work mourns the translucent ranks of risen dead.

The painting depicts the 50th Battalion's most famous battle. On Anzac Eve, 1918, all was chaos as the Germans menaced Amiens from the high ground near Villers-Bretonneux, south of the Somme. Such was its importance, the Allied Supreme

Commander himself, French General-in-Chief Marshal Foch, demanded Villers-Bretonneux be immediately recaptured, before the enemy could consolidate its gains, bring up its artillery, and fortify the town. While the men of the 50th Battalion chiacked, playing leapfrog after taking their breakfast on the banks of the crystal clear Hallue River,[1] a tributary of the Somme, Brigadier Glasgow was told to ready his troops for battle.

Lieutenant-Colonel Salisbury marched his men down to the Somme and marched them up again towards the gunfire and smoke. They shook out into artillery formation against desultory shelling – losing one man killed and four wounded on the way. As the sun set behind them, and after marching 13km, they set down their packs in the woods west of Villers-Bretonneux. They had not eaten since an early breakfast, knew little of the task before them and nothing of the ground over which they would advance. With the enemy less than a kilometre away, at the other end of the same woods, the men of the 50th waited for the word to go. 'These guys are battle-hardened,' historian Dr Aaron Pegram says. 'They've done a pack march, they literally fall on their backs, they have a couple of hours sleep, and they're ready to take the fight to the Germans.'[2] They might have been hardened but Charles Bean feared for the fate of the 'magnificent 13th Brigade … I don't believe they have a chance … went to bed thoroughly depressed'.[3]

The plan was as simple as it was fraught: starting south-west of Villers-Bretonneux, the 13th Brigade would fight its way almost 3km to Monument Wood at the far end of the town. Pompey Elliott's 15th Brigade would envelop Villers-Bretonneux from the north, with the two thrusts joining hands on the other side. Both axes would be guided by fires set in the town by shelling and aerial bombing. However, as at Noreuil, there was no creeping barrage of any consequence. As at Noreuil, the German lines bristled with machine-guns. And as at Noreuil, flares of many colours arced overhead and tracers zipped and cracked as the diggers set off into the night like 'men strolling into fern after rabbits'.[4]

Night Attack by 13th Brigade on Villers-Bretonneux by Will Longstaff
(AWM ART 03028).

And just like Noreuil, the intelligence was flawed. The British reported the woods on the brigade's left 'were practically free from the enemy, the British troops having been told to clear them in the afternoon'.[5] The rivers of angry tracer pouring from the dark woods showed they had not been cleared. The Australians had been ordered to press ahead resolutely, leaving any trouble on the left to the Tommies. However, the weight of fire could not be ignored. Nine men of the 51st Battalion peeled off to strike the Germans with bomb, bayonet and rifle butt; these are the men portrayed in Longstaff's painting. On their left, a platoon of the 50th also plunged into the woods: led by Anzac veteran Lieutenant Percy Nuttall, they captured five machine-guns. On his own initiative, Lance Corporal George Hanneman led his Lewis team on a wide flanking manoeuvre and two more German machine-guns fell silent.[6]

With the flanking fire supressed, though by no means extinguished, onward pressed the 13th Brigade. As they trudged inexorably forward, bullets struck bayonets fixed to slung rifles, showering the men with sparks. Flares momentarily made statues of men. And the town glowed as it burned. A young Tommie corporal stumbled into an Australian aid post, weeping. Was he badly hurt? asked an Australian doctor. 'No, sir,' he said. 'But I can't get the boys to go forward.' Cue a wounded digger: 'Never mind, kid. The boys will hunt Fritz without youse kids.'[7]

The fact it ticked over into Anzac Day during the battle was not lost on the diggers, whose blood was up.[8] When 30–40 Germans sallied out of the wood, enveloping the 51st Battalion's left flank, D Company of the 50th arrived to shoot them down from behind – those Germans not hit fled back into the woods.[9] Elsewhere the battalion's Lewis gunners engaged targets of opportunity and everywhere the men manoeuvred and skirmished and pressed forward under the magnificent leadership of their seasoned officers and NCOs – Villers-Bretonneux was the battalion *in excelsis*.

Much had been learnt in the year since Noreuil. The Lewis gun was king of the battlefield – the men were now expert in its use and aware of its worth. Infantry battalions devoted roughly a third of their fighting strength to fire, carry and feed as many as 30 Lewis guns in battle.[10] Salisbury praised his Lewis gunners' skill, aggression and initiative. He mentioned 'several instances' of Lewis teams pressing forward to engage and subdue machine-gun posts. Lewis gunners supressed the enemy's attempts to bask the field in flare-light, covered the main force's advance and broke up counterattacks. Few Lewis guns were lost in the battle – which Salisbury attributed to the men guarding their guns with their lives, such was the weapon's worth.[11]

By 1918 the Australian doctrine proscribed covering gaps in the line with a crossfire of Lewis guns. This was not possible at Noreuil, because the Germans held the high ground on the right slopes of the valley. But another tactical change employed at Villers-Bretonneux would have saved Captain Todd's A Company from being annihilated if it was in place at Noreuil: attacking battalions were now instructed to overlap each other's flanks. Perhaps the 52nd Battalion's error at Noreuil played a role in the tactical adjustment.[12]

Vietnam veteran Brigadier (Ret) Pat Beale DSO MC has described the victory at Villers-Bretonneux as 'one of Australia's greatest feats of arms'.[13] Foch went further, telling the Australians: 'You saved France. You saved Amiens. Our gratitude will remain ever and always to Australia.'[14] General Monash had nothing to do with the battle but said it was 'the finest thing yet done in the war, by Australians or any other troops'.[15] A highly decorated British general commanding a brigade at Villers-Bretonneux called it 'perhaps the greatest individual feat of the war'.[16] For all the rave reviews, the bare facts are sufficient to honour the great men of Villers-Bretonneux.

The Villers-Bretonneux triumph was the sum of all the men's experience, from Gallipoli to Pozieres to Noreuil and all the great battles that followed. Great battles such as Messines, Zonnebeke and Dernancourt. After Villers-Bretonneux, the 50th fought at Hamel and Peronne. The diggers welcomed new comrades to the field of battle, conducting a joint attack with US troops at Bray on the Somme in August 1918. And it manned frontline trenches at Warneton, Broodseinde, Hollebeke, Corbie, Daours, Gentelles Wood, Cerisy, and Vendelles. From east of Ypres to north-west of Saint-Quentin, 697 men of the 50th were killed in action, sustained mortal wounds, or died on active service. The last two to die in battle, Private John Sherwood, 24, of Port Adelaide, and Private Bill Robertson, 25, of Exeter, were killed on 19 September 1918. They are buried in the Jeancourt Communal Cemetery Extension. About 15km east of Peronne, the cemetery is, like Noreuil, a long way off the beaten commemoration track.[17]

What became of the great men of Noreuil? After suffering such grievous casualties, the battalion was kept out of the line for two months while it was replenished and rebuilt. At its next fight, at Messines, in Flanders, in early June 1917, it lost another experienced officer: Dick Wilton suffered a serious head wound. 'Poor Dick Wilton has lost an eye and also his left forefinger,' Jim Churchill-Smith lamented. 'Bad luck for him. Feel very sorry – a real nice chap.'[18] The tough and wild Broken Hill butcher and original Anzac Herbert Bice was killed at Messines; his grave – '3/4 of a mile NE of Messines' – was never found, so he is commemorated on the Menin Gate Memorial to the missing.[19]

Joe Waine was awarded the Military Cross at Messines that he probably should have received at Noreuil. He survived the war. Promoted to Major after Noreuil, Harry Seager suffered a serious head wound on the Passchendaele Ridge in September 1917. 'I was writing a pigeon message when a shell burst,' Seager wrote. 'The boys thought I would die.' He didn't, but his war was over.[20]

Churchill-Smith also rose to Major and also survived the war, although it was also a close-run thing – he was shot in the head and arm at Zonnebeke.[21] His voluminous diary often refers to Noreuil. For such a small village, it cast a long shadow. At Messines he wrote of a too-thin barrage: 'A fair number of our boys faltered and laid in shell holes. They had had the experience of Noreuil, and those who hadn't had heard all about it.'[22]

Charles Moule was recommended for decorations at Noreuil and Messines, but received nothing. He was awarded the Military Cross for 'conspicuous gallantry and devotion to duty' under heavy artillery fire at Broodseinde in October. The medal didn't do him much good – hit in the knee by the same artillery fire, his leg was amputated and he died the next day. He was 38 and is buried in Nine Elms British Cemetery, Poperinge.

After winning the Military Cross for excelling in the dual role of signals and intelligence officer at Noreuil, Lieutenant Bert Carlton lifted an already high bar at Zonnebeke, where, in charge of the brigade's forward signals station, he was 'shelled out of his position three times ... losing 10 of his party killed and wounded'. Despite these hardships, he maintained communications, repairing lines personally and, as he had at Noreuil, pushing his signals station forward. Carlton won a Bar for his MC, one of only three men of the battalion to achieve the honour.[23]

Two of the NCOs who held C Company together after Captain Armitage was killed, Sergeant James Wilson and Corporal Arthur Verrier, were repatriated early in 1918. Wilson's Gallipoli and Mouquet Farm wounds had caught up with him and Verrier was ruled medically unfit after being shot in the face at Noreuil and in the side at Zonnebeke. Both arrived home with Distinguished Conduct Medals on their chests, as heroes.[24]

Sergeant Andrew Johanson MM, the Anzac who talked Jensen out of throwing his grenades at Noreuil, spent most of the duration recovering from his serious chest wound. He survived the war. Yet another of the brave C Company NCOs, Lance Corporal Harold Pritchard, earned a DCM at Messines to go with the Military Medal won at Noreuil. Promoted to sergeant, Pritchard led a fighting patrol into no-man's land to eliminate a snipers' eyrie. Spraying them with a Lewis gun, he then crawled forward working the bolt on his rifle. Those Germans not killed did not stay and fight.[25]

Lance Corporal Fred Woolfitt, the private who carried on when shot in the hand at Noreuil, was killed at Villers-Bretonneux. He was next to Pritchard when shot in the head by a sniper. 'He was a fine soldier and had received the MM for good work at Noreuil,' Pritchard told the Red Cross.[26]

Still another C Company man who excelled at Noreuil, original Anzac Royce Spinkston, was awarded the MM at Villers-Bretonneux. His citation might have been written for any number of the 50th men that day, such was their mastery of their craft after three years of war. Assuming command of his platoon when his officer was wounded, Sergeant Spinkston 'set a fine example by his courage and coolness ... on one occasion he took out a Lewis gun and engaged an enemy machine-gun at close range, finally silencing it, thereby allowing the line to advance'.[27] Spinkston and his comrades were settling the Noreuil account.

As C Company's sole surviving stretcher-bearer at Noreuil, Private Frank Lee was as lucky as he was brave. After being shot in the face at Broodseinde, and severely wounded in the right foot at Villers-Bretonneux, little wonder Lee let off steam while recuperating from his foot wound in England – he was collectively docked 11 days' pay for twice being absent without leave.[28]

The Indian Anzac Charles Khan resumed his duties as a company cook after recovering from his Noreuil shell wound. He survived the war and was awarded the Meritorious Service Medal. The citation reads: 'This man has proved himself a most willing, conscientious and able worker. His work is always carried out efficiently and his cheerfulness and willingness, even under adverse circumstances, have made his services very valuable to the battalion at all times.'[29]

Some men had premonitions of dying in battle. Not Major Murray Fowler, who after being badly wounded at Mouquet Farm, was not injured again and did not expect to be. 'You have absolutely no thought of being hit yourself and I'm fully convinced, even now, after being hit once … that without doubt, I'm coming home … safe and sound,' Fowler wrote. 'I've often tried to imagine being killed, but no matter how much I try, I can't.'[30] The men were expert at playing the brave soldier boy in their letters home to their families. But their diaries often revealed the truth – many assumed they would not survive the war. They had done the maths. How *could* they survive?

Rare was the intact Noreuil hero when the war ended in November 1918. Stokes mortar specialist Stan Coombs MM was gassed in May 1918, and was subsequently repatriated with pleurisy. Alexander Young MM, the B Company private who scouted 1700 yards (1554 metres) of no-man's land at Noreuil, was shot the day the battalion took over a stretch of trenches at Ypres in January 1918. And, after being knocked out by a shellburst and shot in the shoulder at Noreuil, Sergeant John Yeatman MM took a bullet in the lung in September 1918. Coombs, Young and Yeatman all survived the war.[31]

Noel Loutit added to his impressive list of achievements when, aged 23, he commanded the battalion at the Battle of Zonnebeke in September 1917, while Salisbury was posted to a liaison role. Loutit later commanded the 13th Brigade's training battalion in England and was appointed CO of the 45th Battalion in September 1918. He was leading the 45th in an advance on the Hindenburg Line when a shell splinter punctured his chest, ending his war. The 'Kid Colonel' finished the war with a DSO and bar, three mentions in despatches, and widespread renown for reaching the Third Ridge at Anzac – yet surely his greatest achievement was turning the battle at Noreuil.[32]

Other than leave and brief secondments, Salisbury commanded the 50th Battalion for the remainder of the war. This gave the battalion great stability of leadership when compared with, for example, its parent unit, the 10th Battalion, which had 15 commanding officers. Salisbury received a Bar to his Pozieres DSO for commanding his battalion from a forward, heavily shelled, position at Villers-Bretonneux.[33]

Colonel Pope failed at Noreuil but there was no questioning his bravery – he was severely wounded by a shell while leading his men onto Messines Ridge in June 1917. He was repatriated but, at his request, continued to serve commanding draughts of reinforcements on troopships.[34]

Joergen Jensen remained the only man of the battalion – and one of two in the brigade – to win the Victoria Cross. He found that with honour came responsibility: made a lance corporal immediately after Noreuil, he was promoted to corporal in mid-1917 and temporary sergeant in November. At Villers-Bretonneux Jensen was part of a fighting patrol that closed the trap at the eastern end of the town. When he wasn't fighting Germans he was warring with the military police, leading a party of 50th men that liberated a cache of champagne from a cellar guarded by MPs.[35] Ten days after the Battle of Villers-Bretonneux, while on patrol, he was shot in the head, left arm and left knee. He was repatriated to Australia in August.[36]

Corporal William 'Barney' O'Connor (AWM P09291.020).

Private Jack Campbell's enduring memory of Noreuil was Jensen and his mate Barney O'Connor emerging from the gunsmoke the day after they had been posted as missing. O'Connor, the stockman and fearless horseman from Packsaddle Station, was the battalion's archetypal bushman soldier:[37]

Promoted to corporal, O'Connor was shot in the leg and back at Zonnebeke. After a long stint in hospital he took off for two days and was docked two days' pay. (The modest penalty might have had something to do with the DCM ribbon on his chest.) Corporal O'Connor was killed in action at Villers-Bretonneux. He was 27 and has no known grave. 'I will miss Barney O'Connor,' Private Campbell wrote. 'If anyone got hit he was there to see if he could help. Many a time he took the load off my shoulders the first month I was in France.'[38]

Monument Wood at the far end of Villers-Bretonneux brooded over the 50th men as they dug in. Standing proud among the stumps and matchwood, a single line of surviving pine trees concealed a sniper. A sniper that killed Sergeant Roy Clark, the C Company man who wrote to Captain Armitage's father after Noreuil. 'Clark's helmet was drilled dead-centre,' Corporal Duncan Butler said. 'Two inches either way and the bullet might have glanced off.' Butler saw a reflective glint in the pine tree row. He gave the spot a burst with his Lewis gun and the sniping ceased.[39]

Pat Auld commanded A Company on the right of the 50th's line at Villers-Bretonneux. Auld's axis of attack was furthest from the town and its guiding light. Cresting a low rise, he came upon 20–30 men whom he hailed. They replied with bullets. In the dark and confusion they might be Australians, Auld thought, so he ordered the men with him to hold their fire. 'Not wishing to stop a bullet whether Australian or German – they are equally effective – I jumped down into a small position in front of me, accompanied by my runner,' Auld said. The rest of his men took flight in the other direction as the strangers closed, revealing themselves to be German. 'I fired my revolver into them … which brought a hail of bullets about our ears in return.' Auld had no choice but to surrender.[40] Auld could have done with the navigational skills of master bushman Ted Lamming, who when the night attack was won, led his mates out of the line by following the stars in the sky.[41]

Gilbert Jacob, the private who wrote so lyrically about the colours and sounds and shades of Noreuil, also took up his pen after Villers-Bretonneux. 'It was near dawn when we had dug in, and the great, red fire we had watched was burning low through the misty darkness,' Jacob wrote. 'When the fog cleared we saw the skeleton of the great church that had been burned and the city that was ours. We had made the counter charge we had been ready for for so long. It was Anzac Day.'[42] Jacob was killed near Hamel on 7 July. He was 22. His mother Florence wrote his epitaph: 'Also in memory of his brother 6679 Private GW Jacob 50th Bn Australian Inf 25th September 1917.' George Jacob was 25 when he was killed at Zonnebeke. He is Known unto God.[43]

Thomas and Elizabeth Eglinton of Forest Range, in the Adelaide Hills, sent five sons to war. The youngest, Laurence, 22, was posted to the 50th and was killed at Noreuil. Clarence, 26, joined the 27th Battalion and was killed at the Battle of Menin Road in September 1917. And Thomas, 31, was killed when the 50th was sent back to the Villers-Bretonneux trenches two weeks after the town was recaptured. Wilfred Eglinton was wounded and invalided home and, in a *Saving Private Ryan* prequel, John Eglinton was repatriated for 'family reasons' in late 1918.[44]

Oliver Winter, the Anzac whose boyish visage belied his bayonet work in the Noreuil rubble, was in hospital when the battalion attacked at Villers-Bretonneux. The diagnosis, or non-diagnosis, was pyrexia of unknown origin, in other words a mysterious fever. His brother Albert, also an Anzac and also a Noreuil survivor, was killed at Villers-Bretonneux. Sergeant Albert Winter has no known grave. A third Winter brother, Francis, died of wounds on the Somme in November 1916. In May 1918, while still recuperating from his illness in hospital, Oliver wrote to Salisbury: 'I herewith respectfully beg to apply for discharge from the AIF ... being the only son left in my family, my two other Brothers being recently killed in action.' He told the CO he was a married man (he had wed Ethel, from Catford in south-east London, while on leave) and since enlisting in January 1915, he had 'never had a crime'. Salisbury forwarded the letter to brigade HQ, commenting he was 'agreeable to forward this application for consideration'. And so the letter passed up the chain of command: Brigadier Glasgow was also agreeable, as was 4th Division CO Major-General Ewen Sinclair-MacLagan, and ultimately AIF headquarters in London. Corporal Winter was ordered to Weymouth to await a ship home. He arrived in Australia on 16 September. It appears Ethel took a later passage.[45]

The 50th Battalion was on a train back to the front when the war ended. There had been rumours of an armistice; rumours strong enough to trigger wild booze-ups in the estaminets along the stretch of the Somme where the battalion was billeted. The rumours were confirmed by the scene that greeted the diggers when they clambered out of their cattle-truck carriages at Saint-Quentin. Euphoric Frenchmen kissed the Australians between swigs of *vin ordinaire* from bottles, casks, buckets, canvas bags and steel helmets.[46] The 50th's battalion band played *La Marseillaise*, the Frenchmen wept, the Australians climbed back aboard, and the train retraced its tracks through broken fields littered with dead horses, smashed guns, and bunds of wire that wended across the landscape like giant brown snakes – the Hindenburg Line, laid low and obsolete.[47]

10

... the shallow valley of memory

It takes a tough soldier to stand out in a photograph of 10 Victoria Cross winners. The man with the lantern jaw and defiant mien looks ready to fight the Great War all over again. He resembles Hollywood hard man Lawrence Tierney does the corporal standing in the back row, second right. Tierney was once described as a 'frightening force of nature' and Corporal Joergen Jensen VC was exactly that.[1]

The picture was taken as HMAT *Medic* docked at Port Melbourne in October 1918. Prime Minister Billy Hughes had summoned the heroes home to boost recruiting and the 'Victoria Cross Ship' made good copy. The South Australian heroes Jensen and Roy Inwood (sitting, front left) were ushered onto the Melbourne Express to Adelaide, where they were greeted by a large crowd at North Terrace Railway Station and conveyed to a civic reception in the Town Hall.[2] There were no florid press interviews at the station, town hall or anywhere else: Jensen liked to keep his own counsel. Never mind; he looked fit and strong and recovered from his May head wound.

Corporal Joergen Jensen (back row, second from right) with nine fellow Victoria Cross winners about to dock at Port Melbourne in October, 1918 (AWM 072966).

Migrating alone from Denmark in 1909 and working as a riverboat hand on the River Murray and a labourer in Port Pirie, Jensen was a confirmed wanderer. After his discharge he drifted to Truro at the north-eastern corner of the Barossa Valley, where the Mt Lofty Ranges escarpment drops sharply to the grey plains sweeping all the way to the Murray. Jensen was probably on his way to look for work on the river when he stopped at the Truro pub – and was offered a bar job by the licensee, Katy Harman, alias Miss Katy Arthur. Jensen and Katy Arthur began a relationship.

Unfortunately, 'Miss' Arthur was married with two children. Her husband, Joseph Harman, was unimpressed by his wife's dalliances with the war hero, and filed for divorce, naming Jensen as the co-respondent. The Chief Justice, Sir George Murray, heard the case in the Adelaide Divorce Court on 8

July 1920. His Honour found there had been 'misconduct' and dissolved the marriage. The jilted husband sought costs from Jensen, who told the court Katy had introduced herself as Miss Arthur. When Jensen had discovered her real name, he testified, she told him she had not seen her husband for years. Jensen was under the impression her husband was dead. He was ordered to pay the resurrected Mr Harman's court costs.[3]

Eighteen months later Jensen and Katy, now married and living in Sturt St, Adelaide, were back in court. This time it was the Adelaide Police Court for Jensen to answer a charge of assaulting his wife. 'I'll do for you,' Jensen was alleged to have told Katy when she refused him a bottle of beer. In return, Jensen accused her of threatening him with knives and pelting him with bottles. 'Have you ever called me a ____?' she asked her husband in the court. 'Have you ever called me one?' he fired back to laughs from the gallery. It appeared the marriage was not going well.

'It is only the drink that is his failing,' a tearful Katy told the court. 'He promised to give it up, and he can give it up too.' She was prepared to withdraw the charge if Jensen promised to 'sign the pledge and keep off the drink'. Jensen refused so was given a three-month suspended sentence with a £10 bond.[4] 'It is very hard, Your Honour,' Jensen told Stipendiary Magistrate Sabine. 'I have a lot to put up with.'[5]

Indeed he did. Five months later he was dead. Jensen died 'suddenly' at Adelaide Hospital on 31 May 1922. He was 31. Congestion of the lungs was given as the cause. At his military funeral on 2 June, the route from his Sturt St, city, home to the West Tce Cemetery was lined with mourners, including ranks of silent Sturt St Public School pupils. The coffin, draped in a Union Jack and topped with his medals, was borne by a gun carriage pulled by black horses, and trailed by rank-upon-rank of returned men marching four abreast. Pastor George Walden, who knew Jensen well – Walden had joined the 50th as a chaplain soon after the battalion was formed in Egypt – delivered a graveside eulogy, recalling a modest soldier with little to be modest about, a good comrade and a selfless friend.[6] John Edwards wrote that Jensen's 'geniality and fondness for practical joking made him a general favourite with the troops long before he won his coveted decoration'.[7]

Jensen was the acme of the 50th Battalion's warrior breed but he also represented their campaigns in the war that never ends. His short and troubled life after the war was emblematic of the experiences of many. Wounded and taken prisoner at Noreuil, Reg Sully sent the Red Cross a postcard in June 1918, saying he was 'in good health'. He wasn't. Sully died in Nurse Haigh's Private Hospital, Hutt St, Adelaide, on 21 August 1920. He was 26. 'No doubt his untimely death was brought about by the treatment and hardships he underwent while a prisoner of war,' the *Chronicle* speculated.[8]

Sully might have been badly treated, we don't know; but we do know the German surgeons did their best for Edward Budgen, who had a series of operations to remove shrapnel after being captured at Noreuil. The tough old Anzac, wounded at the Somme and Noreuil, died in August 1925. His death revealed his true age: he had given it as 40 in 1914 – two years over the prescribed upper limit for enlistment at the outbreak of war (how he was accepted is unknown). He must have been 45 or 46 when he joined up, as his West Terrace cemetery tombstone shows he was 57 when he died.[9]

Ted Lamming, the bushman who used the stars to guide men to safety at Villers-Bretonneux, died in December 1921, aged 32, from tuberculosis.[10] George Butler, shot in the thigh at Noreuil and the elbow at Villers-Bretonneux, died in May 1924, aged 26. 'A patient sufferer at rest,' his death notice read.[11] Anzac veteran William Woods, shot in both thighs at Noreuil, was 37 when he died in November 1927.[12] Henry Franklin, one of the seriously wounded men captured by the Germans but made to wait for the wagon that never came, died in February 1928. He was 35.[13] When the Indian Anzac died in 1936, Charlie Khan was borne to his grave by his mates – Keith Tamblyn, Tom Dixon, George Kubank and Stan Coombs were the pallbearers. He died in Renmark Hospital, 'the direct result of war service', the local newspaper reported.[14] Noreuil's fading bugle notes echoed through the decades.

So many dying so young showed it truly was the war with no end, although ascribing any post-war death to a specific battle is an exercise in inexactitude. As the Repatriation Department wrote soon after the Armistice: 'No man who passed through the battle zone returned to the Commonwealth in a normal condition.'[15] They tried to numb their mental torment with alcohol and nicotine and the company of the only ones who understood – their comrades. Noreuil veteran Fred Horley's saloon bar in the Red Lion, at the King William end of Rundle St, was a popular meeting place for the 50th men between the wars.[16] In later years they gathered at the Crown & Sceptre, Earl of Zetland, Strathmore and Richmond hotels.[17]

They convened in the Returned Soldiers Association (later the Returned & Services League) clubrooms that sprang up in the suburbs and country towns after the war. They came together on the sporting field too – the battalion fielded an Australian rules team against the combined Light Horse regiments on Adelaide Oval the day after Anzac Day, 1920. Max Gore and Pat Auld ignored the pain and stiffness of their war-wounded legs to play in a match the battalion lost 6.6 (42) to the Light Horse 8.14 (62). Auld was named the 50th's best player.[18]

They marched on Anzac Day, an occasion observed quite differently than it is today. The 1920 march wasn't a march, it was described as a 'procession'.[19] And it was held the day after Anzac Day, which itself was reserved as a solemn day of church services and reflection (although that might have been because it fell on a Sunday that year). The *Daily Herald* reporter wrote that the procession was a disappointing display of 1500–2000 returned men dressed mostly in mufti. It was too soon for many.[20]

They gathered at battalion reunions, the first of which was held in November 1919, in the Cheer-Up Hut behind Parliament House. The Cheer-Up Society that ran the hut was founded and run by Harry Seager's mother, Alexandrine. The battalion bond was strong a year after the Armistice – the gathering was a sell-out. The 50th's first commanding officer, Fred Hurcombe, spoke, the men discussed forming a battalion cricket side, and one of their most decorated heroes, Harold Pritchard, stepped forward to serve as the 50th Battalion Club secretary.[21]

Volunteering to organise the reunion showed Pritchard was as selfless as he was brave. In June 1938 he wrote to the Base Records Office in Melbourne from his Brisbane hospital bed, requesting a replacement for his lost British War Medal. He had his Messines DCM all right, and his Noreuil MM, and his other medals, but he wanted to reconstitute the set. It appears he was getting his affairs in order. 'I am in a bad stage of Tuberculosis due to war service,' he wrote in June 1938. He died three months later, aged 45.[22]

Their homeland's big skies and broad plains sounded a siren call to free-spirited men after three years of France's smudged landscapes and soft light. Seager farmed sheep on Kangaroo Island and Alfred Salisbury did the same near Goondiwindi in Queensland. Salisbury died of hypertensive renal disease in January 1942, aged 56. Dick Wilton never really recovered from his wounds. Wilton was South Australia's deputy chief engineer and in this role was responsible for the state's network of reservoirs and pipelines. The Premier, Tom Playford, paid tribute to one of the state's most capable public servants when Wilton died in June 1946.[23]

When Germany rose again the Noreuil men answered the call: Jim Downey finished the war as commanding officer of the 2nd Cavalry Division Signals, presumably using the latest in radio technology, not carrying boxes of pigeons into battle as he had in France; Noel Loutit was promoted to brigadier and, as the army's commander of logistics and transport in Alice Springs, kept the road open to Darwin in Australia's darkest hour; David Todd was appointed adjutant of the 4th Garrison Battalion at Keswick Barracks in Adelaide; Seager's keenness for another fight was clear – 'serve anywhere, any capacity' he wrote on his enlistment form – he was made a captain in the Kangaroo Island Detention Company, presumably guarding POWs during the day and farming sheep on weekends; and Joe Waine died mysteriously and a long way from home while serving with the Indian Army – nothing is known of his death other than it occurred on 21 May 1941 at Bhopal, he was

50 years old, and he is buried in Kirkee War Cemetery, Pune.[24]

Peter Clarn was in and out of Keswick hospital for seven years after he took a chunk of shell in the buttock at Noreuil. Too old and too infirm to serve – in uniform at least – in the second war, he bought a food van, which followed the troops on their marches through the Adelaide hills. The Dugout, as he called it, had a happy knack of arriving just as the men stopped for their smoke-oh. He entertained batches of soldiers in his home, gave them crates of beer when they entrained for their voyages to the various fronts, and wrote to them once they were there.[25] Jim Churchill-Smith also saw to the troops' welfare: he was deputy assistant director of the SA Australian Army Canteen Service during World War II. He was 73 when he died in March 1968. The nation owes him a great debt not only for his service but the priceless gift of his war diaries.

How the old men of the battalion must have beamed with pride when one of their own was appointed to command the first South Australian infantry regiment raised in World War II – the 2/10th Battalion. And how they must have nodded their approval at the selection of 'young' Corporal Arthur Verrier, who, aged 21, was shot in the face but held firm at the height of the Noreuil battle. Born of the 10th Battalion, the 50th had now provided a second 10th with a commander, further enmeshing the battalions' blood bonds. Drawing on his combat experience at Noreuil and Ypres, Lieutenant-Colonel Verrier formed a fighting force of which the diggers of the original 10th and 50th were justifiably proud. He led the 2/10th in the Tobruk siege and earned a mention in despatches to go with his Noreuil DCM.[26] 'His capable handling of the battalion, his fairness, impartiality and ready wit made him a natural leader of men,'

2/10th quartermaster and fellow First War veteran Lieutenant-Colonel Frank Allchin wrote.[27]

David Todd's time in German captivity does not appear to have affected his longevity; he was 78 when he died in February 1969. Inveterate wire-jumper John Edwards's Noreuil wounds required surgery after the war but he also lived to a good age. He returned to journalism, first at the *Murray Pioneer*, then the *Whyalla News*, and at the Adelaide afternoon tabloid the *News*, where, as Mr Pim, he filed the *Passing By* column from 1931–51.[28]

Roy Houston was one of many 50th men to serve in the Volunteer Defence Corps (the VDC was Australia's home guard) during World War II and was 85 when he died in 1981. Patrick Tippins, honourably discharged in 1917 when his left index finger was amputated from his smashed hand post Noreuil, tried to join the RAAF, but had to settle for being a lance corporal in 3 Battalion of the VDC.[29]

Roland Carter, the Ngarrindjeri man imprisoned with Muslim troops in Germany, survived his internment, married in 1920, had eight children, corresponded with one of the German anthropologists who interviewed him in the POW camps – when the anthropologist was himself interned in Australia during World War II – and died in 1960, aged 68.[30]

Pat Auld's war wounds and POW privations did not stop him playing A Grade district cricket for Kensington after the war. He was elected president of the 50th Battalion Club and attended the official pilgrimage of veterans to Gallipoli for the 50th anniversary in 1965. He departed for the Middle East in a flutter of official paper, generated by the platoons of army bureaucrats deployed to furnish him with replacements for his medals, which had gone missing some time after Anzac Day, 1964. 'It is essential that, if possible, I should have a complete set to wear on official occasions,' Auld entreated the Central Army Records Office in Albert Park, Melbourne. Reading between the sepia lines in Auld's army record, someone of influence intervened on his behalf, as everything but his Military Cross was quickly replaced – a new MC had to come from England. No matter, Auld furnished the authorities with his itinerary in case the medal did not arrive in time. He was flying Qantas from Sydney to Athens, thence 'a 23-day cruise round the Mediterranean ... calling at 15 places of interest where the wog post offices would not be reliable'. It appeared the 70-year-old Auld's social attitudes were not yet attuned to a nation whose plea for a wave of post-war immigration was heard by most of southern Europe.

In 1967 Auld responded to a call for Gallipoli men to apply for the newly issued Anzac Commemorative Medallion. The former 4th Field Ambulance lance corporal was almost overqualified: the handsome bronze medallion depicted John Simpson Kirkpatrick of the 3rd Field Ambulance and his donkey evacuating a wounded soldier. Many of the surviving 50th men applied for the medal, which was valued, almost coveted, in the veteran community.[31]

Of course, nothing in the remainder of their lives – be it only a few years or many decades – compared with the ordeals of their early adulthood. Max Gore sensed the post-war anti-climax: 'The old camaraderie of the war days had ... vanished with the Armistice. Everything was just mundane, with everybody busy with their own affairs and mostly anxious to get back home as soon as possible.'[32]

Returning to his pre-war job as a bank clerk, Gore quickly became disenchanted. Deploying the same acerbic prose he used to skewer the staff officers who planned the Noreuil battle, he wrote of 'stay-at-homes' and 'cold-footers' and society's selfishness: 'It was sad indeed to observe how quickly the comradeship and selfless devotion towards one another whilst under arms at first wore thin, and then finally disappeared under the stress and strain of what was to become known as the rat race: the effort to get not only a crust but the whole loaf, even if the other fellow starved.'[33]

He left the bank and next we find a Max Gore working a block at Renmark in the Riverland. Apparently, he was not a natural farmer; a provincial quasi-court of two Justices of the Peace fined him £4/8/6 for accidentally flooding a public road. 'The cause of the flooding appeared to be that the defendant had no idea of controlling the water,' the *Murray Pioneer* reported.[34] The flooding was hardly Biblical – a foot deep at the worst, and that in a 'pool'. The priorities were different in peacetime, weren't they?

Gore was restless. It appears he divorced his wife and moved to Perth.[35] He married again and enlisted for a second world war in October 1939, serving as a captain in the 10th Garrison Battalion, a militia unit responsible for coastal defence. He served longer in the second war than he did in the first, and was 50 when he was demobbed in 1944. One of the Noreuil battle's central characters and most important chroniclers was also one of the longest-lived: Gore died in Perth in 1980, aged 85.[36]

Loutit (89), Seager (82) and Auld (78) all lived to grand ages, but no-one came close to Charlie Long: devil's number be damned, 10th Battalion original Private Long, No 666, was 100 when he died in March 1987. Keith Tamblyn might have been the last Noreuil man standing. In 1989 he graciously agreed to submit to more than eight hours of interviews about his war, an ordeal for which he should have been decorated.[37] He died in April 1990, almost exactly 73 years after the battle that changed his life. He was 97.

Roger Freeman's magisterial battalion book ends with a chronological gallery of Anzac Day march and reunion photographs that evoke the same mix of melancholy and sentimentality as do the slide shows at modern-day funerals. In the first photo, of a 1930s Anzac march passing the Bank of Australasia in King William St, Charlie Long breaks protocol to wave to the crowd. Long, Jim Churchill-Smith and others are in uniform, topped with their peaked officers' caps. But look down; their putteed legs are in perfect step. A 1977 march photo shows the 50th men still in step as they march down the hill past Government House – 60 years after the Battle of Noreuil.[38]

The last photo in the sequence shows Red Lion barman Frank Horley, hat on chest, standing silently at the National War Memorial on North Tce. Pip, Squeak and Wilfred on the left breast, RSL badge and Gallipoli medallion on his left lapel, purple and blue battalion tie ... Horley watches over dozens of Anzac Day wreaths as the memorial's girl, student and farmer – representing the state's youth – answer the Spirit of Duty's call. Inside are the names of 141 of Horley's mates and comrades killed at Noreuil or who died in its shadow. We will remember them. How well we do so is another matter.

Gallipoli. Fromelles. Pozieres. Beersheba. Villers-Bretonneux. Even if we don't fully understand what happened at these places, we know the names. We hear the words every Anzac Day. We see the words etched in our memorials. We read the words on book covers: a subject search of the National Library of Australia's catalogue spits out 1012 titles on Gallipoli. Type Noreuil into the same search box and you get ... nothing. We watch Mel Gibson and Mark Lee in *Gallipoli* and Jon Blake and Gary Sweet in *The Lighthorsemen*. More Australians were killed at Noreuil than Beersheba but Noreuil didn't have frenzied horses scenting water through flared nostrils ridden by men with emu feathers in their hats wielding bayonets like swords. (Actually, Noreuil did have this – remember Oliver Winter stalking Germans with his bayonet?)

Noreuil started anonymously. Language difficulties cannot entirely be to blame for the words the diggers themselves used for the battle in their diaries, letters and Red Cross interviews. Families, too, took a while to learn the village's name. Herewith is a selection of Noreuil nom de plumes, substitutes and misnomers: Vimy Ridge, Somme Front, Flers Front, Bapaume Front, Bapaume, Bullecourt, Lagnicourt, Pozieres, Messines Ridge, Noreilles, Nouelle and Mozelle.

By April 1918, the dead men's families well knew the name. Almost eight columns across two pages of *The Advertiser* were needed to accommodate the personal tributes on the battle's first anniversary. Under the heading Heroes of the Great War, relatives, friends and comrades memorialised 72 of the Noreuil dead. Most did so in verse, verse that drew on spiritual faith: 'At that heavenly gate you'll meet us, with your sweet and loving smile, For we are only parted, dearest Herbert, Just for a little while (the family of Herb Winner)'; verse that was frequently pious: 'Our cross, his crown, His duty nobly done (the family of William Bath)'; and verse that was always sad: 'Those who have a father, Love him while you may, He too soon like our dear father, May be called away (Fred Thompson's children Phyllis and Francis)'.

On the eve of the battle Bert Adcock trusted his soul to God and so it came to pass. We know nothing of his death but know he was loved at home; on 2 April 1918, his family included an excerpt of his last letter in its newspaper tribute. In 1922 a son was born to Bert's brother Ralph: Albert Percival Adcock was named in honour of his uncle, Albert Percival Adcock. The following year a John Ross Manthorpe was born and named for Noreuil KIA Sergeant John Ross Manthorpe, presumably an uncle. Each bore their relative's names into a new war 20 years later.[39]

Seventy-two names in the 1918 personal columns dwindled to 23 in the same masthead on 2 April 1927, the 10th anniversary of the battle. Eight men were remembered on the 1937 anniversary. Five years later it was down to three – Harold Harper, Jack Johnson and Fred Thompson, whose son Francis now had two sons of his own, Wayne and Francis junior. Francis faithfully lodged his notice each April: 'fondest memories of dad' he wrote in 1952. Fred Thompson might have been the last to be remembered in the personal pages as the Noreuil dead faded from living memory.

Noreuil lived on in other ways. On 1 April 1918, the Harvey family of George St, Hawthorn, welcomed a daughter, Constance Noreuil. Were these Harveys related to the dead Private Hurtle Harvey?[40] Private George Prest also named a daughter Noreuil. His 27th Battalion fought in the Noreuil sector in March and

April 1917. He might have named his daughter for a lucky escape in the trenches, or perhaps for a friend killed at Noreuil. Or maybe the long rows of 50th Battalion dead made an impression on the wharf labourer from Exeter. Were they friends, relatives or workmates from the Port Adelaide wharves?[41]

French nouns are either masculine or feminine but nuances of a foreign language do not apply when words are transplanted to the new world. Consider the case of Angaston gardener John Wegener, repatriated in late 1917 after being shot in the shoulder at Noreuil. On 13 March 1922, a John Wegener of Angaston christened his newborn son Kevin Noreuil Wegener. Kevin joined up at age 19 in 1941 and served for the duration of World War II. And so the battle lived on in the sons and daughters of the Noreuil men and the Noreuil bereaved.[42]

Names fade away but places endure. Unfortunately, there is next to nowhere named after the Noreuil battle in Australia. Private James Ranclaud of the 43rd Battalion named his Wallaroo house Noreuil in honour of his dead brother William. There's a Noreuil Circuit in Cowaramup, south-west West Australia, and Noreuil Park on the banks of the Murray in Albury, New South Wales. The park was named for an Albury artillery battery's role in repelling a German counterattack two weeks after the Battle of Noreuil. Likewise, *The Noreuil Noose*, an AIF news and gossip sheet printed in May 1917, had nothing to do with the Noreuil battle or the 50th Battalion – the Australian War Memorial ascribes it to the 14th Brigade, an NSW formation that had its HQ at Noreuil during the Second Battle of Bullecourt.[43]

Even the Commonwealth War Graves Commission, which does such a grand job of maintaining almost 3000 cemeteries in France, does the Noreuil men a disservice. Its spiel on the

Noreuil Australian Cemetery begins with: 'Noreuil was the scene of a fierce engagement between Australian troops and the Germans on 15 April 1917.' A quick peek inside the cemetery's walls is all that's required to fix that error in emphasis – 95 of the 220 'identified' burials are men killed on 2 April. The Battle of Noreuil is why the cemetery exists.[44]

The cemetery itself bears witness to the battle's retreat from memory. Its visitors book has only 15 entries for the whole of 2022, including one by Suzanne from the Gold Coast, who 'remembered with love' her great-uncle, Joseph James Earls. COVID-19 is largely responsible for the low number, of course, as an average of about one pilgrim a week made entries in the visitor book from April 2014, to July 2016. Julie, David and Lucas Fraser and Cassandra Harvey, all of Adelaide, paid tribute to their great-uncle, Hurtle Harvey. 'Your sacrifice helped change the world,' Cassandra wrote. Yet even with many of the Covid restrictions lifted, there were only two entries in the first three months of 2023 – from a Manchester/Yorkshire tour group and a couple from Wiltshire. If any Australians visited, they did not write in the book.

The ceremonial record also short-changes Noreuil. The 50th Battalion's battle honours, conferred by King George V in 1927, are, in order of precedence: Pozieres, Bullecourt, Messines 1917, Polygon Wood, Passchendaele, Ancre 1918, Villers-Bretonneux, Amiens, Hindenburg Line and France & Flanders 1916–18. Noreuil doesn't even warrant a mention in the battalion's secondary battle honours: Somme 1916 & 1918, Ypres 1917, Menin Road, Hamel, Albert 1918, Epehy and Egypt 1916. Presumably whoever allocated the honours determined that Noreuil was covered by the Hindenburg Line and Bullecourt awards. (On a separate point, Bullecourt is a spurious battle honour – the battalion played no part in First Bullecourt [11 April, when it was at Vaulx-Vraucourt] or Second Bullecourt [3 May, when it was resting and refitting at Buire on the Ancre].) Noreuil is absent from the colours and the honours, even though one in five of the battalion's dead fell at Noreuil or died from wounds sustained in a battle, which, as a feat of arms, stands alongside Villers-Bretonneux, if not above it.[45]

Relics of the battle and battalion are few. In 1918 the Australian War Records Section collected uniforms of various ranks to be preserved and displayed after the war, which is how Lieutenant-Colonel Salisbury's breeches and tunic are part of the Australian War Memorial's collection. His uniform is not on permanent display, but Jensen's medal set is – donated to the museum in 1987, it sits with those of 65 other Victoria Cross winners in the Hall of Valour.

Personal mementoes survive in dusty drawers and packing cases, fraying at the edges and fading into sepia. A century after the uncle he never knew was killed at Noreuil, World War II RAAF pilot Robert Oswald Jose gestured at a portrait of Wilfrid Oswald Jose (yes, he was given Wilf's middle name) on his mantel. A portrait crowned with a Rising Sun badge, an Australia badge, and two of Lieutenant Jose's tunic buttons, all attached by his sweetheart, Barbara South, before the dashing young soldier sailed off to glory and death. 'When he was killed a lot of people said how it was an extra blow to them to lose such a good friend,' Robert said. Robert's son Nick said Wilf lived on in his family's thoughts. 'There's a strong sense of his presence,' Nick said. 'And that sense of the great potential lost in a life cut short.'[46]

Armitage appeared bound for greatness too. He had to settle for playing a part in the renaissance of Australian remembrance in the 1970s: Armitage is one of the principal figures in Bill Gammage's *The Broken Years*, the seminal study of the diggers' fears, loyalties and motivations in World War I.

A memorial to the last of the Noreuil 141, Corporal Will Spurling, the thrice-wounded C Company Lewis gunner who died in a British hospital in August 1917, is symbolic. In a sandy siding 150km east of Adelaide, beside a long-closed branch of the broad gauge railway to Barmera (also closed), sits a derelict building. A plaque on a boulder tells the story: 'The Spurling Memorial Hall was erected in 1920, in memory of Corporal William Alfred Spurling of Copeville. Killed in action 1917.' Copeville, population 34, is a long way from Noreuil. It's a long way from anywhere. The hall is missing a wall and the 'g' in Spurling's name has weathered away, yet here he is; a man from a forgotten battle lingering on a forgotten frontier of Australian farmers' ongoing campaign with unforgiving country. What hopes they had for this place. What hopes Spurling had for this place. But the railway came and went, the silos were shuttered, dreams died, and Spurling never came home.

Each Anzac Day we stand and stare at the names on the war memorials. At Norwood (Harold Armitage and George Watt). Nairne (Ernie Goodes and both the Earls). Naracoorte (the Bostons, Bill Hoggarth and John Mehaffey) and scores of other places. We remember them in the avenues of honour, such as the one at Rose Park (Harold Hughes and Frank Lillecrapp). In churches such as Christ Church North Adelaide and in St Peter's Cathedral (Wilf Jose). In their workplaces: bank manager Charles Bulbeck is on the Savings Bank's honour roll in its old

King William St building. They are remembered on honour boards in RSL bars such as the one that heaves at half-time of North Adelaide Football Club's home games (John Dwiar, Frank Kingsley and Hurtle Whaites). We intone 'We Will Remember Them', but they are gone from living memory. Even if they are not well remembered, at least their names are recorded. But rarely do the memorials say where they were killed.[47]

Noreuil has come full circle. Starting anonymously, it has withdrawn to the shallow valley of memory. Yet there might be a twist in this story of fading echoes of forgotten valour. When the Unknown Soldier was interred in the Australian War Memorial's Hall of Memory on Remembrance Day, 1993, prime minister Paul Keating said: 'He is all of them. And he is one of us.' We will never know who the Unknown Soldier is. That is as it should be, but it doesn't stop us wondering. We might even imagine that he was a 50th Battalion man. Well, there is every chance he was. Because the Unknown Soldier was retrieved from Adelaide Cemetery at Villers-Bretonneux. And if he's a 50th man, then he might be a Noreuil man. Known unto God? Maybe God is trying to tell us something, as the soldier was exhumed from Grave No 13 – the 50th belonged to the 13th Brigade, its 13 Platoon was wiped out, and it marched 13km up the hill to fight at Villers-Bretonneux. And, God knows, the 50th was unlucky at Noreuil.[48]

Epilogue

April 2, 2023. Cocks crow, startled doves flutter, an icy wind blows ... the cliches are as thick as the low cloud over Noreuil 106 years to the morning of the battle. Atop the southern ridge the wind reminds you of the continent on which you stand: it's a northerly and it's literally polar.

Five deer take flight across the sodden beet fields as you pick your way down the cloying mud path to the south-west corner of the village: the ground tramped by Jim Churchill-Smith's D Company on this morning in 1917. The treeless fields are bereft of cover. It's Sunday, so the pealing bells of Saint-Brice church guide the way, the church's steeple poking out of the hidden valley. The Australians had no such beacons – the church, town hall and any other structure of significance had been shelled to rubble or dynamited by the Germans.

Walking the ground reveals much about the battle. Starting where they started, near the Vaulx-Lagnicourt Rd, the ground rises imperceptibly for the first 100m or so, to a peak of 107m above sea level. Aha, Noel Loutit laid his start tape on a plateau, not a round-topped ridge as in the mind's eye of one's imagination. Then the ground drops steadily for the next 800m to the L'Hirondelle River at the edge of the village, at an altitude of 82m.

From the start line, the low ridge hides the village. And the track on the 50th's left flank only achieves its 'sunken' designation about two-thirds of the way down the hill, where the gentle slope becomes sharper. Soon the banks on both sides are 2m high. Scrubby plum or prunus trees show their first flush of white blossom. Beneath them are tangles of blackberry and bursts of thistle. There is no trace of the barricaded bunker in the road. However, the rain has revealed a relic: a shrapnel ball on the track – probably Australian and probably from the too-thin barrage, 106 years ago today.

The cemetery is next, on the right of the road. Typical of the Commonwealth War Graves Commission graveyards, it is enclosed by a low stone wall, is dominated by a cross inlaid with a huge sword, and is immaculate. The east-west rows of headstones are missing a few teeth courtesy of post April 1917 shelling. Gun-metal shoots sprout from rose bushes and a softer cushion of spongy lawn could not be imagined.

Presently we see Tom Boston, alongside an unknown Australian soldier – his brother Angus? Fourteen other 50th Battalion men have identified graves: Harold Armitage, Wilf Bidstrup, Joe Earls, Arthur Funnell, Charles Hendry, Bill Hoggarth, Wilf Jose, Sydney Kennewell, John Manthorpe, Arnold McFarlane, Tom Rule, Arthur Benton, Herbert Jennison and Fred Thompson.[1] Another 82 are remembered in the 'Special Memorial' headstones arrayed in alphabetical order in tight ranks at the far end of the rectangular, tennis-court-sized plot. Two-hundred-and-forty-four Commonwealth soldiers are buried here: how 50th men comprise all but one of the 83 Special Memorial headstones makes no sense, but that's nothing unusual for this place, this battle and this war.[2]

Treading this sacred ground, I think of my late friend Jack Thomas, veteran of Syria, of Java, of the Burma Railway and the Japanese coal mines. I remember an official trip to the Australian Ex-Prisoners of War Memorial in Ballarat, country Victoria, in 2017. Aged 96, Jack was loath to travel from Adelaide to Ballarat for the anniversary of the Fall of Singapore, but his responsibility to his dead friends weighed heavily; after the memorial service the official bus lingered while Jack, in blistering heat, oversaw his helper attach poppies to each of his friends' names on the memorial. So many names. At Ballarat I told Jack about Noreuil. About the triumph. The guts and glory. The blunders. The waste. The dead. Later appeared an unfamiliar hand in my notepad: 'I can only feel the sorrow of it,' Jack had written. 'Tread softly for you step on my grave.'[3]

Noreuil Australian Cemetery, 2 April, 2023 (Andrew Faulkner).

Across the road from the cemetery, the tiny Chapel of the Seven Sorrows stands sentinel at the edge of the town. It is absent from the 50th Battalion men's accounts, so was probably demolished by the Germans before the battle and, like the rest of the town, rebuilt after the war. The railway embankment is long gone – the branch line closed in 1969.[4] Then we come to the 100m-wide river flat, which was enfiladed by the machine-guns on the left. This is where Wilf Bidstrup and so many others died. We cross the L'Hirondelle, which, even after days of unceasing drizzle, is little more than a trickling brook, and enter the village.

Noreuil, population 141 (the same number as the 50th's death toll), is a triangle of small and neat houses, coddled gardens and farm sheds of varying dimensions.[5] On this frigid Sunday morning, farmers yarn in a barn next to the town hall. (The farmers live in the towns – at nearby Croisilles a tractor is parked outside the pub at lunch-time.) Across the road, the churchyard is lined with espaliered walnut trees, hard-pruned and full of sap rushing to budburst. The word Noreuil is a grouping of the Gallo-Roman 'place planted with walnut trees' and the Latin for 'small walnut grove'. The church's bells are pealing but its doors are locked: the Sunday service rotates among the local villages and today it is Neuville-Vitasse's turn. A formidable poilu stands guard atop the town's Great War memorial plinth. Not a soul is seen on the climb to the top of the town, up where D and C companies burst into the open ground and wheeled right to the objective.

Retracing our steps, we turn left to follow A Company's advance down the valley. Arriving at the fork in the Queant Rd, we veer right. More than a century later, the road's right bank tapers just as Max Gore described, getting lower and lower until disappearing. Conversely, Loutit's relief force had good protection from the high bank on the top side of the road. It is easy to see how A Company was divided before it was conquered – because the isosceles triangle of fire-swept ground is much larger than one might imagine: each of the forks are more than 300m long, the triangle completed at the eastern end by 150m of the objective road.

Hawks circle and crows pick over piles of manure ready to be spread in the fields. Doves fleeing from the unexpected walker do so with a distinctive and pronounced whirring flutter: the noise that led the diggers to call the Priesterwerfer mortar bombs 'turtledoves'? At the battle's apex, the crossroads in the valley, we turn right up the hill: the road to the German machine-gun nest that dominated this part of the battlefield. Partway up the track an artillery shell case sits on the right side of the road. Then a strange encounter – a man and his dog, an Alsatian, loom on the misty horizon. Like the doves, they are puzzled by the intruder: the dog is quickly put on a short leash and the strangers pass with a nod and a *Bonjour, monsieur* from muffled mouths.

Further up, sapling thickets on high banks mark the probable site of the machine-gun post. From this eyrie, the Germans overlooked the valley to the crossroads and the whole of the triangular field, which stands out today because it is fallow grey in a sea of green. You don't need to stand here to know this to be true, Gore's account and all the other testimonies make this truth self-evident, but walking the ground confirms this tragic fact.

An associated tragic fact appears further up the hill. Like the track on the far left, the track on the far right flank emerges onto a plateau. A plateau across which the 52nd Battalion advanced a few hundred metres to dig in well short of where it should have been. The going was good but Lieutenant-Colonel Pope's error was very bad indeed for David Todd's A Company. And the Lagnicourt church bells toll.

Returning to the valley, passing the man and his dog on their return journey, we pick our way up the objective road. At the far corner of the triangle, we turn to see the man and his dog disappearing over the opposite ridge where wind turbine blades wave from Lagnicourt. It's misty and cold and the cloud hugs the ground yet you can see for many kilometres even though there is no-one to see. Two cars parked at the site of Joergen Jensen's VC stunt disgorge no-one.

Turning back towards the village, the upper track of the triangle reveals little; there is no trace of the serendipitous shallow trench into which D and C companies plunged and held against the odds. Neither can Todd's dugout be found. Or dugouts of any description. Time has reclaimed the landscape.

And the cold has won the day. We set a course for Le Canberra pub in Bullecourt, in search of hot coffee. The straight 1km road from Ecoust-Saint-Mein to Bullecourt should offer a different perspective of the Noreuil battlefield. A balcony view from the high ground to the north. Slowing to absorb the scene, we see … nothing. Not even the church spire can be seen from the road running along the northern extremity of the battle. There is only the fields trailing down the hill and the fields stretching up the opposite slope. Noreuil has vanished.

Four days later our train from Arras to Amiens to Paris is cancelled by a strike. Fortunately there is a direct fast train to Paris. Even more fortunately, the line passes within 4km of Noreuil. So we should be treated to one last look at the battlefield from the railway embankment, albeit a fleeting one as the train gobbles up the 160km journey in 49 minutes. However, as we near Noreuil the train slows from 150km/h to 5km/h. This is a peculiar event for the (strikes aside) highly efficient French train network. As the carriage crawls along at walking pace, it feels like *they* don't want us to leave. And then, as we pass Noreuil, in the final act of this ghostly, haunted epic, the village is veiled by a thick curtain of fog. More than 100 years later, Noreuil refuses to release all its secrets. Deserted, shrouded and forgotten ... Noreuil is Australia's Brigadoon.

Noreuil Honour Roll

Killed in action at Noreuil or died of wounds sustained at Noreuil

Private Albert Adcock, 21, Croydon, SA: KIA, 2 April, Noreuil Australian Cemetery (Special Memorial)*

Lance Corporal Gerald Ahern, 20, Thebarton, SA: KIA, 2 April, Noreuil Australian Cemetery (Special Memorial)

Captain Harold Armitage, 22, Millicent, SA: KIA, 2 April, Noreuil Australian Cemetery

Private Clarence Ash, 21, Unley, SA: KIA, 2 April, Noreuil Australian Cemetery (Special Memorial)

Private William Ball, 27, Semaphore, SA: KIA, 2 April, Noreuil Australian Cemetery (Special Memorial)

Private John Bath, 37, Renmark, SA: KIA, 2 April, Noreuil Australian Cemetery (Special Memorial)

Private William Bath, 21, Parkside, SA: KIA, 2 April, Noreuil Australian Cemetery (Special Memorial)

Private William Batt, 21, Bolivar, SA: DOW, 8 April, St Sever Cemetery Extension, Rouen

Private Percy Beauchamp, 22, Goodwood, SA: KIA, 2 April, Noreuil Australian Cemetery (Special Memorial)

Private Prince Begley, 28, Adelaide, SA: KIA, 2 April, no known grave

Private Arthur Benton, 22, Adelaide, SA: KIA, 2 April, Noreuil Australian Cemetery

Lieutenant Wilfred Bidstrup, Hyde Park, SA: 27, KIA, 2 April, Noreuil Australian Cemetery

Private Angus Boston, 28, Naracoorte, SA: KIA, 2 April, Noreuil Australian Cemetery (Special Memorial)

Corporal Thomas Boston, 25, Naracoorte, SA: KIA, 2 April, Noreuil Australian Cemetery

Lance Corporal John Brakenridge, 31, Port Pirie, SA: KIA, 2 April, no known grave (probably buried in Noreuil Australian Cemetery)

Lance Corporal Charles Bulbeck, 28, Maylands, SA: KIA, 2 April, Noreuil Australian Cemetery (Special Memorial)

Private Richard Button, 28, Yahl, SA: KIA, 2 April, Noreuil Australian Cemetery (Special Memorial)

Sergeant Henry Cheney, 26, Mitcham, SA: KIA, 2 April, no known grave (probably buried in Noreuil Australian Cemetery)

Private Oscar Chenoweth, 39, Kangarilla, SA: KIA, 2 April, Noreuil Australian Cemetery (Special Memorial)

Private John Cherpiter, 33, Adelaide, SA: KIA, 2 April, no known grave

Private Joseph Cox, 22, Milparinka, NSW: KIA, 2 April, Noreuil Australian Cemetery (Special Memorial)

Private Norman Currie, 23, Mylor, SA: KIA, 2 April, Noreuil Australian Cemetery (Special Memorial)

Private Henry Dougal, 34, Adelaide, SA: KIA, 11 April, Vaulx Hill Cemetery

Private William Dullea, 22, Saddleworth, SA: KIA, 2 April, Noreuil Australian Cemetery (Special Memorial)

Private John Dwiar, 27, Kadina, SA: KIA, 2 April, Noreuil Australian Cemetery (Special Memorial)

Private Joseph Earls, 31, Callington, SA: KIA, 2 April, Noreuil Australian Cemetery

Private Leslie Edgar, 24, Adelaide, SA: KIA, 2 April, Noreuil Australian Cemetery (Special Memorial)

Private Laurence Eglinton, 23, Forest Range, SA: 2 April, Noreuil Australian Cemetery (Special Memorial)

Lance Corporal Dudley Evans, 21, Goodwood, SA: DOW, 19 April, St Sever Cemetery Extension, Rouen

Private John Fanning, 24, Murray Bridge, SA: DOW, 18 June, St Sever Cemetery Extension, Rouen.

Private John Fitzpatrick, 21, Gawler, SA: KIA, 2 April, Noreuil Australian Cemetery (Special Memorial)

Lance Corporal Percy Foster, 25, Lucindale, SA: KIA, 2 April, Noreuil Australian Cemetery (Special Memorial)

Private William Foster, 26, Renmark, SA: KIA, 2 April, Noreuil Australian Cemetery (Special Memorial)

Private Douglas Freeman, 19, Gawler, SA: KIA, 2 April, Noreuil Australian Cemetery (Special Memorial)

Lance Corporal Arthur Funnell, 23, Norwood, SA: KIA, 2 April, KIA, April 2, Noreuil Australian Cemetery

Private Herbert Gale, 22, Edwardstown, SA: KIA, 2 April, Noreuil Australian Cemetery (Special Memorial)

Private Peter Gascoigne, 24, Loxton, SA: KIA, 2 April, Noreuil Australian Cemetery (Special Memorial)

Lance Corporal Norman Gates, 24, Natimuk, Vic: KIA, 28 March, Vaulx Hill Cemetery

Private Andrew Gay, 35, Nonning, SA: DOW, 9 April, Aveluy Communal Cemetery Extension

Private Ednie George, 19, Kent Town, SA: KIA, 2 April, Noreuil Australian Cemetery (Special Memorial)

Lance Corporal Arthur Gilbert, 25, Broken Hill, NSW: KIA, 2 April, Noreuil Australian Cemetery (Special Memorial)

Private Clifford Goode, 23, Richmond, SA: KIA, 2 April, no known grave

Lance Corporal Ernest Goodes, 24, Harrogate, SA: KIA, 2 April, no known grave

Private James Graham, 34, Brinkworth, SA: KIA, 2 April, no known grave

Private Oswald Griffen, 22, Riverton, SA: KIA, 2 April, Noreuil Australian Cemetery (Special Memorial)

Private Robert Haines, 25, Alberton, SA: KIA, 2 April, no known grave

Corporal Harold Harper, 22, Adelaide, SA: KIA, 2 April, Noreuil Australian Cemetery (Special Memorial)

Private Hurtle Harvey, 20, Kadina, SA: KIA, 2 April, Noreuil Australian Cemetery (Special Memorial)

Sergeant Charles Hendry, 23, Port Adelaide, SA: KIA, 2 April, Noreuil Australian Cemetery

Private John Hepworth, 25, Colton SA: KIA, 2 April, Noreuil Australian Cemetery (Special Memorial)

Private Nicholas Herring, 20, Lobethal, SA: KIA, 2 April, Noreuil Australian Cemetery (Special Memorial)

Private George Hinderwell, 22, Hindmarsh, SA: KIA, 2 April, no known grave

Private John Hogan, 34, Port Augusta, SA: KIA, 2 April, Queant Road Cemetery

Lieutenant William Hoggarth, 27, Hawthorn, SA: KIA, 2 April, Noreuil Australian Cemetery

Private Harold Hollis, 26, Exeter, SA: DOW, 14 April, St Sever Cemetery Extension, Rouen

Private Walter Holman, 30, St Peters, SA: KIA, 2 April, no known grave

Private Harold Hughes, 23, Eastwood, SA: KIA, 2 April, Noreuil Australian Cemetery (Special Memorial)

Private John Hunt, 22, Dandenong, Vic: KIA, 2 April, Noreuil Australian Cemetery (Special Memorial)

Sergeant William James, 25, Broken Hill, NSW: KIA, 2 April, Noreuil Australian Cemetery (Special Memorial)

Private Frederick Jeffries, 28, Adelaide, SA: KIA, 2 April, Noreuil Australian Cemetery (Special Memorial)

Private Herbert Jennison, 21, Warnertown, SA: KIA, 2 April, Noreuil Australian Cemetery

Private Allan Johnson, 25, Houghton, SA: KIA, 2 April, Noreuil Australian Cemetery (Special Memorial)

Private Douglas Johnston, 24, Oakbank, SA: DOW, 5 May, Cambridge City Cemetery

Lieutenant Wilfrid Jose, 22, North Adelaide, SA: KIA, 2 April, Noreuil Australian Cemetery

Sergeant Hedley Joyce, 25, Paruna, SA: KIA, 2 April, Noreuil Australian Cemetery (Special Memorial)

Private Robert Kemsley, 33, Prospect, SA: KIA, 2 April, Noreuil Australian Cemetery (Special Memorial)

Private Sydney Kennewell, 22, Gawler, SA: KIA, 2 April, Noreuil Australian Cemetery

Private Herbert Kernick, 37, Bundanoon, NSW: KIA, 2 April, Noreuil Australian Cemetery (Special Memorial)

Private Frank Kingsley, 23, Prospect, SA: KIA, 2 April, Noreuil Australian Cemetery (Special Memorial)

Private William Lawrance, 22, Port Pirie, SA: KIA, 2 April, Noreuil Australian Cemetery (Special Memorial)

Corporal Hedley Leverington, 25, Payneham, SA: KIA, 2 April, Noreuil Australian Cemetery (Special Memorial)

Private Frank Lillecrapp, 23, Rose Park, SA: DOW, 4 April, Pozieres British Cemetery

Private Karl Ljung, 24, Birkenhead, SA: KIA, 2 April, Noreuil Australian Cemetery (Special Memorial)

Private Sydney Mace, 31, Murnpeowie, SA: KIA, 2 April, no known grave

Private Henry Mahoney, 24, Gawler, SA: KIA, 2 April, no known grave

Corporal Halcro Main, 32, Adelaide, SA: DOW, 12 April, St Sever Cemetery Extension, Rouen

Lance Corporal Ralph Mann, 29, Adelaide, SA: DOW, 2 April, Bapaume Australian Cemetery

Sergeant John Manthorpe, 21, Unley, SA: KIA, 2 April, Noreuil Australian Cemetery

Private Edgar Maxwell, 25, Saddleworth, SA: KIA, 2 April, Noreuil Australian Cemetery (Special Memorial)

Corporal Arnold McFarlane, 31, Port Pirie, SA: KIA, 2 April, Noreuil Australian Cemetery

Private Charles McIvor, 50, Port Augusta, SA: KIA, 2 April, Noreuil Australian Cemetery (Special Memorial)

Private Roderick McLeod, 39, Poonindie, SA: KIA, 2 April, Noreuil Australian Cemetery (Special Memorial)

Private Patrick McNamara, 38, Jamestown, SA: KIA, 2 April, Noreuil Australian Cemetery (Special Memorial)

Private Lachlan McQueen, 22, Stepney, SA: KIA, 2 April, Noreuil Australian Cemetery (Special Memorial)

Sergeant John Mehaffey, 23, Naracoorte, SA: KIA, 2 April, no known grave

Private Jack Mills, 28, Mypolonga, SA: DOW, 11 April, St Sever Cemetery Extension, Rouen

Private James Mochrie, 23, Adelaide, KIA, 2 April, Noreuil Australian Cemetery (Special Memorial)

Private Douglas Moore, 22, Meadows, SA: DOW, 16 April, St Sever Cemetery Extension, Rouen

Private Victor Moore, 19, Exeter, SA: KIA, 2 April, Noreuil Australian Cemetery (Special Memorial)

Private John Mullins, 24, Unley, SA: KIA, 2 April, Noreuil Australian Cemetery (Special Memorial)

Private Thomas Murrin, 34, Yelta, SA: KIA, 2 April, Noreuil Australian Cemetery (Special Memorial)

Corporal James Murray, 22, St Peters, SA: KIA, 2 April, no known grave (probably buried in Noreuil Australian Cemetery)

Private John Neddermeyer, 30, West Thebarton, SA: KIA, 2 April, Noreuil Australian Cemetery (Special Memorial)

Private Ernest Newton, 21, Broken Hill, SA: KIA, 2 April, Noreuil Australian Cemetery (Special Memorial)

Private Andries Norman, 29, Gladstone, SA: DOW, 3 April, Pozieres British Cemetery

Private Ernest Norman, 25, Mt Gambier, SA: KIA, 2 April, Noreuil Australian Cemetery (Special Memorial)

Private Theodore Norman, 32, Clarence Park, SA: KIA, 2 April, Noreuil Australian Cemetery (Special Memorial)

Private John O'Rielly, 21, Tailem Bend, SA: KIA, 2 April, Noreuil Australian Cemetery (Special Memorial)

Private Bertram Osborne, 18, Balhannah, SA: DOW, 9 April, St Roch Communal Cemetery, Valenciennes

Private Edward O'Toole, 43, St Peters, SA: KIA, 28 March, Vaulx Hill Cemetery

Sergeant Joseph Peebles, 35, Broken Hill, NSW: KIA, 28 March, no known grave

Private William Potts, 27, Balhannah, SA: KIA, 2 April, Noreuil Australian Cemetery (Special Memorial)

Private William Ranclaud, 20, Wallaroo, SA: KIA, 2 April, no known grave

Private Allan Reid, 21, Birkenhead, SA: KIA, 2 April, Queant Road Cemetery

Lance Corporal Horace Richardson, 21, North Adelaide, SA: DOW, 20 April, St Sever Cemetery Extension, Rouen

Private Stephen Roach, 34, Broken Hill, NSW: KIA, 2 April, Noreuil Australian Cemetery (Special Memorial)

Private William Roberts, 39, Woods Flat, SA: DOW, 4 April, Pozieres British Cemetery

Lieutenant Esson Rule, 22, Burra, SA: KIA, 2 April, Noreuil Australian Cemetery

Private Thomas Russell, 33, Port Adelaide, SA: KIA, 2 April, no known grave

Lance Corporal Harold Scott, 24, Broken Hill, SA: KIA, 2 April, no known grave

Private Alan Shadgett, 23, Parkside, SA: KIA, 2 April, Noreuil Australian Cemetery (Special Memorial)

Lance Corporal Cornelius Shea, 26, Crystal Brook, SA: KIA, 2 April, Noreuil Australian Cemetery (Special Memorial)

Lieutenant Alfred Sheard, 27, Wayville, SA: DOW, 29 March, Aveluy Communal Cemetery Extension

Private Patrick Sheehan, 33, Kingswood, SA: DOW, 3 April, Pozieres British Cemetery

Private Amyas Smith, 24, Echunga, SA: KIA, 2 April, no known grave

Corporal Will Spurling, 24, Copeville, SA: DOW, 16 August, Melcombe Regis Cemetery, Weymouth

Private Percy Stagg, 24, Yeelanna, SA: KIA, 2 April, Noreuil Australian Cemetery (Special Memorial)

Private Howard Stark, 20, Naracoorte, SA: KIA, 2 April, Noreuil Australian Cemetery (Special Memorial)

Sergeant Henry Steuve, 23, Broken Hill, NSW: KIA, 2 April, no known grave

Private John Stewart, 27, Cheltenham, SA: KIA, 2 April, no known grave

Private Richard Tavender, 19, Angaston, SA: KIA, 2 April, Noreuil Australian Cemetery (Special Memorial)

Lance Corporal John Taylor, 19, Portland, SA: KIA, 2 April, Noreuil Australian Cemetery (Special Memorial)

Private Frederick Thompson, 26, Birkenhead, SA: KIA, 2 April, Noreuil Australian Cemetery

Private Hugh Thompson, 20, Northfield, SA: KIA, 2 April, Noreuil Australian Cemetery (Special Memorial)

Private Frank Tiver, 20, Burra, SA: KIA, 2 April, Noreuil Australian Cemetery (Special Memorial)

Private Walter Trehearne, 23, Minlaton, SA: KIA, 2 April, Noreuil Australian Cemetery (Special Memorial)

Private Ernest Truan, 23, Veitch, SA: KIA, 2 April, no known grave (probably buried in Noreuil Australian Cemetery)

Private Alfred Tucker, 22, Curramulka, SA: KIA, 2 April, Noreuil Australian Cemetery (Special Memorial)

Lance Corporal Gethen Turpin, 19, Port Adelaide, SA: KIA, 2 April, Noreuil Australian Cemetery (Special Memorial)

Corporal Bewick Vincent, 26, Southwark, SA: KIA, 2 April, Noreuil Australian Cemetery (Special Memorial)

Private Herbert Wall, 19, Salisbury, SA: KIA, 2 April, Noreuil Australian Cemetery (Special Memorial)

Private William Walsh, 37, Adelaide, SA: KIA, 2 April, Noreuil Australian Cemetery (Special Memorial)

Private Charles Washington, 26, Adelaide, SA: KIA, 2 April, Noreuil Australian Cemetery (Special Memorial)

Private William Watson, 38, Sydney, NSW: KIA, 2 April, Noreuil Australian Cemetery (Special Memorial)

Private George Watt, 30, Norwood, SA: KIA, 2 April, Noreuil Australian Cemetery (Special Memorial)

Private Hurtle Whaites, 23, Prospect, SA: KIA, 2 April, Noreuil Australian Cemetery (Special Memorial)

Private Thomas Williams, 21, Rockhampton, Qld: KIA, 2 April, Noreuil Australian Cemetery (Special Memorial)

Lance Sergeant Sydney Wills, 26, Broken Hill, NSW: DOW, 3 April, Pozieres British Cemetery

Private Herbert Winner, 21, Gilberton, SA: KIA, 2 April, Noreuil Australian Cemetery (Special Memorial)

Lance Corporal Thomas Wood, 30, Peterborough, SA: KIA, 2 April, Noreuil Australian Cemetery (Special Memorial)

Private Joseph Woodgate, 22, Aldgate, SA: KIA, 2 April, Noreuil Australian Cemetery (Special Memorial)

*The 'special memorial' men are those known to be buried in Noreuil Australian Cemetery, but whose graves were destroyed. Their headstones line the eastern end of the graveyard.

Acknowledgements

Authors, like defeats, are orphans; and while writing is indeed a solitary pursuit, this story of the victory at Noreuil has many fathers. The first of many debts to be acknowledged is that owed to Peter Brune, who filled many roles – advisor, advocate, amateur agent ... Peter read the manuscript, suggested the title and provided sage counsel and companionship over a cleansing beer.

I have been blessed for 30 years to retain the friendship of my university lecturer and one of the finest writers I know, Dr Nigel Starck, whose encouragement, sound judgment, and perspicacious annotations have shaped this book. The debt owed to Nigel can never be repaid.

To the men who trod the Noreuil ground before me: In *Hurcombe's Hungry Half Hundred*, the late Roger Freeman did more than memorialise the men of the 50th Battalion, by collecting their letters, diary entries and photos, he gave them deserved immortality. We often express our regret at not recording soldiers' stories for posterity – well Roger did just that, and we as a nation owe him an eternal debt; Peter Edgar's *To*

Villers-Bretonneux contains a forensic dissection of the Noreuil battle, and is much more than a book about Brigadier Glasgow and the 13th Brigade. It was a valuable reference point and is highly recommended.

Advice on military minutiae came from a platoon of experts, whose complement included (apologies for the absence of post-nominals, I don't have the space): Brigadier Dave McCammon, Colonel Peter Scott (Ret) – who generously read much of the book and gave precious feedback -- Colonel Steve Larkins (Ret), Lieutenant-Colonel Fred Fairhead (Ret), Sergeant Robert 'Dogs' Kearney (Ret), Sergeant Ed Czerwinski (Ret) and the late Private Jack Thomas. Jack's observations reinforced the poignancy of the Noreuil tragedy.

I am deeply appreciative for the support of Dr Peter Stanley and Dr Aaron Pegram: Peter for encouraging me to press on into the largely forgotten front of the 'outpost villages'; and Aaron for his most generous help with battlefield maps and documents relating to the Noreuil POWs.

I am grateful to the following for their help, be it by answering my questions, giving me direction, providing information about their soldier relatives, or simply listening to long dissertations about a little-known battle: Colin Abel, the late Dr Alan Brissenden, Colin Bungay, Rhys Crawley, David Cree, Bill Denny, Ken Duthie, Keith Harrison, Jo Hook, Michael Kelly, the Lucas family, Dr Sharon Mascall-Dare, Katy Macmillan, Robin Marlin, Anthony Medhurst, Professor Robin Prior, Sharyn Roberts, Des Ryan, Richard Sims, Doug Strain, Dr David Sweet, Michael von Berg, Dr Bernard Whimpress, Suzanne Wilson (St Peter's Cathedral), members of the 2/3rd Machine-Gun Association and all my friends at the Royal

Australian Regiment (SA). I am bound to have missed someone and for that I apologise.

To Denny Neave and his Big Sky Publishing team: Thank you for taking a punt on an obscure battle. Allison Paterson has been a delight to work with during the production process. It's such a comfort to have a safe pair of hands at the other end of the line. And thank you to copy editor Jenny Scepanovic for turning around the manuscript in near-record time.

To my sagacious travel agent, amateur battlefield archaeologist (she found the shrapnel ball in the sunken road), IT consultant, and Thesaurus in human form, thank you, Melanie Reid.

This book is the story of a battalion. A battalion from my home state and a battalion born of the Fighting 10th, which was the focus of the first part of my Arthur Blackburn biography. In this book about Noreuil, I was motivated by finishing that story; the story of the men of Anzac who died on a forgotten front two years after the Landing. As such, I have not given due regard to the unit that attacked on the left flank on April 2, 1917. And so a blank page awaits the West Australians of the 51st Battalion, which, like the 50th, comprised Anzacs and reinforcements alike (acknowledging that a 51st unit history was published in 2000). All the battalions who stormed the fortress villages beneath the Hindenburg Line in 1917 deserve the same. As Peter Stanley told me when I started this book: *that no-one has heard of these battles is the very reason we need to tell these stories and remember these men.*

Bibliography

Australian War Memorial

1DRL/0428 – Australian Red Cross Society Wounded and Missing Enquiry Bureau files, 1914–18 War

AWM30 B11.1 – Prisoner of war statements

AWM25 861/9 PART 317 - Field Returns. 50th Australian Infantry Battalion. January–June 1917

AWM38 3DRL 606/148/1 – 1917 – Charles Bean notebooks

AWM4 unit war diaries, 1914–18 War

    10th Infantry Battalion

    27th Infantry Battalion

    49th Infantry Battalion

    50th Infantry Battalion

    51st Infantry Battalion

    52nd Infantry Battalion

    13th Machine Gun Company

    13th Infantry Brigade

    4th Division

    1st ANZAC Corps

AWM Collections

Harold Armitage diaries/letterbooks, volumes 1–5, 1DRL/0053

Henry Cheney papers, 1DRL/0199

My Landing on Gallipoli, Miles Beevor, MSS0761

Service dress tunic: Lieutenant AG Salisbury, 50th Battalion, REL34024.001

Keith Tamblyn interview, SO1201

Sergeant H Steuve commemorative brooch, REL/12996

The Noreuil Noose, AWM079584

Sinking of the SS *Barunga*, A01043

Roll of honour

Honours and awards

Embarkation roll

National Archives of Australia

B2455 – First Australian Imperial Force Personnel Dossiers

State Library of South Australia

South Australian Red Cross Information Bureau, 1916–19

James Churchill-Smith diary

SA Newspapers: Pen Names of South Australian journalists and cartoonists

Virtual War Memorial

Biographical files

War memorial files

Will Spurling diary

Robert Haines diary

Newspapers

The Border Watch (Mt Gambier)

The Chronicle

The Daily Herald

The Express and Telegraph

Port Pirie Recorder and North Western Mail

The Advertiser

The Daily Observer (Tamworth)

The Herald

The Journal (renamed *The News* in 1923)

Murray Pioneer and Australian River Record

The Narracoorte Herald (in the late 1800s the town changed its name to Naracoorte, but the paper retained the double r spelling until 1948)

The News (*The Journal* prior to 1923)

The Observer (Adelaide)

The Register (Adelaide)

South Eastern Times (Millicent)

The Southern Cross

The Sunday Mail (Adelaide)

The Transcontinental (Port Augusta)

Magazines/Periodicals/Leaflets/Manuals

50th Battalion AIF Club Annual Reunion Smoke Social program 1935

St Peter's School Magazine

Guidons, colours, ensigns and banners – St Peter's Cathedral

British General Headquarters, Instructions for the Training of Platoons for General Action, Issued by the General Staff, February 1917

Australian Dictionary of Biography

Roland Carter

Harold Pope

Alfred Salisbury

Alexandrine Seager

Books

Allchin, Frank, *Purple and Blue, the history of the 2/10th Battalion, AIF (The Adelaide Rifles)*, Griffin Press, Adelaide, 1958

Beale, Pat, *Legends of war, the AIF in France, 1918*, Australian Scholarly Press, Melbourne, 2017

Bean, Charles, *Official history of Australia in the war of 1914–1918, vol I: the story of Anzac from the outbreak of war to the end of the first phase of the Gallipoli Campaign, May 4, 1915*, Angus and Robertson, Sydney, 1940

Bean, Charles, *Official history of Australia in the war of 1914–1918, vol II: the story of Anzac from 4 May 1915, to the evacuation of the Gallipoli Peninsula*, Angus and Robertson, Sydney, 1924

Bean, Charles, *Official history of Australia in the war of 1914–1918, vol III: the Australian Imperial Force in France, 1916*, Angus and Robertson, Sydney, 1940

Bean, Charles, *Official history of Australia in the war of 1914–1918, vol IV: the Australian Imperial Force in France, 1917*, Angus and Robertson, Sydney, 1941

Bean, Charles, Burness, Peter (Ed), *The Western Front Diaries of Charles Bean*, NewSouth Publishing, Sydney, 2018

Beeston, Joseph Lievesley, *Five months at Anzac*, Angus & Robertson, Sydney, 1916 (courtesy Project Gutenberg Australia)

Butler, AG, *Official history of the Australian Army Medical Services, 1914–1918, Vol II, the Western Front*, AWM, Canberra, 1940

Bibliography

Edgar, Peter, *To Villers-Bretonneux, Brigadier-General William Glasgow DSO and 13th Australian Infantry Brigade*, Australian Military History Publications, Sydney, 2006

Faulkner, Andrew, *Arthur Blackburn VC, an Australian hero, his men, and their two world wars*, Wakefield Press, Adelaide, 2008

Freeman, Roger, *Hurcombe's Hungry Half Hundred, a memorial history of the 50th Battalion, AIF, 1916–1919*, Peacock Publications, Adelaide, 1991

Gore, Maxwell, *The long dim tunnel, an autobiography* (unpublished manuscript cited in Edgar)

Holloway, David Clare, *Combat colonels of the AIF in the Great War*, Big Sky, Sydney, 2014

Kearney, Robert, *Fallen Saints*, St Peter's College, Adelaide, 2015.

Lock, Cecil, *The Fighting 10th*, Webb & Son, Adelaide, 1936

Lupfer, Timothy T, *'The Dynamics of Doctrine: The Changes in German Tactical Doctrine During the First World War' Leavenworth Papers, No. 4*, Combat Studies Institute U.S. Army Command and General Staff College, (Fort Leavenworth, KS : 1981)

Maughan, Barton, *Australia in the war of 1939–45, Vol III, Tobruk and Alamein*, AWM, Canberra, 1966

McMullin, Ross, *Pompey Elliott*, Scribe, Melbourne, 2002

Mitchell, GD, *Backs to the wall*, Allen & Unwin, Sydney, 2007

Pegram, Aaron, *Surviving the Great War, Australian prisoners of war on the Western Front, 1916–18*, Cambridge University Press, Cambridge, 2020

Sadler, Peter S, *The Paladin, a life of Major-General Sir John Gellibrand*, Oxford University Press, South Melbourne, 2000

Stanley, Peter, *Men of Mont St Quentin, between victory and death*, Scribe, Carlton North, 2009

Stanley, Peter, *Lost boys of Anzac, first to join, first to fight, first to die*, NewSouth Publishing, Sydney, 2014

Wigmore, Lionel, *They dared mightily*, AWM, Canberra, 1963

Wrench, CM, *The fighting 9th, In and out of the line with the Ninth Battalion AIF*, Boolarong Publications, Brisbane, 1985

Websites

26th Reserve Division (German Empire), 2023, Wikipedia https://en.wikipedia.org/wiki/26th_Reserve_Division_(German_Empire)#cite_note-1914-18.info-1

ABS – Commonwealth population – its distribution and fluctuation, 2012, Australian Bureau of Statistics, Canberra https://www.ausstats.abs.gov.au/ausstats/free.nsf/0/E460415E64A5C941CA257AEF00178694/$File/13010_1901_1918%20section%204.pdf

Adelaide hotels – Hindley St, 2014, LocalWiki, Adelaide https://localwiki.org/adelaide-hills/Adelaide_Hotels_-_Hindley_Street

British Library – Prisoners of War, 2022, British Library, London https://www.bl.uk/world-war-one/articles/prisoners-of-war

Captain Randall Lance Rhodes – WWI & 2, 2018, Adelaide, Rhodes family – https://captainlancerhodes.wordpress.com/

Commonwealth War Graves Commission, 2023, Commonwealth War Graves Commission, Maidenhead, Berkshire https://www.cwgc.org/

Department of Veterans' Affairs – Australian internees and prisoners of war in World War I, 2021, Department of Veterans' Affairs, Canberra https://anzacportal.dva.gov.au/wars-and-missions/ww1/personnel/australian-pows#4

Department of Veterans' Affairs – Battles of Bullecourt, 2020, Department of Veterans' Affairs, Canberra https://www.dva.gov.au/newsroom/media-centre/media-backgrounders/battles-bullecourt#:~:text=First%20Battle%20of%20Bullecourt%2011%20April%201917%204th,largest%20number%20captured%20in%20single%20battle%20during%20WW1

Department of Veterans' Affairs World War II nominal roll, 2023, Department of Veterans' Affairs, Canberra https://nominal-rolls.dva.gov.au/ww2

Sir John Monash Centre, Australian National Memorial, 2018, France, Department of Veterans' Affairs, Canberra https://sjmc.gov.au/

Laws of War: Laws and Customs of War on Land (Hague, II), 29 July 1899, 2008, Yale Law School, New Haven, Connecticut https://avalon.law.yale.edu/19th_century/hague02.asp –

Line from Boisleux to Marquion (in French), 2022, Wikipedia https://fr.wikipedia.org/wiki/Ligne_de_Boisleux_%C3%A0_Marquion

Scottish Prisoners of War 1914-18, 2023, National Records of Scotland, Edinburgh https://www.nrscotland.gov.uk/research/learning/first-world-war/scottish-prisoners-of-war-1914-1918

World War I vets popularised the most important accessory in a gentleman's wardrobe, 2016, Business Insider, New York https://www.businessinsider.com/watches-after-wwi-the-male-accessory-2016-5

YouTube

The Great War in Numbers, 1917: Germany's Last Chance to Save the War, 2022, War Stories, https://www.youtube.com/watch?v=D9OjOY4LPSM

Why The Allies Couldn't Overcome German Trenches in Spring 1917 (WWI Documentary), 2022, The Great War YouTube channel – https://www.youtube.com/watch?v=2foTijS7NyQ

Podcasts

The Old Front Line podcast

True Blue History podcast

Tales From the Battlefield podcast

Fieldwork

Visits to Noreuil (2016, 2018 and 2023) and Villers-Bretonneux (2015 and 2018).

Endnotes

Chapter 1

1   Henry Cheney papers, AWM

2   St Peter's School Magazine – WK Thomas & Co, Adelaide, 1914 (quoted in *Fallen Saints*)

3   The Advertiser, 2/9/1915, p9

4   The Register, 25/6/1915, p8

5   According to Bean in Vol I of his Official History (p351), C Company was to the right of D Company.

6   There were some gaps. Some were later filled by the brigade reserve, the 12th Battalion.

7   10th Battalion embarkation roll

8   Bridley's medal was not promulgated until 1916

9   Miles Beevor's My Landing on Gallipoli

10 Five Months at Anzac, Beeston, J

11 Lock, The Fighting 10th, p227 (The original 10th had eight rifle companies – A to G.)

12 AWM collections – biographical material accompanying Salisbury's donated uniform

13 Bean Vol I, p263

14 Harold Pope ADB entry.

15 Armitage diary, AWM, p29/30

16 Hoggarth served the duration of the campaign

17 ADB says Salisbury was evacuated in November

18 Faulkner, Arthur Blackburn VC, p81

19 Barrett and Murrin NAA files
20 Tamblyn interview AWM
21 Winter picture ex VWM

Chapter 2

1   Auld in Freeman, p6
2   Lance Rhodes memorial website
3   Seager in Freeman, p4-5
4   Enlistment papers did not record birth dates, only ages, with months expressed in fractions of 12 (ie, 20 years and 11/12 months if the soldier was 21 next month)
5   Harvey's NAA file; AWM embarkation roll
6   JE Edwards letter, Transcontinental, 2/6/16, p2
7   Donald Kerr in Freeman, p8
8   Auld in Freeman, p8-9
9   Anonymous letter, Port Pirie Recorder and North Western Mail, 5/6/16, p1
10 Armitage diary/letter book, AWM (Freeman, p11)
11 Gore in Freeman, p11
12 AWM honours and awards
13 Murrin NAA file
14 Tamblyn AWM interview
15 The Western Front Diaries of Charles Bean, Peter Burness (Ed), p118
16 Bean Vol III, p447n
17 Pompey Elliott, Ross McMullin, p234
18 Armitage diary/letter book, 1916-18, p48-49, AWM

Chapter 3

1   Armitage diary/letter book, 1916-18, p101
2   "The French civilians ... were evicted by force. They had no choice in the matter. They were removed and taken into German-held territory and their property was simply destroyed." Dr Spencer Jones, University of Wolverhampton in The Great War in Numbers, 1917: Germany's Last Chance to Save the War. https://www.youtube.com/watch?v=D9OjOY4LPSM
3   Bean Vol IV, p178-186
4   50th Battalion diary
5   Each company comprised four platoons of approximately 40 men (Instructions for the Training of Platoons for General Action, Issued by the General Staff, February 1917)

6   Armitage diary/letter book, 1916-18, p101; Scotch maker Johnnie Walker's slogan was "still going strong", while Viceroy Tea's catchphrase was "going stronger".

7   Herring NAA file

8   Possibly Sylvera as the name is indistinct in Vincent's NAA file

9   Vincent in Freeman, p124

10   Houston in Freeman, p126; the battalion marched from billets at Buire-sur-l'Ancre (west of Dernancourt) to the front via Martinpuich, Eaucourt L'Abbaye and Bapaume.

11   More tracks than roads, they ran through fields that had inched higher over centuries of fertilisation and cultivation. The banks on these sunken roads were commonly three metres high so they made good trenches.

12   Gates Red Cross file (he was reinterred at Vaulx Hill Cemetery)

13   Sheard Red Cross file

14   The urgency was no doubt rammed home when the "commander-in-chief", either Nivelle or Haig (the brigade diary does not say which), visited Glasgow's HQ on 30 March.

15   Coad NAA file

16   Churchill-Smith diary, Vol 2, p19, State Library of SA

17   Khan NAA file; 50th Battalion Field Returns

18   Churchill-Smith diary, The Western Front, Vol II, p20

19   Gore in Freeman, p100

20   50th Battalion diary, 30/3/17

21   Armitage diary/letter book, 1916-18, p61, AWM; "The 50th ... properly should have been termed the second of the 10th" – 'RF' in 50th Battalion Smoke Social 1935

22   The Advertiser, 2/4/18, p4

23   The LOB group is not listed in the Field Return.

24   D and C companies would attack on 180 yard fronts, while A Company had a 360 yard front.

25   Jacob in Freeman, p97

26   Hamlet, Act 1, Scene 1

27   Mt Lofty is the highest feature in the ranges overlooking Adelaide.

28   Jacob in Freeman, p97

29   13 Brigade War Diary

30   Churchill-Smith, Seager and Jacob in Freeman, p95-99

31   Alfred Marsh in Frederick Douglas's Red Cross file

32   Bean writing in The Register, 15/6/17, p8

33 Churchill-Smith diary, Vol II, p57
34 Haines diary, VWM
35 Bean notebook no 148, 1917, p36
36 Churchill-Smith diary
37 Bean Vol IV, p220n
38 Sheehan Red Cross file
39 Prime was from Bowmans in South Australia's Mid-North region.
40 Bennett, Prime and Rehn accounts from AWM30 B11.1, prisoner of war statements.
41 Bidstrup Red Cross file; Bean notebook
42 Fisher in 50th Battalion Smoke Social
43 Register, 11/4/25, p13
44 Jacob in Freeman, p97
45 Washington Red Cross file
46 Bean notebook, p35
47 AWM28 (honours and awards); Jensen's NAA file; Wigmore, They Dared Mightily, p78/79
48 AWM28; Woolfitt NAA file
49 Foster Red Cross file
50 Spurling diary, VWM
51 Kearney, *Fallen Saints*, p192
52 March's 1967 letter to Ivan Jose in Falling Saints
53 Listed as 'Thomas Lee' in the AWM's honours and awards
54 Bean notebook, p30; Armitage wrote Churchill-Smith as "Smith" and Waine as "Wane"
55 Bean, Vol IV, p215
56 AWM honours and awards
57 Douglas Red Cross file
58 AWM30 B11.1; Wood was a Lewis gun sergeant in D Company; Green had been cut off and captured after taking a bullet through his left foot (Express and Telegraph, 20/8/17, p1)
59 Bean notebook, p37
60 AWM30 B11.1

Chapter 4
1 Todd NAA file; AWM honours and awards
2 AWM honours and awards
3 Gore in Freeman, p100

4   Goodes Red Cross file

5   Harper and Shea Red Cross files

6   Taylor Red Cross file

7   Gore in Freeman, p100

8   Jacob in Freeman, p97

9   Fisher, 50th Battalion AIF Club, p28

10 Gore in Freeman, p100

11 Taylor Red Cross file

12 Mehaffey SA Red Cross file

13 'RF' in 50th Battalion Smoke Social 1935

14 POW statements, AWM30 B11.1

15 Gore in Freeman, p101; Fisher 50th Battalion AIF Club, p31

16 Bean Vol IV, p214; Tamblyn AWM interview

17 Gore in Freeman, p101

18 'RF' in 50th Battalion Smoke Social 1935

19 Tamblyn AWM interview

20 Tamblyn AWM interview

21 Todd Red Cross file; another runner was dispatched but was killed on his way back to battalion HQ (Bean Vol IV, p217n)

22 POW statements, AWM30 B11.1

23 Gore letter, p102

24 A Company's platoons became mixed in the confusion of battle – Barnard, Blake and Brown, for example, belonged to 1 Platoon, not Gore's 2 Platoon.

25 James biography, VWM

26 13 Machine Gun Company war diary, April 1917

27 Bean, Vol IV, p219n

28 POW statements, AWM30 B11.1

29 POW statements, AWM30 B11.1

30 Robinson in Freeman, p219

31 POW statements, AWM30 B11.1

32 Tamblyn Red Cross file

33 Ruediger Red Cross file

34 Bean notebook, p13-18

35 Bean, Vol I, p261

36 Edgar, To Villers-Bretonneux, p128

37 Sometimes killing prisoners was officially sanctioned. A July 1916, British memo on clearing trenches stated: "Captured Germans might be able to overpower their guards and then shoot our leading lines in the back." (Typed

report on clearing captured German trenches proposing throwing down phosphorous P Bombs and not taking prisoners as a means of clearing dugouts – Montgomery-Massingberd papers -- @SimonJHistorian tweet, 23/9/22)

38 Gore in Freeman, p209-10
39 Jacob in Freeman, p98
40 Bath NAA file

Chapter 5

1 Sassoon, Memoirs of an Infantry Officer, p77
2 https://en.wikipedia.org/wiki/Granatenwerfer_16; AWM collection, REL35049
3 Bean notebook, p33
4 50th Battalion Smoke Social 1935
5 Bean Vol IV p216
6 Bean notebook, p31
7 The Register, 11/4/25, p13; Hudson NAA file
8 The Advertiser, 3/4/29, p10
9 Spurling in Freeman, p128; Spurling diary, VWM
10 Clark in Freeman, p103
11 Bean notebook, p33
12 Some accounts have Armitage saying this to Wilson before he was hit (Fisher in 50th Battalion AIF Club, p26, states that Armitage told Wilson: "Now, mind. Watch the right flank, and hold on, whatever happens."). But Bean was adamant that Armitage "spoke to Wilson after this" – Bean underlined the word "after" – and also asserted this version of events in The Register (15/6/17, p8).
13 Clark in Freeman, p103
14 Bean Vol IV, p216
15 Battalion HQ was in the "vicinity" of the north-east edge of Vaulx-Vraucourt (50th Battalion diary, 1/4/17)
16 AWM honours and awards
17 Bean Vol IV p217; Seager in Freeman, p96; Rule was recommended for a Military Cross for his "coolness and bravery under fire" at Mouquet Farm.
18 AWM honours and awards; Yeatman served on Gallipoli with the 9th Light Horse Regiment
19 Bean notebook, p5
20 After the war Bean handed the 'furthest inland' palm to 10th Battalion Private Arthur Blackburn.

21 Bean notebook, p5-7 and 31-32

22 Bean notebook, p8

23 Main's first name is given as 'Halcro' in some documents and 'Halero' in others – the confusion is possibly due the similarity of the cursive 'c' and 'e'.

24 AWM honours and awards

25 Mullins Red Cross file

26 Todd Red Cross file; Grant NAA file

27 The 13th Machine Gun company lost five men killed and six wounded in the battle (unit diary).

28 The Journal, 4/8/17, p14

29 Bean notebook, p8

30 Bean Vol IV, p218n

31 Lock, p227; Seager, Alexandrine, ADB

32 Bean notebook, p34-35; Bean wrote in the Official history (p218) that "Salisbury was satisfied that the line could be held as it was".

33 51st Battalion unit diary, April 1917, p10

34 AWM honours and awards; Young NAA file

35 Intelligence, Headquarters, 1st ANZAC Corps, April 1917, Part 1, p6

36 Stanley Barnard Red Cross file; Stanford's wound required his left foot to be amputated (Stanford NAA file)

37 Bean notebook, p15

38 Bean notebook, p37; Salisbury's report on attack on Noreuil; 4 Australian Division diary, April, p4

39 Headquarters 4th Australian Division diary, April 1917, p3

40 Jacob in Freeman, p98

41 AWM Official History, Medical, p119-127

42 Spurling diary, p20

43 Jack Campbell in Freeman, p153

44 Willmott in Freeman, p103

45 Joyce Red Cross file

46 'Gone west' being the soldier's euphemism for dying.

47 Bean took his figures from Salisbury's official report of the action.

48 Appendix 2, 13 Infantry Brigade war diary, April 1917

Chapter 6

1 Report on Attack on Noreuil and Ground to North-East, 50th Battalion War Diary, April 1917

2 Spurling diary, VWM

3   The battalion's Field Return lists 194 men wounded before, during, and after the 2 April battle (excluding wounded POWs and men who died of their wounds). It is, however, understandably dotted with errors, with dead men listed as wounded and captured, and many names misspelt.

4   The Field Return states the unit's 'total rationed' complement was 23 officers and 831 other ranks on 1 April. It was standard practice to leave 10 per cent of the unit out of the battle as a nucleus around which the battalion would be reformed in the event of catastrophic casualties.

5   The Brigade's losses were probably in excess of 700 – twice as many reported by Brigade Major Morell. Bean stated that the 51st Battalion lost 205 killed, wounded or captured, the 52nd Battalion 25, the 49th Battalion seven, the 13th Machine Gun Company 11 and the 13th Light Trench Mortar Battery three (Bean Vol IV, p219). As the 50th Battalion example shows, these numbers were probably low of the mark.

6   https://www.ausstats.abs.gov.au/ausstats/free.nsf/0/E460415E64A5C941CA2 57AEF00178694/$File/13010_1901_1918%20section%204.pdf

7   Harvey brothers Red Cross and NAA files; The Herald, 4/8/17, p3

8   The "enemy determinedly resisted", Haig wrote of the 2 April offensive, but "met with heavy casualties". (The Daily Observer, Tamworth, 5/4/17, p2)

9   Mann is buried in Bapaume Australian Cemetery

10   Red Cross files

11   Brakenridge Red Cross file

12   AWM Collections, Studio portrait of four members of the 50th Battalion, AIF (P10608.001)

13   Begley NAA file

14   Dwiar and O'Rielly Red Cross files

15   Marsh and 'Simmons' are mentioned in Joyce's Red Cross file.

16   'Left out of battle' groups gave the battalion a nucleus of men around which the battalion could re-form if it was wiped out.

17   Churchill-Smith diary 1916/17, p25

18   Tucker Red Cross file

19   Hughes NAA file, p19

20   Joyce, Hughes, Tucker and Turpin Red Cross files

21   Auld in Freeman, p120

22   Churchill-Smith diary

23   Weatherill NAA file

24   Evans Red Cross file

25   Johnston Red Cross file

26   50th Battalion Field Return, p108

27 47 of the 141 were aged 21-23.

28 Ages were given in years and months at enlistment. Dates of birth were not recorded.

29 Russell NAA file

30 Chronicle, 26/5/17, p38

31 The men's occupations can be found in their National Archives files and on the roll of honour circulars filled out by their next of kin.

32 Armitage diary/letter book, 1916-18, p102; 50th Battalion Field Return

33 Jacob in Freeman, p98

34 Armitage diary/letter book, 1916-18, p28

35 Bidstrup Red Cross file

36 Armitage was piqued that Churchill-Smith was decorated for his work at Mouquet Farm.

37 Churchill-Smith diary, Vol IV, p237

38 When he enlisted in September 1916, Wall gave his age as 24. Yet the AWM roll of honour and Commonwealth War Graves Commission record him being 19 when he was killed.

39 Beauchamp Red Cross file.

40 Woodgate Red Cross and NAA files

41 Backs to the Wall, Mitchell, GD, p115; Mitchell received the Distinguished Conduct Medal for a famous incident at Bullecourt in which he covered his battalion's withdrawal before shouldering his Lewis gun and strolling through murderous fire to his lines. (See Bill Gammage's VWM biography of Mitchell.)

42 Gore in Freeman, p100; Gore was promoted to Captain on 29 March 1917, but he was in captivity when the rank was confirmed.

43 Gore, The Long Dim Tunnel, p197 (quoted in Edgar, p137)

44 Clark in Freeman, p103

45 Report on attack by 13th Australian Infantry Brigade on village of Noreuil and high ground to north and north-east (AWM23, 13th Brigade diary, April 1917)

46 Salisbury after-action report; Seager in Freeman, p 96; Tamblyn AWM interview; Churchill-Smith in Freeman, p99

47 Report on attack by 13th Australian Infantry Brigade on village of Noreuil and high ground to north and north-east (AWM23, 13th Brigade diary, April 1917)

48 Leavenworth Paper, p11-13

49 https://www.youtube.com/watch?v=2foTijS7NyQ

50 https://en.wikipedia.org/wiki/26th_Reserve_Division_(German_Empire)#cite_note-1914-18.info-1

51 Leavenworth Paper, p11

52 Bean Vol IV, p251

53 Churchill-Smith in Freeman, p99

54 'RF' in the 50th Battalion Smoke Social 1935

55 Ecoust-Saint-Mein has since absorbed Longatte

56 Bean Vol IV, p207

57 Edgar, p139

58 4th Division diary, April 1917, p41

59 Edgar, p138

60 13th Australian Infantry Brigade, Order No 58, 30/3/17

61 Report On Attack By 13th Australian Infantry Brigade On Village of Noreuil and High Ground To North And East

62 52nd Battalion diary, 2/4/17

63 Bean Vol IV, p219n

Chapter 7

1 The Overway was on the north-east corner of Hindley and Morphett streets (being at the start of the bridge – or "overway" -- across the Torrens River). It now trades as the Rosemont.

2 The Register, 11/6/17, p4; https://localwiki.org/adelaide-hills/Adelaide_Hotels_-_Hindley_Street

3 Jensen NAA file

4 Jensen was among the scores of men promoted immediately after Noreuil to fill vacancies created by the casualties. He was made Lance Corporal on 4/4/17 and Corporal on 15/7/17. The Buckingham Palace investiture was on 21/7/17.

5 The Register, 11/6/17, p4

6 Jensen NAA file. He was posted to the 13th Training Battalion at Codford, 20km north-west of Salisbury, from mid-July to early October.

7 Salisbury in recommending Bishop for the MM

8 AWM honours and awards

9 AWM honours and awards

10 Armitage diary/letter book, 1916-18, p67

11 Gore in Freeman p73. Gore blamed the 49th's CO, ex-10th Battalion officer Francis Lorenzo, for unjustifiably pushing his men for promotion. In the event, Gore received the MC for his fighting at Mouquet Farm and Flers. He "saved the flank of the battalion from being turned" at Mouquet Farm. The MC was conferred in June 1917, two months after he was captured.

12 Bean notebook, p36

13 Bean wrote that "about 60" men of the 50th were captured. The Germans claimed 300 Australians surrendered, but said most were cut down by 'friendly' machine-gun fire, leaving only 60 to make it safely to the German rear (Bean, Vol IV, p220; Register, 5/4/17, p7).

14 Carter ADB entry

15 Carter Red Cross file

16 Mawby Red Cross file

17 Gore in Freeman, p210

18 Osborne Red Cross file

19 Osborne NAA file

20 Powell Red Cross and NAA files

21 Budgen Red Cross and NAA files

22 Budgen Red Cross file

23 Holthouse in Freeman, p212

24 Holthouse in Freeman, p214

25 Molloy POW statement

26 Swanston POW statement; Swanston NAA file

27 Starr POW statement

28 Jacob Red Cross file; Ross Jacob landed at Anzac with the 10th Battalion, was transferred to the 50th upon its formation, and was given command of the 10th in February 1917.

29 Douglas POW statement

30 Tamblyn AWM interview

31 Murphy POW statement

32 Pegram, Surviving The Great War, p55

33 Murphy POW statement

34 Tamblyn AWM interview

35 Some POWs said they were at Lille for 10 days and others said it was six.

36 https://avalon.law.yale.edu/19th_century/hague02.asp

37 Pegram, p57

38 The Germans told the Australians the treatment were reprisals for the British and French using German POW labour in the same way. See https://www.bl.uk/world-war-one/articles/prisoners-of-war

39 Whether Murphy had been trained as an army cook is unknown.

40 Gore in Freeman, p215

41 Occasionally salted herrings were issued in lieu of the horse meat and sometimes a 4lb can of black pudding was shared by 40 men. A small portion of marmalade was issued every other day. (Murphy POW statement)

42 Wheeler POW statement

43 The dead were from the 15th and 48th battalions and 4th Machine-Gun Company.

44 Pegram, p62

45 Schneidemuhl is now called Pila and is in north-western Poland.

46 Murphy POW statement and NAA file (neurasthenia was a catch-all term for general malaise, often caused by emotional disturbance, especially shellshock or post-traumatic stress)

47 https://www.nrscotland.gov.uk/research/learning/first-world-war/scottish-prisoners-of-war-1914-1918

48 Marks POW statement

49 Brown POW statement

50 Robinson in Freeman, p219

51 Rampton and Brown POW statements

52 Tamblyn in Freeman, p205

53 Gore in Freeman, p216-17

54 Todd POW statements; Couston NAA file

55 Edwards POW statements; Gore in Freeman, p219

56 Pegram, p117

57 Barnard, Blake, Douglas, Garrard, Goldsworthy, Hart and Medhurst joint POW statement.

58 Marks, Masters, Murphy and Reynolds POW statements.

59 Pegram, p98

60 Official History, Vol XI – Australia During the War, p706/707

61 https://anzacportal.dva.gov.au/wars-and-missions/ww1/personnel/australian-pows#4

62 Pegram, p98

63 Gore in Freeman, p218

64 Henning Red Cross file

65 Clifford POW statements

66 Robinson in Freeman, p219

Chapter 8

1 Stanley, Lost Boys of Anzac, p163-167; Official History Vol XI, p231

2 https://www.dva.gov.au/newsroom/media-centre/media-backgrounders/battles-bullecourt#:~:text=First%20Battle%20of%20Bullecourt%2011%20April%201917%204th,largest%20number%20captured%20in%20single%20battle%20during%20WW1

3   See Stanley, p167/168

4   Christ Church, North Adelaide

5   The Journal, 12/4/17, p1 (The Journal (1912–1923) was the former name of The News)

6   The Narracoorte Herald, 9/3/17, p4 (both the town and the paper were originally spelt Narracoorte)

7   The Narracoorte Herald, 4/5/17, p4

8   The Narracoorte Herald, 27/4/17, p3

9   The Narracoorte Herald, 8/5/17, p2

10   Medhurst SA Red Cross file

11   Sewing kits

12   The Border Watch, 24/5/16, p2 (Pasfield fought with the 43rd Battalion)

13   Button NAA file

14   The Advertiser, 26/3/17, p7

15   The Advertiser, 4/4/17, p1

16   Bean Vol IV, p219n

17   The Advertiser, 4/4/17, p7

18   Chronicle, 14/4/17, p49

19   Wheeler Red Cross file; Wood Red Cross file

20   Norman was with A Company, so the fact he was collected by stretcher-bearers suggests he was hit early in the battle, before A Company was cut off.

21   Express and Telegraph, 2/5/17, p4

22   The Advertiser, 3/5/17, p9

23   Express and Telegraph, 17/8/17, p1; A fourth son, Bombardier Thomas Dullea, survived the war; Saddleworth was in almost permanent mourning – Edgar Maxwell's brother Bombardier Norman Maxwell died from appendicitis in Rouen in December 1916.

24   The Advertiser, 3/5/17, p9; McQueen was listed as 'Sergeant-Major' McQueen. He had achieved non-commissioned rank but reverted to private after a minor indiscretion in England.

25   The Chronicle, 5/5/17, p44-46

26   Southern Cross, 11/5/17, p14

27   Richardson NAA file

28   Griffen brothers' NAA and Red Cross files and roll of honour entries

29   Haines diary, VWM, and Haines NAA file

30   South Eastern Times, 15/5/17, p2

31   Graham SA Red Cross file and NAA file, CWGC website

32   Gethen Turpin Red Cross and NAA file; Richard Turpin NAA file

33 Goodes NAA file, Churchill-Smith diary; see Lost Boys of Anzac, p230-240

34 Daily Herald, 15/6/17, p5

35 Funnell NAA file

36 McFarlane NAA file

37 Hendry NAA file

38 Tavender NAA file and SA Red Cross file; AWM roll of honour; VWM;
    Daily Herald, 27/4/17, p7; Tavender's first given name was Richard but all
    the newspaper articles referred to him as Roger.

39 AWM collections REL/12996

40 Batt NAA file

41 Before the war wristwatches were seen as fey or affected, even effeminate,
    but their convenience in the trenches transferred into post-war civilian
    life. See https://www.businessinsider.com/watches-after-wwi-the-male-
    accessory-2016-5

42 Sheehan NAA file

43 Stagg NAA file

44 McQueen and Hoggarth NAA files

45 The Cheney family lost a second son. Lieutenant Edward Cheney MC, the
    50th Battalion's inaugural RSM, died of shell wounds on 12/3/1918. Edward
    won his MC at Mouquet Farm and was fortunate to miss the Battle of
    Noreuil when with the 13th Training Battalion while recovering from illness.

46 Jose NAA file

47 Ranclaud NAA file

48 Mullins Red Cross and NAA files

49 Tiver Red Cross and NAA files

50 https://www.awm.gov.au/collection/A01043

51 Evans's Roll of Honour certificate, Red Cross file, and NAA file

52 Kennewell NAA file

53 Roberts NAA file; The Advertiser, 28/1/22, p8

54 AWM Official History, Vol XI, Australia During the War (7th Edition, 1941),
    p838

55 AWM Official History, Vol XI, Australia During the War (7th Edition, 1941),
    Appendix 13

56 Gay NAA file

57 Johnston died of his wounds at 1st Eastern General Hospital, Cambridge, on
    5/5/17

58 Johnston NAA file

59 Manthorpe SA Red Cross and NAA files

60 George NAA file
61 DVA World War 2 Nominal Roll; the VWM records Peter as being born in 1922.
62 So described by a Renmark businessman advocating on her behalf.
63 Bath NAA file
64 Mahoney is commemorated at the Villers-Bretonneux memorial for the missing but his NAA file refers to him being buried at Noreuil Australian Cemetery. For his crimes, which included being AWOL in Cairo and near Etaples on the French coast, he was sentenced to field punishment, docked pay, and stripped of his lance-corporal stripe.
65 John and William Dwiar NAA files, Red Cross files, and SA Red Cross files
66 Stagg NAA file
67 Percy Foster roll of honour circular

Chapter 9
1 Gilbert Jacob in Freeman, p153
2 Pegram on the True Blue History podcast, 25/4/2022
3 Bean diaries, 24/25 April 1918; as the Australians marched, British and German crews fought history's first tank versus tank battle, south of Villers-Bretonneux (Bean Vol V, p564-565).
4 Bean Vol V, p582
5 Bean Vol V, p580; McMullin, Pompey Elliott, p410 (McMullin goes further, highlighting the scandalous claims of a British general that the woods had been cleared and the 13th Brigade "was not interfered with from this wood at all".)
6 Nuttall was awarded the Military Cross and Hanneman the Military Medal
7 The 52nd's RMO Captain Forsyth in Bean Vol V, p586; the British units on the Australian flanks comprised many young reinforcements.
8 "The troops themselves were very conscious of the date." (Pegram in the True Blue History podcast, 25/4/2022)
9 50th Battalion war diary, April 1918, Appendix 6, p2
10 In an 8/9/1918 diary entry, Bean quotes Monash saying: "So long as they have 30 Lewis guns it doesn't matter very much what else they have." (Also quoted by Stanley in Men of Mont St Quentin, p43)
11 50th Battalion unit diary, May 1918, Appendix 8
12 Bean Vol V, p576
13 Beale, Legends of War, p33
14 Foch speech at Amiens Cathedral service, 8/9/18 (quoted in The Fighting 9th by CM Wrench, p436)

15 Sir John Monash Centre website (Monash was commanding the 3rd Division and was not appointed Australian Corps commander until May 1918.)

16 Brigadier-General George Grogan VC, DSO and Bar in McMullin, p422

17 AWM roll of honour

18 Churchill-Smith diary, Vol II, Western Front, p30 (In Arthur Blackburn VC I wrote that Wilton lost his eye at Noreuil, not Messines – I regret the error and am glad to correct it here.)

19 Bice NAA file

20 Seager in Freeman, p114

21 Churchill-Smith NAA file

22 Churchill-Smith in Freeman, p108

23 The other two were Churchill-Smith and Lieutenant James Loudon

24 Wilson and Verrier NAA files

25 Pritchard DCM citation, AWM honours and awards

26 Woolfitt Red Cross file. Other soldiers gave different accounts of Woolfitt's death but Pritchard's appears the most reliable.

27 AWM honours and awards

28 Lee NAA file

29 AWM honours and awards

30 Fowler in Freeman, p238; as battalion adjutant and later 2IC, Fowler was less exposed to danger than company commanders, for example. He was, however, frequently under fire and was awarded the Military Cross for his bravery and exemplary staff work at Noreuil, Messines and Ploegsteert Wood in 1917 (AWM honours and awards).

31 Coombs, Young and Yeatman NAA files

32 Loutit NAA file; Holloway, Combat Colonels of the AIF in the Great War, p155, 156, 337 (Holloway found that only four Australian World War battalion commanders were younger than Loutit.) Bean initially determined that Loutit made it the furthest inland on 25 April, but later decided the honour belonged to 10th Battalion comrade Arthur Blackburn.

33 AWM honours and awards

34 Pope ADB entry

35 Murray Pioneer, 9/6/22, p14

36 Wigmore, p79; Jensen NAA file

37 AWM Last Post ceremony 13/11/22 (YouTube)

38 Campbell in Freeman, p152

39 Butler in Freeman, p150 (Butler received a Military Medal for his bravery at Villers-Bretonneux)

40 Auld in Freeman, p210

41 Freeman, p264

42 Jacob in Freeman, p153

43 AWM roll of honour; Commonwealth War Graves Commission

44 Thomas Eglinton VWM entry

45 Oliver Winter NAA file

46 Joe Scales in Freeman, p205

47 Passing through the Somme for the last time, in early 1919, Lieutenant Ernest Hodge likened the barbed wire to brown snakes. (Freeman, p231)

Chapter 10

1 David Kehr, New York Times, 5/7/2005

2 The Observer, 19/10/18, p34

3 The Register, 9/7/20, p5

4 The Express and Telegraph, 14/12/21, p1

5 Daily Herald, 15/12/21, p8; The Register, 15/12/21, p11; Other sources give Katie's name as Katy, Katey or Kati and her husband's surname as Herman.

6 The Register, 3/6/22, p10; Chronicle, 10/6/22, p36

7 Murray Pioneer, 9/6/22, p14

8 The Express and Telegraph, 23/8/20, p2; Chronicle, 4/9/20, p19

9 Edward Budgen, VWM

10 The Express and Telegraph, 19/12/21, p2; Freeman p264

11 The Advertiser, 26/5/24, p8; Border Chronicle, 30/5/24, p2; Butler had spent two years in the Bedford Park Sanatorium for consumptive soldiers

12 William Woods NAA file

13 The Narracoorte Herald, 7/2/28, p2

14 Murray Pioneer and Australian River Record, 6/2/36, p10

15 Interim Report upon the Organisation and Activities of the Repatriation Department, 8 April 1918, to 30 June 1919, p5 (quoted in Vol III of the Official Medial History, p797)

16 Horley was a career barman who worked at the Criterion and a string of country and interstate pubs. The secret to being a good barman, he said, was "tact and a good temper". (The Advertiser, 13/7/45, p8; The News, 25/4/39, p4)

17 Freeman, p265

18 The Advertiser, 27/4/20, p8

19 RSL SA states the "Commemorative March is not a 'parade' and does not prioritise recognition of the living".

20 Daily Herald, 27/4/20, p2; however the following year's march (1921), was "splendid" and "stirring", the Express and Telegraph reported (26/4/21, p1). The Daily Herald was a union paper so might have been inclined to talk down the march.

21 The Advertiser, 24/11/19, p2; The Register, 25/11/19, p8; It appears this attempt to form an association foundered, but the club was revived in 1927 thanks to the efforts of Max Gore (Murray Pioneer, 5/8/27, p9). Other prime movers were Murray Fowler, Noel Loutit, Harry Seager and Royce Spinkston. The association continued until about 1980, when declining membership prompted an amalgamation with the 10th Battalion Association (Allchin, Purple and Blue, p88).

22 Pritchard NAA file

23 The Chronicle, 27/6/1946, p29. Wilton was 53 or 54.

24 VWM profiles; Department of Veterans Affairs World War II nominal roll

25 The Advertiser, 16/6/41, p11

26 AWM Official History, World War II, Vol III – Tobruk and El Alamein, p221 and 226-8

27 Allchin, Purple and Blue, p189

28 Murray Pioneer, 21/9/21, p9; News, 8/9/39, p4; State Library of SA, SA Newspapers: Pen Names of South Australian journalists and cartoonists

29 Veterans Affairs World War II nominal roll, 50th Battalion Field Return, Tippins NAA file

30 VWM profiles, NAA records, Red Cross files, Carter's ADB entry and dates of death in Freeman.

31 Auld NAA file

32 Gore in Freeman, p241

33 Gore in Freeman, p258

34 Murray Pioneer, 8/2/24, p11

35 The Advertiser, 25/9/35, p11

36 Gore NAA file; Department of Veterans' Affairs World War II Nominal Roll

37 Tamblyn interview, AWM

38 Freeman p266-275

39 The Advertiser, 2/4/18, p4; Albert Percival Adcock's and John Ross Manthorpe's World War II nominal roll entries (Department of Veterans' Affairs).

40 The Advertiser, 13/4/18, p6

41 Prest NAA file; The Advertiser, 27/3/45, p8; 27th Battalion war diary (AWM); At least 10 of the Noreuil dead came from the Port Adelaide area.

42 John and Kevin Wegener's NAA files: Department of Veterans' Affairs World War II nominal roll.

43 AWM079584 (AWM Collection)

44 However, a panel in the far corner of the cemetery states: "Noreuil was captured by Australian troops in April 1917, lost a year later and retaken in August 1918."

45 Freeman, pV; the battalion colours themselves have had a troubled life – laid up in Adelaide's Anglican Cathedral, St Peter's, in 1927 by Murray Fowler, in 1973 they were sent to St David's Cathedral in Hobart, the army logic being that the most recent unit with the 50th appellation was a Tasmanian militia outfit. A campaign to return them to Adelaide was successful and they were reinstalled in St Peter's on 7 November 1993.

46 The Sunday Mail, 23/4/2017, p26-27; Robert Jose died on 23/1/2020, aged 95.

47 The memorials are listed on the VWM site.

48 Noreuil's church is named for Saint Brice – the Saint's holy day is 13 November.

Epilogue

1 On his 2 April, 2023, visit, the author counted 10 men of the 50th with headstones. A second walk of the rows also yielded 10 names. Yet the Commonwealth War Graves Commission tally is 15. Another of Noreuil's mysteries …

2 Rifleman John Devonshire of the 12th Battalion, Rifle Brigade, is the only non-50th Battalion soldier in the Special Memorial section. Devonshire died on 4/6/1917; the 82 includes William Marshall, killed in action at Villers-Bretonneux on Anzac Day, 1918 (See Chapter 17)

3 Jack Thomas died on 12 December 2021, aged 101.

4 https://fr.wikipedia.org/wiki/Ligne_de_Boisleux_%C3%A0_Marquion

5 Population figure from the Paris School of Advanced Studies of Social Sciences

About the Author

Andrew Faulkner is an Adelaide-based journalist and author. His first book, *Arthur Blackburn VC: An Australian hero, his men, and their two world wars*, was shortlisted for the 2009 National Biography Award. *Stone Cold: the extraordinary true story of Len Opie, Australia's deadliest soldier*, was shortlisted in the 2016 NIB Literary Awards. He wrote about cricket and Australian Rules football for The Australian from 2007-2020 and in 2019 co-authored *For Cap and Country*, a collection of interviews with Australian international cricketers. He enjoys working on his cousin's cherry orchard, keeping wickets for Kensington District Cricket Club, and listening to The Fauves.

Index

Index

Index